P9-APZ-188

This book provided courtesy of

The Parkland Group, Inc.

1375 East Ninth Street
Suite 1350
Cleveland, OH 44114

216/621-1985

Contact the Parkland Group for additional copies

CORPORATE INTENSIVE CARE

Why Businesses Fail
and
How to Make Them Succeed

Larry Goddard

York Publishing Co.
Shaker Heights, Ohio 44120

This book is available at a special discount when ordered in bulk quantities. For information, contact:

York Publishing Co.
16781 Chagrin Boulevard, #336
Shaker Heights, Ohio 44120 U.S.A.
Phone 216/491-0231
Fax   216/491-0251

This publication is designed to provide accurate and authoritative information in regard to the subject matter covered. It is sold with the understanding that the publisher is not engaged in rendering legal, accounting, or other professional service. If legal advice or other expert assistance is required, the services of a competent professional person should be sought. The author and publisher do not assume and hereby disclaim any liability to any party for any loss or damage caused by errors or omissions in this book, whether such errors or omissions result from negligence, accident or any other cause.

Library of Congress Cataloging-in-Publication Data
Goddard, Larry
    Corporate Intensive Care
    Why Businesses Fail and How to Make Them Succeed

    Includes bibliographical references and index.
    ISBN 0-9634940-0-7
    1. Corporate Turnarounds - United States - Management
    2. Corporate Reorganizations - United States I. Title

Editors: Bryan Aubrey and Laura Stone Bell
Cover Design: Roberta Dickinson
Interior Design: Jerry Pignolet/NewsLetter Group

©1993 L.V. Goddard
All rights reserved.
Printed in the United States of America.

This publication may not be reproduced, stored in a retrieval system, or transmitted in whole or in part, in any form or by any means, electronic, mechanical, photocopying, recording, or otherwise, without the prior written permission of York Publishing Co., 16781 Chagrin Blvd., #336, Shaker Heights, Ohio 44120.

Printing number

10 9 8 7 6 5 4 3 2 1

92-062451
CIP

*To my wife, without whose love, support and guidance
this book would not have been possible.*

CONTENTS

PREFACE

Underperforming and distressed businesses are consuming a vast amount of the United States resources and energy: During the period 1980 through 1990, business bankruptcy filings increased 62 percent[1]! While these statistics show huge increases in bankruptcy filings, no records exist to measure the extent and breadth of underperforming businesses not in bankruptcy. My experience as a turnaround and workout consultant has caused me to believe that these statistics dwarf those of bankruptcy. I have also been struck by the inefficiency of the available systems for dealing with a distressed business. Chief Executive Officers are usually trained to run successful businesses: Very few have had experience managing distressed businesses. When a company experiences a life-threatening crisis, availability of the most vital resource, cash, is scarce. In most cases, the communications between a

[1] *The 1991 Bankruptcy Yearbook and Almanac*, New Generation Research, Inc., Boston, Ma.

distressed company, its secured creditors and unsecured creditors deteriorates to a point where very little constructive action is taken to remedy the situation. In the minority of cases where communications are adequate, the parties rarely agree on a strategy to restore the business to health. The result often is that help is not readily available for a distressed or underperforming business, at a time when it is most needed. The owners and managers of a business in these circumstances can find this to be a frustrating and frightening experience. The costs to the individuals, corporations and institutions involved, as well as to society at large, can be staggering.

Corporate Intensive Care is based on more than 16 years of experience as a principal and advisor in more than 40 corporate turnarounds. The purpose of this book is to provide a tool for all parties involved with a distressed business, whereby they can obtain an improved understanding of the process, and facilitate a maximization of the outcome. Interested parties usually include owners, managers, employees, secured lenders, unsecured lenders and creditors, attorneys, potential investors, acquirers and accountants. The step-by-step method and approach outlined in this book has been developed by my firm, The Parkland Group, Inc., and has proven to be extremely successful.

As with a medical emergency, someone trained and experienced in *corporate first-aid* has a significantly greater likelihood of reviving the *corporate patient*. Quick and decisive action by an experienced and knowledgeable *corporate physician* can make a significant difference to the outcome. A corporate Chief Executive of a distressed company, like a medical doctor, needs to have a well-developed *bedside manner*. He needs to instill confidence in his employees, creditors, shareholders and other stakeholders, and must clearly communicate the philosophy and direction of the company. He needs to convey sensitivity and concern—but must always be ready to make bold decisions. The skills needed to run a distressed business can be very different from those needed for a healthy one. As such, applying the techniques and approaches outlined in this book will greatly help the CEO in managing such a business back to health.

The major warning signs of impending business failure include:

- A worsening cash position resulting in an inability to keep lender or supplier obligations current, or to maintain adequate inventory levels

- Deteriorating sales, margins and profits

- Deteriorating accounts receivable aging

- Increasing quality problems, returns of goods and customer complaints

- Increasing production lead-time and delivery times

- Employee and management turnover and dissatisfaction

- Reduced responsiveness to customers

- Excessive work hours for management and staff, and sharply reduced vacation time

Any Chief Executive who sees an increasing number of the above items become a reality in his company should take the time to realistically assess the health of the company.

The experience of our firm has indicated that, for companies that diligently implement a turnaround and workout program, the probabilities of success are favorable. The surviving company is often very different from how it started out, but it can survive and, in time, thrive. Implementing a turnaround is not easy. The conditions and circumstances leading up to the crisis usually accumulate over a lengthy period of time, and they are rarely undone overnight. Nevertheless, an analytical, methodical and persistent application of turnaround techniques almost always results in an improvement of the company's situation, and often will return it to good health. It is unusual to find an immediate quick fix. Successful turnarounds are, to use a baseball analogy, usually achieved with a lot of *singles*, rather than one *home run*. Most companies need some outside help in achieving the turnaround. An experienced bankruptcy attorney must be consulted throughout the process to ensure you stay within the law, and that you take maximum advantage of bankruptcy laws. Some situations require a new CEO with good turnaround skills, or the services of an experienced turnaround consultant, who can help management analyze the extent and severity of the problems, and assist in developing and implementing the turnaround strategy. The involvement of a turnaround consultant often facilitates a calmer, more effective assessment and resolution of the problem, because the consultant can approach the issues without an emotional bias. The consultant can also help to reduce tension by using his credibility with all parties as the foundation for finding compromise solutions.

If the problems faced by the business are of such a magnitude that a successful turnaround is unrealistic, this conclusion must be reached as quickly as possible. In these situations, the liquidation or sale of the business (or major parts thereof) might be the optimum solution. The longer the delay in making this decision, the more ongoing operating losses will eat into the ultimate proceeds all parties will receive.

The content of this book will be of maximum benefit to those who are directly involved in turning around an *underperforming* or *distressed* company. However, there are many disciplines, ideas and concepts that can be used to improve companies that may not be in *life-threatening* situations. The book has been primarily modelled around a medium-sized manufacturing/sales organization. However, most of the concepts could easily be applied or adapted to a wholesale, retail or service organization. The methods and approaches described apply equally to the turnaround of a business that has just been acquired, or to one that has found itself in difficulty during its continuing operations.

The following is a brief description of the sections of the book:

Introduction—provides a description of the experiences of the Chief Executive Officer of the fictional company Excalibur, Inc., as he arrives at the realization that his business is in far worse condition than he had previously been willing to contemplate.

Part 1: Why Businesses Fail—The three sections provide an analysis of the reasons for business failure; a description of the Corporate Treadmill Test, an early warning indicator of business distress; and a method for measuring the financial health of a business, and for pinpointing the specific problem areas.

Part 2: How to Make a Business Succeed—describes the three phases of a corporate turnaround and workout program.

1. *Vital Signs*—a diagnostic review of the business to determine its strengths and weaknesses, the extent and severity of its problems, and to provide the information necessary to develop a turnaround program.

2. *Corporate CPR*—the emergency remedial procedures necessary to stabilize the business in a crisis.

3. *Recuperation*—strategies to rebuild the business to sustainable financial and operating health.

Conclusion—provides an assessment of the status of Excalibur, Inc., the fictional company described in the Introduction. This section also contains a description of the steps taken by Excalibur to deal with its crisis.

In practice, the three phases of Part 2 do not necessarily occur in strict sequence. While one would ideally like to complete the diagnostic review before commencing remedial treatment, circumstances often dictate that some forms of

Corporate CPR and Recuperation strategies begin before the Vital Signs Phase is completed.

My very warm thanks are extended to Willy Bagg, Brian Bash, David Brown, Edwin Daniels, Chet Dickey, Gregg Foster, Mitch Frankel, William Hale, Joe Laskowski, Kevin McHugh, Curt Oliver, Tony Potelicki, Howard Rosenberg, Ruth Rosenberg, Bill Schonberg, Dr. Kevin Trangle, Dick Warren and Rick Wright for reviewing the manuscript. Their comments and support have been invaluable to the development of this project. Thanks also to Laura Bell and Bryan Aubrey for their insightful editorial comments. I have a special debt of gratitude to my dedicated and tireless secretary, Shelly Soukup, for her patience and painstaking commitment through innumerable redrafts of this book, over several years.

There are very few experiences more exciting and ultimately rewarding than *turning around* an underperforming business. The stakes are very high, but the thrill of seeing your corporate patient reviving is one of the greatest satisfactions imaginable.

Wishing you a speedy recovery.

Larry Goddard
January, 1993

About the Author

LARRY GODDARD, a member of the Turnaround Management Association, is the founder and chairman of The Parkland Group, Inc., an advisory and investment banking firm based in Cleveland, Ohio, devoted to assisting underperforming businesses return to financial and operating health. Parkland provides services in the areas of turnaround consulting, crisis management, restructuring of debt, raising of equity, and the sale of underperforming businesses, product lines or divisions. Parkland has pioneered in the development of low-cost alternatives to Chapter 11 for distressed businesses.

Born in South Africa and qualified as a Chartered Accountant and Chartered Business Valuator in Canada, Larry Goddard has spent the last 16 years as a principal or adviser in more than 40 turnaround situations. During this time, he spent four years as an accountant and consultant with Price Waterhouse, eight years as the Chief Executive Officer of Waco International Corporation, a U.S. manufacturer and distributor of construction equipment, and four years as an adviser and investment banker to underperforming businesses. During his tenure as CEO of Waco International, Goddard led the turnaround of what started as an $8 million regional business incurring significant losses, to a $100 million profitable national business with branches and plants in more than 25 U.S. cities.

INTRODUCTION

Peter Jones has been the Chief Executive Officer of Excalibur, Inc. for 15 years. The company manufactures and sells bicycles and other sports equipment. He started the company after being employed for five years as sales manager for a major competitor.

The initial capital for the business was obtained from a bank loan, secured by a second mortgage on Jones' house. Because of his expertise as a salesman, the business grew rapidly, achieving sales of $20 million in its tenth year of operations. Sales growth then began to slow down significantly, reaching only $22 million for the most recent fiscal year. Since its inception, the growth of Excalibur was financed by additional bank loans, secured by the company's inventory and receivables, *and Mr. Jones' personal guarantee.*

Except for its first year of operations, the business earned healthy profits in all of the first ten years. For the most recent five years, Excalibur, Inc. broke even in two, and incurred losses for the other three. Peter Jones was becoming increasingly concerned about the business: The losses of the last few years were taking their toll. He was not enjoying his work any more, and for the first time in his life, he did not look forward to going to work.

Jones tried to identify the reasons for the lack of profitability in the business. He could think of the following explanations:

- Several foreign competitors entered the market about five years ago, and have been offering good quality products to Excalibur's dealers at very low prices.

- Paul Smith, who was Excalibur's Sales Manager, resigned three years ago, and started his own competing company. His close relationship with most of Excalibur's major customers enabled him to win a significant percentage of the company's business. Excalibur was forced to respond by trying to win market share from other competitors, and inadvertently triggered a price war.

- While competitive forces were squeezing Excalibur's margins, its raw material and operating costs were continuing to rise. In particular, group medical and workers' compensation insurance premiums had risen significantly.

- The addition to the plant that was built four years ago in anticipation of the continued growth in revenues increased the company's debt and related interest cost significantly. A large part of that plant is now underutilized, but the company is still carrying the burden of utility costs, property taxes and maintenance costs.

The following week, the company missed (for the first time) its federal payroll withholding payment. The Controller

2

notified Jones that if they made the payment, they would not have enough funds that week to meet payroll and the bank principal and interest payment. Jones, distracted and distressed by the loss of a large order, concluded that he would rather miss the government payment than a bank payment. He made this decision because he had already had several meetings with bank officials, who had expressed serious concern about the company's deteriorating performance. Jones had assured the bank that the business was sound, and that he was about to launch a new product line that would recapture significant market share and profits.

The next pay period, the Controller advised Jones that, not only did they now not have the funds to make withholding obligations, they would also probably not be able to make the next bank payments.

Jones called a meeting of all of Excalibur's senior management. When everybody was assembled in the conference room, he closed the door and said in a solemn voice, "You are all aware that cash has been a little tight for a while. In the last few months, this situation has become a lot more serious, to the point where we have not been able to make payroll withholding and bank payments. As a personal guarantor of these obligations, I am beginning to become extremely concerned about this situation, and I would like to hear what you think the problems are."

As the meeting unfolded, he heard the following:

- The Credit Manager reported that a major customer had not paid its large balance outstanding due to quality problems with the products. The customer had shipped the goods back, and had given the order to a competitor. When questioned, the Production Manager explained that the quality issues resulted from problems with the new paint system, which the manufacturer refused to repair because

3

Excalibur had not made the last three payments for the new system.

- The Sales Manager reported that sales were down significantly for the month because a supplier of parts needed for a large order would only ship with a C.O.D. payment, due to Excalibur's exceeding its credit limit and being behind on payments.

- The Engineering Manager reported that development costs on the new product had skyrocketed due to a miscalculation that had been made about safety standards, and the launch date for the new line would be delayed at least six months.

After listening intently to each manager's explanation, Jones said, "These are all valid explanations, but they relate more to specific problems than to a broader explanation of why we have not earned a profit for the last five years."

The Sales Manager raised his hand. "Peter, I believe the problem stems from the fact that we don't make enough profit on our sports equipment line," he said. "Prior to introducing that line five years ago, we always made money with our bicycle line. Since then we've been losing money. Doesn't it stand to reason that the sports equipment is the problem?"

"Is this true?" Jones asked, turning to the Controller. "Is the sports equipment line losing money?"

"I can't tell you," the Controller sheepishly replied.

"Why not?" Jones retorted.

"Because we make both product lines in the same plant, and our accounting system does not give us an accurate picture of costs or profitability by product line," the Controller responded.

"So how do we know if we're making or losing money on a particular product?" Jones asked.

"Well, when we introduced the line five years ago, we did an estimated costing of each product, and we priced the products to produce our required gross profit margin. Since

4

then, we periodically update the significant costs for the more popular products," the Controller replied.

"So aside from these estimates, we don't really know what it costs us to make our product?" Jones asked rhetorically. "If this is the case, how do we know we are making the products efficiently?"

At that point, the Production Manager interrupted. "Peter, we've been making bicycles for 15 years, and sports equipment for five. Most of our workforce has been with us for more than ten years. We are probably the most efficient plant in the country in these products. You see how hard everybody works."

While the discussion continued, Jones' mind began to wander, "If we don't really know what our costs should be, and we don't have a system to track actual costs, how can we know if we are efficient? That's like asking somebody to go out and run a four-minute mile without giving him a stop watch to time himself!"

He began to realize the severity of the problem he was facing. His business was losing money and he did not have the tools to identify where the losses were occurring, nor did he have the systems to implement and monitor corrective action. For quite some time, he had been aware that things were deteriorating, but he now acknowledged to himself that he had been avoiding facing the reality of how bad the company's condition actually was. He could also see that the substantial time he had spent on non-company business over the last few years had really begun to hurt the operations. Several things had gone wrong that he wasn't even aware of. Of the problems he was aware of, he had ignored most of them, hoping they would *go away*. It was now clear to Peter Jones that his management team was not strong enough to manage this declining business, and that he had not focussed enough attention on the issues either.

After the meeting, a depressed Jones called the Controller into his office to decide what to do about the bank payment. He really did not want to miss the payment, but it appeared he had no choice. All the time the threat of the personal guarantee was pounding in his brain. The Controller asked if he should phone the bank officer and explain. Jones decided against this, because he did not know how to explain the situation in a way that would avoid confirming the bank's already negative view of the company.

One week later, the bank officer called and asked Jones why they had not received the payment. Jones said he would look into the matter and report back. The next day, he called to explain that there had been some temporary cash problems, and that the payment would be made up the next month. The bank officer reluctantly agreed to this arrangement, but warned Jones that the bank was getting concerned.

The following month Excalibur did not have the funds to make the bank payment. Further, several suppliers had placed the company on C.O.D. payments only, the company had discontinued making payments on any of its past due accounts payable, and a demand letter had been received from the IRS. The bank officer, now extremely angry, called Mr. Jones to advise him that the bank's senior management was upset, first, at the company's poor performance, and second, and more seriously, at the apparently misleading information they had been receiving about the company's status.

Peter Jones telephoned his friend and attorney, David Cartwright, to seek his advice.

At a meeting later that day, Jones gave Cartwright a bleak picture of Excalibur's situation. Cartwright was surprised.

"I know business hasn't been great, but you've always indicated the situation is under control. What about that great new product you've been telling me about?" he said.

"Dave, I hate to admit this," Jones replied, "but I think I've been asleep at the switch. When I really analyze the situation, it's obvious that the business has had serious problems for years. I knew things weren't quite right, but I didn't want to think about it. I kept telling myself that the slowdown in sales was an industry-wide problem, and that our new product would remedy that. Now, I find out that the new product doesn't meet government safety standards, and that the launch will have to be delayed for six months."

"Can you identify the causes of the problem?" Cartwright followed up.

"No! Our accounting system stinks, and I'm beginning to realize that some of my key managers are in over their heads," Jones confessed. Becoming more agitated, he continued, "Dave, I've never had any experience with this type of situation. What should I do? Maybe I should file Chapter 11 immediately! What do you think?"

Cartwright replied in a reassuring tone, "I want you to calm down. There is absolutely no point in panicking; you need to think clearly. I'm going to make an appointment for both of us to see a good friend of mine, George Simon, who is one of the best bankruptcy attorneys in town. This doesn't mean that I think you should file Chapter 11; it's because I believe it's important in these situations to be guided by an experienced bankruptcy attorney who can counsel us as to the best strategy."

"That's fine with me," Jones responded, "but time is of the essence."

Cartwright stood up and said, "I'll call George at home now, and see if he can see us tomorrow."

At the meeting the next day, Jones explained the situation to Simon. After listening intently, Simon responded, "I am going to give you three pieces of advice: Firstly, Chapter 11 will not solve your problem. You do not have the cash resources to file, and based on the facts you have described, it is unlikely that you will retain control of your business at the conclusion of a Chapter 11 case. Secondly, you've got to advise your bank of your situation. Lastly, you need help in understanding exactly what the problem is, and in developing a remedial plan. I'm going to give you the name of a consultant I have worked with in the past who has been extremely successful in helping people in situations similar to yours. His name is Charlie Benson, and I suggest you call him right away. After you have figured out what the business status is, we'll get together again and develop a strategy that makes business and legal sense."

In the elevator on the way down from the meeting, Jones asked Cartwright, "You don't really think I need outside help, do you?"

"Pete," Cartwright responded, "as your attorney and friend, this is one time in your life when I think that this is a problem that is beyond your field of expertise. Focus on saving your business, not preserving your ego!"

That afternoon, Jones made two calls: the first to Steve Kramer, the loan officer at ABC Bank to set up a meeting for the next day; the second call was to Charlie Benson, the turnaround and workout consultant recommended by George Simon.

At 10:00 a.m. the next day, Jones arrived at ABC Bank's headquarters to meet with Steve Kramer. As Kramer came out to greet him, Jones sensed a stiffness in Kramer's demeanor toward him, although he tried to convince himself he was only imagining it. Jones opened the conversation. "Steve, I appreciate your meeting with me at such short notice. As you are aware, we've been having some problems at Excalibur lately. At first, I genuinely believed that the problems were minor and of a temporary nature. Now, I realize they're more serious. However, with your cooperation, I believe that I can deal with this situation within a few months."

Kramer interrupted, "When you say, with our cooperation, what specifically do you mean?"

"Well, I was thinking that if ABC could increase my line by another $500,000 for six months, that would give me the time to fix the business, and also launch our new product," Jones responded.

"Peter, I'd really like to help you," Kramer replied, "but it's out of my hands. Our senior management has decided to transfer your account to our workout department."

"Oh!" Jones stammered, "What exactly does that mean?" He did not understand the significance of this step.

"What it means, Peter, is that your loan is in default and the bank is now concerned about our ability to fully recover on your loans, and a decision has been made that we do not want to continue our relationship with Excalibur," Kramer explained.

Jones was shocked. He could not believe the bank was abandoning him when he needed them most. He was sure that he could correct the problems, if only they would advance the additional $500,000.

Before Jones could respond, Kramer continued, "Because of this situation, I'd like to introduce you to Ted Rogers, one of our workout officers who has been assigned to Excalibur. If it's alright with you, I'll ask Ted to join us now."

Barely hearing what Kramer had said, Jones nodded, and Kramer left the room. For the next ten minutes, Peter Jones, unable to concentrate clearly, began to consider the consequences of financial ruin.

When the door opened again, Ted Rogers introduced himself and indicated that Steve Kramer had been called away to attend to some other business. Rogers wasted very little time on pleasantries and advised Jones, "The bank is extremely concerned about the situation at Excalibur, and we want you to find another bank."

Jones attempted to repeat his appeal for the bank's temporary financial support. But before he could finish, Rogers interrupted, "ABC Bank is seriously concerned about recovering its existing loans to Excalibur. Under the circumstances, we certainly would not entertain advancing any additional funds."

Jones started to get the message. "Look," he said, "I acknowledge that I let things get out of control, and that I was wrong in not keeping the bank informed. However, I want you to know that I am going to correct this problem, and I intend to repay every penny I owe the bank. I would also like you to know that I now realize I need some help in achieving this: I'm going to retain a turnaround and workout consultant, Charlie Benson, to assist me."

"I'm pleased to hear that you are going to get some help. Most CEOs in your situation wait until it's too late to seek help. I know Charlie Benson, and have worked with him on several cases that had favorable results," Rogers responded. "While I am sure that the bank will not advance you any more funds, we may be willing to give you some time to work your problems out."

"What does that mean," Jones inquired, sensing, for the first time, an easing in Rogers' tone.

"Well, if you and Benson can develop a turnaround and workout plan that makes sense, we may be willing to forbear on your default for a while, to give you time to get straightened out. Bear in mind, I can't make any commitments until I see your plan, and there will likely be some fees and costs involved," Rogers explained.

Feeling a little less overwhelmed, Jones shook Rogers' hand and headed for his meeting with Charlie Benson. As he steered his car through traffic, he realized that he was about to begin a new challenge, perhaps the biggest of his life, to save his business and preserve his family's financial well-being and security.

From a review of the above facts, it is clear that Excalibur, Inc. is experiencing extreme distress. The company has been deteriorating for five years, and has now reached a point where its resources have been depleted to where it can no longer meet its obligations.

The above description is fictional. However, the circumstances described above for Excalibur are typical of very real situations facing many businesses in today's economic climate. As the world has become one marketplace, business conditions have become tougher and more competitive for most companies. Many have adapted well and have thrived, but others—too many, unfortunately—have experienced declines similar to Excalibur's. The excessive leverage available in the 1980s has contributed to this by giving businesses easy access to capital to fund rapid growth and acquisitions, often beyond the company's capabilities to manage. Most importantly, many companies simply do not have the information and early warning systems to identify potential problems before they become debilitating.

When a business finds itself in this situation, a key determinant in its ultimate survival will be how it manages all phases of the crisis. The one common ingredient in most of these situations is mistrust. As the company's performance deteriorates, it often slips in meeting its obligations to lenders, suppliers, customers and even employees. With progressive deterioration, mistrust sets in, and management's credibility begins to evaporate. The Chief Executive in this situation must find ways to restore the trust, at least to a level sufficient to buy enough time to identify and implement solutions to the problems. For the company to survive, it will need to immediately commence a *Turnaround and Workout* program that will entail:

1. Thoroughly identifying and quantifying the full extent and severity of the company's problems, resulting in a comprehensive understanding of the areas of difficulty, and possible solutions.

2. Developing a short-term turnaround and workout strategy that will enable the company to continue operating while it searches for the longer-term strategies that can result in a healthier, profitable business.

3. Developing and implementing the medium-term strategies that will enhance the profitability and finances of the organization, so that it will be able to return to a situation where it can meet all its ongoing obligations, and provide an acceptable return to its shareholders.

Most *turnarounds* are accompanied by *workout* activities. Turnaround generally refers to steps taken to change the operations of the business to improve its profitability, e.g., reduce expenses, eliminate unprofitable products. Workout refers to the negotiations that result in a change in the company's obligations, e.g., extended or reduced payments to lenders and creditors and conversion of debt into equity. In the earlier stages of distress, turnaround activities are usually more applicable than workout. As the distress progresses and worsens, more extensive workout strategies need to be introduced.

Without a concerted Turnaround and Workout program, it is highly unlikely that Excalibur, Inc. will be able to withstand the pressures of meeting its obligations, and it will ultimately face bankruptcy. This alternative could be a very costly and stressful route for the company, its Chief Executive, lenders, creditors, shareholders and employees. Much of these costs, and the stress associated with them, can be avoided by a well thought out and executed Turnaround and Workout program. This book is devoted to providing Chief Executives with the basic road map should they find themselves in a situation that resembles Peter Jones' dilemma at Excalibur. Understanding the turnaround process is also useful and helpful to the lenders, creditors, employees, attorneys, accountants and other professionals of underperforming or distressed businesses.

The experiences of Peter Jones and Excalibur are representative of similar situations occurring throughout the United States and the world. Most companies, in such circumstances, do not have many life support systems they can turn to for help. We do not have mechanisms in place that can train management to deal with distressed situations, nor are there resources readily available to facilitate crisis management. For example, very few business school programs offer comprehensive courses in corporate turnarounds. To date, we have felt the effects of this in the real estate industry, through the savings and loan crisis, which has cost this country hundreds of billions of dollars. We are now only beginning to feel the impact of this in other business areas, as the weight of the excessive leverage of the 1980s starts to drag down companies, large and small.

The business community in Japan, on the other hand, has developed an informal support system for companies that experience hard times.

> "More than ever, the fabled *Keiretsu*, or business families, that form the backbone of Corporate Japan are rising to the defense of their weaker members with financial backing, management savvy, or favorable contracts...
> ...Each case shows the *Keiretsu* fulfilling one of their key missions: To provide a safety net when corporate relatives start to teeter. There's little doubt that this is helping cushion the impact of Japan's recession and that more such cases are in store."
>
> *Business Week*, October 26, 1992

Because such support systems are not readily available to U.S. businesses, it is even more important for them to identify impending problems early and to take decisive corrective action, so that they can survive without relying on outside help.

Many owners and managers, when they read or hear about companies facing the problems like Excalibur's, might reassure themselves that their problems are not as serious—and they do not need to take the kind of drastic steps that Peter Jones is surely going to need. On the contrary, if they have even slight nagging suspicions that their business is underperforming, it could well be that, with time, they will be closer to Excalibur's situation than they would ever like to admit. This is the time to act: Every day that passes without recognition of the problems, no matter how small they may seem at the time, contributes to reducing the chances of a successful turnaround later. Early intervention offers a greater array of turnaround options, and significantly increases chances of success. The techniques described in this book offer all businesses, underperforming or not, an effective approach to performing an *annual physical* of the company's fiscal health.

If management of today does not quickly learn turnaround skills, the demise of the companies over which they preside will, paradoxically, become the opportunity of the 1990s, when acquirers pick off the jewels at bargain-basement prices and implement the changes that their predecessors did not. The victims will be the employees and creditors of these businesses.

While, in the short run, this is not a favorable situation for the country as a whole, in the long run it will likely result in a stronger national economy—because the surviving companies will be healthier and better run. That is, until the herd mentality again triggers a rush for banks to lend money to people unqualified to use it, and the process starts all over again.

The remainder of this book provides an outline of steps that a Chief Executive Officer of an underperforming business should follow to understand *why his business is failing, and how to make it succeed.* Specifically, *Corporate Intensive Care* describes a new and unique way to examine a business, assess its health, identify problem areas and implement practical and realistic solutions. In addition, the Conclusion reveals how Peter Jones and Excalibur respond to their challenge.

Part one

WHY BUSINESSES FAIL

Section I:

REASONS FOR BUSINESS FAILURE

While it is clear from the description in the Introduction that Excalibur, Inc. is in serious trouble, what is not so apparent are the exact causes. While Peter Jones might feel a very real need to take immediate action, without an in-depth understanding of the fundamental reasons for the poor performance, his actions may prove futile or, even worse, detrimental to the business. As such, it is extremely important that the Chief Executive of an underperforming company take the time to evaluate the real reasons or causes why the business is not meeting expectations. Efforts should then be devoted to correcting causes, rather than symptoms.

My research over the last 16 years has led me to the conclusion that the reasons why most businesses fail fall into the following eight categories. In many underperforming businesses, more than one of these reasons will be prevalent. However, one reason will usually be dominant.

Undermanaged

Many people find it easy to blame the demise of a business on *bad management*. However, my research has shown that a more prevalent cause is *undermanagement*. Bad management usually results from one or more *wrong* actions that lead to the company's ultimate downfall. While bad management actions are indeed the cause of many business failures, many, if not most, are caused by inaction, i.e., they fail because management undermanaged the company by not doing enough *right things*. While very different concepts, both can be devastating to the health of a business.

In every business, senior management sets the direction and strategy, installs information systems, procedures and controls, selects the resources needed, motivates and communicates. A company that is undermanaged will have fallen short in one or more of these areas.

Symptoms of an undermanaged company include no comprehensive and understandable business plan and strategy, a lack of timely decision-making, high turnover of capable employees, inadequate or untimely management information, limited knowledge about customers and market conditions, an inadequate or unrealistic assessment and projection of cash needs, excessive corporate politics and inadequate delegation of authority.

Overcommitted

Management's ability to function with a clear, purposeful and effective focus is impacted by the number and complexity of areas and projects it is pursuing. A business that is overcommitted will be growing faster or tackling more product lines, divisions, branches or projects than is within the company's ability to plan, manage, control and finance.

Symptoms of an overcommitted company are the lack of a clear core business, operating executives managing more than one business unit, extensive vertical or horizontal integration, lack of time or interest from senior management

18

(which could manifest in unreturned phone calls, non-attendance at meetings, receiving and taking excessive calls during meetings) and lack of response to deterioration in performance.

Overcosted

The total cost of a business is a melting pot, arising from a multitude of individual decisions relating to the acquisition of materials, labor and overhead expenses. A company that is overcosted will not have pursued the optimum costs at every level of the buying or spending decisions.

In the case of materials, parts or finished goods, overcosting can result from poor design of products, a lack of aggressive buying practices, excessive waste or scrap or the lack of pursuit of substitute materials for its products. Inefficient labor costs can result from excessive pay scales, inadequate training, inadequate incentives or motivation, inflexible union rules, duplication of effort, underutilized personnel, unnecessary tasks, reports and meetings or too many layers of management. Overheads can grow from a lack of commitment to a *lean and mean* operation, e.g., company-owned cars for executives, first-class travel, club memberships, cellular telephones, unmonitored entertainment. The costs of materials, labor and overheads are always affected by inefficient, inadequate or less than state-of-the-art methods, procedures, equipment, or efficiency tracking and monitoring systems.

Symptoms of an overcosted company are an inadequate costing and reporting system, inadequate budgeting, lack of forecasting and comparison to actual results, ineffective or nonexistent efficiency tracking systems and related incentive plans, backlog build-up, missed delivery schedules, excessive returns, low bid success rate, production bottlenecks, excessive out-of-stock occurrences or downtime, excessive rework and the lack of a constant pursuit of cost measurement and improvement.

In general, overcosting is one of the easiest areas to improve: Once overcosting can be identified and measured, a strategy can usually be implemented to lower costs.

Inadequate margins

Margins are a function of both costs and selling prices. While costs predominantly are internally impacted, selling prices are substantially affected by external forces. The unpredictable and uncontrollable forces of competition, customers' needs and desires, and other outside influences, such as industry and general economic conditions, play a significant role in establishing selling prices. While external influences are significant, inadequate margins can often result from internal inadequacies.

Many businesses do not have mechanisms to assist them in striving for the highest selling price possible, resulting in money *being left on the table*. This usually results from inadequate information about market sensitivity and margins achieved for each product sold, together with the lack of an incentive system to motivate management and sales personnel to pursue higher prices. Industry and general economic conditions are external forces that can have a significant impact on margins. When revenues or margins decline on an industry-wide basis, even the best management will have difficulty counteracting this.

Symptoms of inadequate margins are salesperson compensation tied to gross revenues, rather than margins, inadequate margin reporting system, and turbulence in the industry, e.g., competitor bankruptcies, acquisitions, significant excess capacity. In most businesses, margins can be improved by more effective margin management and incentive programs, together with appropriate sales, advertising and promotion strategies. Notwithstanding this, industry and general economic conditions will always have an overriding influence on margin potential.

Underdeveloped or declining franchise

A company's franchise is its following in the marketplace: Its name and reputation, and its historical relationships, will determine whether it has a positive market franchise. A well-developed franchise results from a customer base that is solid, dependable and has a favorable impression of the company, its products and service.

A business that does not pay close attention to its customer needs, does not place the highest priority to quality or does not have a clear strategy for winning and keeping customers is unlikely to have a strong franchise. As hard as it is to build a good franchise, it is even harder to recapture one that is declining. General Motors, once the undisputed leader in the automobile industry in the U.S., is living through this, because it allowed its franchise to erode in the face of foreign competition. In this case, internal inadequacies (product quality) resulted in an external problem.

Other contributors to franchise erosion include uncompetitive pricing in relation to value, outmoded product design and ineffective advertising, promotion or sales efforts. Many newer businesses or products fail before their franchises can be developed to the point where they can generate enough sales volume to sustain the business, e.g., DeLorean automobile. The cost of building a franchise can be extensive, and the time span for success is very hard to predict.

Symptoms of an underdeveloped or declining franchise are excessive reliance on one or a few significant customers, erratic or declining sales revenues, excessive discounting, sales strategy based on price rather than value, lower quotation/bid and order levels and inadequate product differentiation and recognition.

Achieving a turnaround of these problems is a difficult and often slow process, the magnitude of which should not be underestimated.

Undercapitalized

Another reason often cited for a business failure is excessive debt. While this is true in some situations—for example, if a purchaser overpays for a business and manages to finance the overpayment with debt—in the vast majority of cases, excessive debt is a *symptom* rather than a *cause*.

Any of the reasons for business failure included herein could result in excessive debt, but debt is rarely the single cause. Excessive debt, however, is often the condition that exposes the company's distress, which may explain why it often bears the blame.

It is true, however, that the higher the proportion of borrowed funds to total capital, the more likely it is that the company will experience distress. High debt levels increase cash outflow—to service interest and principal payments, and also usually result in less cash reserves to respond to emergencies.

Higher debt can result from inadequate initial capitalization; excessive shareholder withdrawals from the business in the form of remuneration, expenses or dividends; ongoing operating losses; and aggressive growth by acquisition or internal development that outpaces the cash generated internally by the business, or overpayment for acquisitions or assets acquired. The highly leveraged LBO acquisitions of the 1980s provide numerous examples of transactions that are experiencing difficulty because of some of these factors.

Symptoms of an undercapitalized company are stretched payments to suppliers, a high debt/equity ratio, excessive debt principal repayments, use of lines-of-credit to make principal payments, declining availability on credit lines and defaults on lender covenants.

Undercapitalization can be corrected by infusion of additional shareholders equity, restructuring of existing debt and capital structure or by the sale of assets without a proportionate reduction in earnings.

Inefficient asset management

The ultimate determination of a company's performance is the amount of profit it earns in relation to the amount of assets employed to earn those profits. Businesses that do not use their assets efficiently are wasting their shareholders' resources. If this persists, at some point in time the company's cash resources will become strained. Without corrective strategies, the viability of the business will be jeopardized.

Symptoms of inefficient asset management at a macro level are inadequate returns on assets from individual divisions, branches, product lines or customers. Micro-level symptoms include high or increasing days' sales in accounts receivable, low or declining inventory turnover and unutilized or underutilized assets.

Asset efficiency can be measured and monitored by the *Return On Assets Managed*. See Part 1: Sections II and III for further discussion of how to apply this important ratio.

External

Businesses can find themselves subjected to external threats totally beyond the control of management, such as shifts in market demand resulting in obsolescence of, or changed demand for, products, e.g., Singer sewing machines; bankruptcy of a major customer; recession; environmental crises, e.g., John Manville/asbestos; or catastrophic occurrences, e.g., Union Carbide/Bhopal, Johnson & Johnson/Tylenol. While these threats may have little or no relationship to the company's current operations, they can sometimes be of sufficient magnitude to jeopardize the financial survival of even a healthy company.

While many external events can legitimately be attributed to conditions beyond the control of management, there are circumstances where an argument can be made that management should have had the foresight to contemplate, and plan for, the possibility of the event.

ACTION STEPS

> Critically evaluate why your business is under-performing

> Focus on treating *causes* rather than *symptoms*

> Be realistic: Don't accept easy rationalizations to explain problem areas

> Seek the assistance of people you trust, and who are qualified, to help you make this determination. Include in this group people who are unbiased, and who will *tell it to you like it is*

> Determine if you need outside expert help. This includes legal, financial, and operations

> Don't procrastinate: If your business is underperforming, commence a turnaround or workout program immediately

Section II:

CORPORATE
TREADMILL TEST

U nderstanding the reasons why businesses fail provides a Chief Executive Officer with a framework from which to appreciate why his business might be underperforming. This affords a solid foundation on which to base the appropriate remedial strategies. However, a business can avoid the unpleasant and expensive task of a turnaround if it has an effective early warning indicator for impending corporate distress.

Consider this analogy: About three years ago, I visited my doctor for a complete physical, which included a treadmill stress test. At the conclusion of the test, my doctor pronounced, "Your arteries should be good for at least another two to three years!" He went on to explain that the treadmill test checks for blocked arteries that could prevent the flow of blood and oxygen to the brain. Based on the results of my test, he was able to predict that my arteries would not restrict blood flow for at least two to three years. For weeks after that visit, I kept thinking, "Wouldn't it be great if a similar test could be developed for businesses!" So, I set out to analyze what factors could restrict the blood flow of a business. That is, what could cause a business to run out of money?

Our subsequent research indicated that there are at least eight types of cash outflows that can drain a company's resources, and a business must ensure that it generates enough internal profitability (measured by its Return On Assets) to fund all of these eight outflows. We were able to develop this knowledge into a very effective test that we named *The Corporate Treadmill Test*. Similar to the test for human health, this test can predict when a business is heading for *Corporate Cardiac Arrest*. The test has also proven to be an extremely valuable tool for enhancing the performance of businesses, because it highlights the problem areas on which to focus.

With an early warning gauge like the Corporate Treadmill Test, potential problems can be identified early in the declining process. This affords the opportunity to apply turnaround strategies that may not be available at the later stages of decline, and provides the CEO with a wider array of strategies to pursue. If the decline of the business is only identified when the business is in, or close to, a crisis, the turnaround options can be severely restricted.

Why is the Corporate Treadmill Test so helpful?
Because it answers the important question of:

How much profit is enough?

Earning a profit, while an essential goal for any business, is not necessarily sufficient to ensure the long-term health of the business. In fact, profitable businesses can, and often do, go bankrupt—because they do not earn *enough* profit to generate the appropriate level of cash to be able to meet all of the company's required or committed disbursements. The Corporate Treadmill Test tells management how much profit it will need to *survive and thrive* in the long-term.

What is also unique about the Corporate Treadmill Test is that, in addition to determining how much profit the business as a whole must achieve, it also determines target profit levels for operating divisions and product lines. With this information, management can translate corporate goals into operating strategies at a micro level.

Positive cash flow

A major goal for all businesses should be to achieve *Positive Cash Flow* over an extended period of time. Positive Cash Flow is defined as being able to generate enough operating profit to fund all of a business' required or committed expenditures. If the business is not generating Positive Cash Flow, it will not be able to continue to operate indefinitely with only internally generated or borrowed funds—and will eventually need to look to its shareholders, or other sources, to invest further funds. If a business fails the Corporate Treadmill Test, it will likely not be able to maintain Positive Cash Flow without a significant change in strategy or business circumstances.

Committing capital

Many businesses unwittingly trade their way into bankruptcy, without there initially being apparent signs of extreme problems. Most businesses are extremely complicated, and the final performance of the company is a melting pot of a multitude of transactions and decisions. Very few business executives have the tools to put into perspective how their day-to-day decisions will affect the *survival* of their businesses. The Corporate Treadmill Test provides the executive with a tool to distill all of these actions into an understandable format. This process can be more easily appreciated if you think along the following lines.

Almost every business or business decision starts with a decision to commit capital to a venture. This fact may not always be immediately apparent but, at some stage of the decision process, capital must be committed. Often, the biggest problem is the manager doesn't realize he's committing capital. For example, many new ventures are financed by leasing equipment or facilities; because the manager does not have to make an immediate investment of cash, the impact of the capital committed is downplayed. Once a manager commits capital to a venture, he then has to find a source for the capital, decide how he is going to use it, and consider the other consequences that will result. Everything from then on is dependent on, and must be measured in relation to, that capital investment.

Many managers mistakenly believe a business is driven by its Profit and Loss Statement

---

"If only I can achieve my sales and profit target, everything else will take care of itself," they believe. In fact, a business is driven by its Balance Sheet; once you commit to the company's assets and liabilities, the Balance Sheet **dictates** what you need from your Profit and Loss Statement. If you manage your Balance Sheet well, you will place less demands on your Profit and Loss Statement. The makeup, size and characteristics of your assets and liabilities will establish your cash outflows, thereby determining the extent of profits needed. Not understanding this is one of the most significant causes of business failure.

In order to achieve Positive Cash Flow, a business must generate sufficient internal profitability to cover all of its required or committed expenditures, which includes at least eight components (see box on adjacent page).

Should internal profitability, defined as earnings before interest, depreciation and taxes (abbreviated to EBDIT), not

Eight cash outflows

1. Interest on all interest-bearing debt
2. Additional interest on increased lines of credit or new term loans to finance growth
3. Principal repayments for term loans
4. Additional principal repayments on new term loans to finance growth
5. Working capital requirements to fund growth in inventories, receivables, and growth or replacement of fixed assets—less the portion of such expenditures that can be financed by additional supplier credit, lines of credit or additional term loans
6. Amounts required, if any, to repay past-due debts
7. Dividend requirements on shareholder preferred or common stock
8. Taxes that will have to be paid on earnings

be enough to cover the above expenditures, the business will experience Negative Cash Flow. If such circumstances occur, the business will have two choices:

- Seek an infusion of cash—this can be done by using already available cash or lines of credit (non-interest or interest-bearing), seeking new debt facilities, or raising new equity funds. The availability, pricing, terms and conditions of such a cash infusion will depend on the financial condition of the business.

- Modify the business strategy to improve cash flow— this can be done by finding ways to increase EBDIT[2],

[2] EBDIT can be enhanced by increasing unit sales, increasing selling prices, reducing cost of sales and reducing operating expenses.

by reducing the amount of the cash expenditures or obligations[3], or by the sale or liquidation of assets.

If a business experiences continued Negative Cash Flow, and neither of these two choices are effectively implemented, the decline of the organization will commence because it will not have the funds to properly operate its business. Because of most companies' ability to *borrow from Peter to pay Paul*, businesses are often able to juggle their obligations for quite some time—and this decline does not become readily evident—sometimes for many months, often several years.

Example

Assume you decide to start a new business venture, and determine you will need $1,000,000 of capital to invest in machinery, inventory, receivables and other equipment. Assume $400,000 of this is borrowed, with $300,000 provided by shareholders equity and the remaining $300,000 being provided by supplier credit.

The assumptions for this company's balance sheet and a projected Profit and Loss Statement are on page 31.

On page 32, Figure 1 reflects a model of the Corporate Treadmill Test for this hypothetical company, reflecting the eight different types of cash outflows. It shows that, based on the projections reflected above, the business in this example fails the Corporate Treadmill Test and, therefore, will not survive in the long run unless it improves its profitability or changes

---

[3] Cash expenditures or obligations can be reduced by reducing the amount of capital that needs to be employed through better asset management (e.g., just-in-time inventories), increasing the proportion of non-interest-bearing debt to total debt (e.g., by negotiating longer payment terms with suppliers), lowering the interest rate on borrowing funds, reducing principal payments on borrowed funds, reducing future working capital and fixed asset expenditure needs (through efficiency and better planning, delayed expenditures or reduced growth rate), increasing financing available for working capital or capital expenditures, reducing taxes payable and reducing shareholder dividend requirements.

NEW BUSINESS VENTURE
EXAMPLE ASSUMPTIONS
OPENING BALANCE SHEET

Total Assets Employed		**$1,000,000**
Financed by: Accounts Payable to Suppliers		300,000
Interest-bearing Debt	- term loan	300,000
	- line of credit	100,000
		400,000
Shareholders' Equity		300,000
		$1,000,000

· To fund the company's projected growth in sales, its working capital and fixed assets are expected to grow at 25%, but will attract additional supplier credit and lender debt of 15%.

· The initial term loan is to be repaid in six annual installments of $50,000.

· An additional term loan of $30,000 will be obtained to finance growth in fixed assets, and will have to be repaid in six annual installments of $5,000.

· Shareholders require a dividend of 16.6% on their invested equity.

PROJECTED PROFIT AND LOSS STATEMENT

Sales	$4,600,000
Cost of Sales	3,450,000
Gross Margin	1,150,000
Division/Branch Operating Expenses	(750,000)
Division/Branch Contribution	400,000
Head Office/Corporate Expenses	(150,000)
Earnings before Interest, Depreciation, and Taxes (EBDIT)	250,000
Interest	(45,000)
Depreciation	(60,000)
Earnings before taxes	145,000
Income Taxes	(50,000)
Net Income	**$ 95,000**

Figure 1: CORPORATE TREADMILL TEST
EXAMPLE

		ROAM
Assets managed	[a] $1,000,000	
Projected earnings before depreciation, interest and taxes (EBDIT)	[b] $250,000	25.0%
Deduct required or committed expenditures:		
1. **Interest** cost on borrowed funds $400,000 @ 10%	40,000	
2. Additional **interest** on increased lines of credit and term loans to finance growth $100,000 @ 10% for half year	5,000	
Total interest cost	45,000	(4.5%)
3. **Principal** repayments of existing borrowed funds	50,000	
4. Additional **principal** repayments on new term loans to finance growth	5,000	
Total principal	55,000	(5.5%)
5. **Working capital and capital expenditure** needs to fund growth	250,000	
Less: Additional lender and supplier credit available	150,000	
	100,000	(10.0%)
6. Amounts required to repay **past-due debts**	0	(0.0%)
7. **Dividends** to be paid to shareholders of 16.6% on equity contribution of $300,000	50,000	(5.0%)
8. **Taxes** payable[5]	50,000	(5.0%)
Total required or committed expenditures (Target)	[c] 300,000	(30.0%)
Negative Cash Flow	[b-c] $50,000	(5.0%)

Note: The amounts in this example are hypothetical and used to demonstrate how the Corporate Treadmill Test is calculated. **In this example, the business fails the test by 5 percent and would, therefore, need to generate a Return On Assets Managed of 30 percent to pass.** In practice, the actual amounts must be calculated for every business and may differ significantly.

[5] While not applied here, taxes is a circular calculation as follows: Taxes = (total required or committed expenditures-interest-depreciation) x tax rate.

its strategy. Based on an assumed projection that the business will generate a Return On Assets Managed (ROAM[4]) of 25 percent [250,000/1,000,000], the Corporate Treadmill Test indicates that this business will operate at a negative cash flow of 5.0 percent of its assets managed. Under these circumstances, the business will not be able to continue funding its normal operations indefinitely. When this happens, the decline of the business commences, and results in a continual juggling of resources to keep operations going. This process can go on for quite some time before the corporate arteries are completely blocked and *corporate cardiac arrest* sets in. Because this process can take quite a long time, sometimes as long as five years, to become apparent, management is often lulled into believing all is well. I have heard many managers derive comfort from the fact that they have juggled their cash for several years, and it comes as a complete shock to them when corporate cardiac arrest happens. As with human health problems, the variety and effectiveness of remedial procedures for an underperforming business are significantly more extensive and attractive if the condition is detected early.

If the required or committed expenditures of the business are expected to differ significantly after the forthcoming year, the Corporate Treadmill Test should be calculated for each of those years, and the business may need to generate differing ROAMs to achieve Positive Cash Flow.

Denial

With a diagnostic test like the Corporate Treadmill Test, management denial remains a major obstacle to recovery. Even when they are aware of a life-threatening condition, many managers refuse to accept the reality of the situation and believe that the turnaround is just around the corner. Such denial must be overcome for the Treadmill Test to become a valuable tool to facilitate the restoration of business health.

[4] ROAM is calculated as: (EBDIT/(Total assets+accumulated depreciation)) x (100). To the extent the market value of assets differ significantly from their original cost, market value should be used as the denominator in the ROAM calculation.

If management were to conduct the Corporate Treadmill Test prior to committing capital for any project, it would be forced to re-evaluate the plan if it failed the test. In reality, however, the enthusiasm for the new venture often is the driving force, and a sober examination of the true viability of the venture is often brushed aside. This is another form of denial and analogous to somebody deciding to enter a marathon race without having done any training.

Opportunities for improvement

As in a medical situation, a failed Corporate Treadmill Test gives management an early warning system to identify critical success factors, and to make necessary adjustments to the plan to achieve the desired result. In the above example, management would have to restructure its strategy to at least eliminate the 5.0 percent cash deficit. There are several areas that can be worked on (see table on page 35). Aim to make a lot of small improvements in several areas.

Figure 2 is a diagrammatic presentation of the Corporate Treadmill Test. This shows the three sources of funds—equity investment from its shareholders, interest-bearing debt from outside lenders, and non-interest-bearing debt from its suppliers and other creditors. The organization then commits these funds into *Assets Managed*, which generally comprise cash, inventories, accounts receivable and fixed assets. The business then (one hopes) earns, through its operations, a *Return* on the Assets Managed, which increases the Assets Managed by the amount of the Return. Such Return is then disbursed in the form of the eight required or committed disbursements—interest and loan principle to lenders, dividends to shareholders, payments on past-due obligations to creditors, taxes to the IRS, with the remaining cash and Assets Managed reinvested into new Assets Managed to fund growth in working capital and fixed assets (including replacement of obsolete or worn-out equipment). If the Return on the Assets

Improving results of the Corporate Treadmill Test

Improve EBDIT

- Improve the operating profitability of the business by increasing sales volume or margins, or by reducing costs or expenses

Reduce assets managed

- Reduce the amount of capital employed, i.e., reduce the amount of assets needed—less inventory, smaller building, less expensive machinery, etc.
- Lower future working capital and capital expenditure needs—through reduced growth rate or improved asset management

Reduce cash disbursements/target ROAM

- Increase the proportion of non-interest-bearing debt (accounts payable) to total debt
- Lower the interest cost on borrowed funds
- Lower principal repayments on borrowed funds
- Increase financing available on working capital and capital expenditures
- Reduce taxes payable—through improved tax planning
- Lower shareholder dividend requirements

Managed is not sufficient to satisfy all required or committed disbursements, the business will incur a working capital shortage[6], and will experience severe difficulties if it can't find

---

[6] In addition, the mix of the Assets Managed generated by a business needs to be balanced correctly, to produce the right amount of cash needed to satisfy all disbursements. Working capital that can't be converted to cash could result in illiquidity.

Figure 2: CORPORATE TREADMILL TEST
Diagram

This diagram is provided to show the concept of the progression of the funds in a business, i.e., received from the sources of funds; applied to assets managed; expanded by earning a return on assets managed; disbursed back to the sources of funds or reinvested into assets managed. The diagram is not drawn to scale.

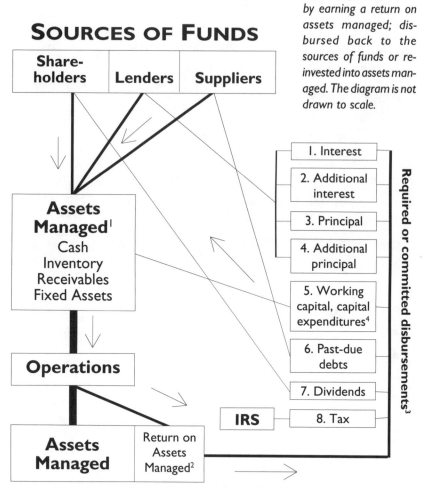

SOURCES OF FUNDS

| Share-holders | Lenders | Suppliers |

1. Interest
2. Additional interest
3. Principal
4. Additional principal
5. Working capital, capital expenditures[4]
6. Past-due debts
7. Dividends
8. Tax

Assets Managed[1]
Cash
Inventory
Receivables
Fixed Assets

Operations

IRS

Assets Managed
Return on Assets Managed[2]

Required or committed disbursements[3]

---

1 Assets Managed also includes other assets (e.g. prepaids, employee advances) and intangible assets (e.g. goodwill, covenant not to compete).
2 Return on Assets Managed is earnings before interest, depreciation and taxes (EBDIT) generated from the Assets Managed.
3 If required or committed disbursements exceed Return on Assets Managed, the business ultimately will run out of cash, i.e., fail the Corporate Treadmill Test.
4 Working capital and capital expenditures needed to fund growth are shown net of additional financing that can be generated thereon from lenders and suppliers.

new sources of funds, improve its returns, or change its business strategy to reduce disbursements.

Every business situation will result in a different Corporate Treadmill situation, and the components and dynamics of every situation must be carefully evaluated. The mix and terms of the company's Sources of Funds will have a strong impact on the result. The lower the percentage of interest-bearing debt to total assets employed, the greater the cash flow is likely to be. Debt that involves little or no principal repayments also facilitates cash flow. These two factors will significantly impact cash flow related to debt service.

The need to commit funds to working capital growth or capital expenditures also has a significant impact on cash flow. Businesses that have low requirements to reinvest their cash into working capital or capital expenditures are known as *cash cows*, because they facilitate the generation of cash rather than the consumption of cash.

In a turnaround situation, the situation is usually complicated by the need to repay often large amounts of old or past-due debts (both interest-bearing and non-interest bearing). As such, a large proportion of available cash needs to be devoted to repaying such debt. This often necessitates a Return on Assets that is even higher than would be sufficient in a non-turnaround situation.

In practice, being able to accurately quantify and predict all these items is easier said than done. However, without a diligent projection of all these factors, and an appropriate model with which to evaluate them, the chances of the venture's survival are significantly reduced. Many times, in business, your toughest issue is identifying the problem while you still have time to do something about it. Most problems are solvable, if you know about them. If you consciously and regularly apply the Corporate Treadmill Test to all your business ventures, existing and planned, you will quickly get a sense of whether you're headed in the right direction, or whether corrective action is needed.

Cash disbursements vary with type of debt

The type of debt used to leverage the business has a significant impact on cash flow. There are several types of debt, each with different cash flow consequences.

CASH FLOW CONSEQUENCES

Type of debt	Examples	Interest	Principal
Non-Interest-Bearing	Accounts Payable and Accrued Liabilities	No	No
Interest-Bearing	Revolving Line of Credit	Yes	No
	Term Loan (including leases)	Yes	Yes

Clearly, non-interest-bearing debt (that is not past-due) is the lowest-cost form of financing, and revolving lines of credit are the least cash-burdensome of the interest-bearing funds. Because of this, the type and mix of debt can have a material impact on cash flow.

Assets utilized determine type of debt, cash and shareholder equity requirements

While the above table would seem to indicate that all businesses should utilize only trade credit and revolving lines to finance their business, the type of assets utilized in the business will have a large impact on the type and extent of funding available.

With traditional asset-based financing, lenders generally lend differing percentages on the various types of assets. In addition, suppliers will usually extend credit to finance a portion of a company's inventory requirements. To the extent assets cannot be leveraged, the remaining funds predominantly need to be generated from shareholder funds, or quasi-shareholder funds, e.g., mezzanine debt.

	SOURCES (approximate % of funds available, in relation to asset cost)			
USES OF FUNDS	Accounts Payable	Revolving Line of Credit	Term Loan	Share-holder Funds
Inventory	35-60%	40-65%		-25-25%
Accounts Receivable		60-85%		15-40%
Land & Buildings			55-85%	15-45%
Machinery & Equipment			30-60%	40-70%
Other assets, start-up costs, operating losses, intangibles	0-40%			60-100%
Cash				100%

From the above two tables, it can be seen that the types of assets employed by a business will have a significant impact on 1) how much the business can be leveraged, 2) the likely cash consequences that will result from interest and principal payments, and 3) the amount of funds shareholders will have to contribute.

Businesses with term loans as the predominant source of capital will have higher cash obligations (interest and principal) than those that are financed more by supplier credit (no cash cost) and revolving lines of credit (interest only). Firms whose major asset is inventory will generally have lower shareholder equity requirements than those who have a substantial amount of accounts receivable, fixed assets or intangible assets. Because of the ability to finance inventory from two sources (i.e., suppliers and lines of credit), it is not unusual for minimal or zero shareholder funds to be required to finance inventories. All other assets will generally require some degree of shareholder funds.

Most businesses do not have much choice in the type of financing they can obtain—which is substantially determined by the use to which the funds will be put.

Examples

The predominant asset in a retail business is inventory, a high proportion of which can usually be financed by supplier credit, with a substantial portion of the remainder coming from bank revolving lines of credit. With more non-interest-bearing funds, higher asset turnover and no principal repayments, cash flow and shareholder equity needs can be lessened.

An automobile rental company's primary asset is cars, which are generally financed by term loans (or leases, which in reality is similar to a term loan). Because of the longer-term nature of these assets and principal repayments, cash flow and shareholder equity requirements are greater.

Because of the nature of their respective assets, these businesses will have significantly different cash out-flows relating to debt service and capital expenditures, and will, therefore, require differing levels of profitability (i.e. Return On Assets Managed) and shareholders' equity to ensure the maintenance of Positive Cash Flow. Failure to appreciate and react to the significance of this important reality can make the difference in the ultimate survival of a business.

Figure 3: **CORPORATE TREADMILL TEST**
INDIVIDUAL DIVISIONS OR BRANCHES

	Target EBDIT[1]	Assets[2]	Target ROAM[3]
Company Target (Fig. 1)	$300,000	$1,000,000	30%
Add/(Deduct) Head Office	150,000[4]	(100,000)[5]	
Division/Branch Target	**$450,000**	**$900,000**	**50%**

[1] Earnings before interest, depreciation and taxes.

[2] Assets are at gross original cost before accumulated depreciation.

[3] Return On Assets Managed (ROAM) = EBDIT/ASSETS. Target of 30% for overall Company was determined on Figure 1.

[4] $150,000 of head office and corporate expenses added back to arrive at Division/Branch target EBDIT of $450,000.

[5] $100,000 of head office and corporate assets (e.g., central warehouse building and inventory, corporate equipment and furniture, intangibles and other assets) deducted to arrive at Division/Branch assets.

Divisions and product lines

One of the most significant benefits of the Corporate Treadmill Test is that it allows management to evaluate the performance of individual divisions or product lines. When the Corporate Treadmill Test has determined the target Return On Assets Managed for the business as a whole, you can then work backward to determine the Return On Assets Managed required from individual divisions, branches or product lines in order to achieve the overall target.

Figure 3 sets out the calculation to determine the target Return On Assets Managed required from individual divisions or branches of the business referred to in Figure 1. In that example, in order to achieve the overall company target Return On Assets Managed of 30 percent described in the example above, individual divisions or branches should achieve an average Return On Assets Managed of 50 percent.

With this information, management would be able to evaluate all existing and prospective divisions and branches to determine if they meet or exceed the Division/Branch Target. If they do not meet the target, a determination should be made about whether there are opportunities to improve the Return On Assets Managed of the underperforming divisions or branches. Without compelling evidence to justify their retention, underperforming divisions or branches should be sold or liquidated. While, in the long run, financial considerations are very important, in the short run, non-financial factors may impact the decision to retain or divest. For example, even though a branch or a region may be underperforming, its retention may be essential to provide the appropriate level of service to customers who operate in several regions. Alternatively, an underperforming product may be retained because it helps to sell more profitable products. It is also important to ensure that your calculations only allocate to the discontinued units' overhead that will be eliminated along with the unit. If you eliminate the unit but not the overhead, you will not have achieved very much.

Figure 4 contains the calculation to determine the target performance for individual product lines. Because the only asset that can usually be specifically allocated to individual product lines is inventory, this calculation, called Gross Margin/Return On Inventory (GM/ROI), is different from Return On Assets Managed, and is calculated as follows:

$$\frac{\text{Gross Margin Dollars}}{\text{Inventory}}$$

In the example on Figure 4, individual product lines would have to achieve a GM/ROI of 300 percent for the overall company to achieve its target Return On Assets Managed of 30 percent. Again, with this information, management would be able to evaluate all existing and prospective product lines and individual products to determine if they generate enough return to facilitate achieving the overall company target.

42

Figure 5 sets out an example of how to determine whether individual product lines pass the Corporate Treadmill Test. In this example, it can be seen that the Division as a whole and two of the three product lines fail the test. However, this analysis provides management with the information needed to redirect its strategy to improve its test score. In this example, management should focus its attention on improving the

---

Figure 4: CORPORATE TREADMILL TEST
INDIVIDUAL PRODUCT LINES

Division/Branch Target EBDIT (Fig. 3)	$450,000
Add: Division/Branch Operating Expenses	750,000
Division/Branch Target Gross Margin	**$1,200,000**
Division/Branch Inventory	**$400,000**
Target Gross Margin/Return On Inventory (GM/ROI) for Individual Product Lines	**300%**

Figure 5: CORPORATE TREADMILL TEST
COMPARING INDIVIDUAL PRODUCT LINES

	Product 1	Product 2	Product 3	Division total
Sales	1,050,000	2,090,000	1,460,000	4,600,000
Cost of Sales	731,000	1,600,000	1,119,000	3,450,000
Gross Margin	319,000	490,000	341,000	1,150,000
Inventory	150,000	172,500	77,500	400,000
GM/ROI	213%	284%	440%	288%
Target GM/ROI*	300%	300%	300%	300%
Treadmill Test	**Fail**	**Fail**	**Pass**	**Fail**

* If any product lines require abnormally large required or committed expenditures (e.g. working capital growth, capital expenditures or term loan repayments) the target GM/ROI for that product line might need to be higher than the average established in Figure 4.

Gross Margin and reducing the inventories of the two product lines that failed the test.

Options for improving underperforming product lines

- Increase sales volume through improved sales, marketing or merchandising techniques
- Increase margins by raising prices, increasing operating efficiencies or reducing purchasing costs
- Reduce inventory levels through improved inventory management techniques

---

Even though Product 3 passed the test, every effort should still be devoted to improving its GM/ROI further. Should Product 1's GM/ROI not be able to be significantly improved, serious consideration should be given to its elimination, unless compelling reasons exist not to do so.

The GM/ROI calculation can be very helpful in improving overall corporate performance, because the identification of underperforming product lines gives management a tool to target product lines that need to be improved or eliminated. Armed with this information, significant improvements can almost always be achieved.

As stated earlier in this section, any divisions, branches or product lines that do not pass the Corporate Treadmill Test should be carefully examined—without compelling evidence to justify their retention, these should be sold or liquidated.

Having an accurate awareness of the real reasons for the company's downfall provides a more realistic picture of whether a turnaround is achievable, and facilitates remedial treatment that is directed at the specific major problems. The knowledge of where to focus will save a lot of time and effort, and will significantly increase the chances of saving the company. With this information, attention should be directed toward areas that can be improved in a time frame and at a cost that is compatible with the company's capabilities. Resources directed at problem areas that cannot realistically result in significant improvements within the required time frame will reduce the chances of a turnaround, and can quite likely reduce the ultimate value of the company or its remaining assets.

ACTION STEPS

> Complete a Corporate Treadmill Test analysis for your business as whole, and for individual divisions, business units and product lines

> If any areas fail the test, explore ways to change the business strategy so that it can pass the test

> If it still cannot past the test, develop a plan to sell or liquidate that area of the business—unless there are compelling reasons not to do so

> For areas of the business that pass the Corporate Treadmill Test, continue to pursue ways to improve ROAMs in those areas

> Always look for ways to reduce the target ROAM required to pass the test

> Determine if your business has enough shareholder equity to fund the type and amount of assets to which you have committed capital

Section III:

MEASURING FINANCIAL HEALTH

W hen a business is underperforming, it is important to pinpoint the specific areas that are contributing to the lack of performance. This involves a financial evaluation from several different points of view. Most businesses have divisions and products that are more profitable than others. Almost all distressed companies have significant areas that are losing money. In addition, they may have departments or cost centers that have excessive costs or are inefficient. If a business is losing money overall, it is possible that the net loss is made up of a combination of profitable and unprofitable divisions, branches, products, departments or cost centers. To identify where the profitable and unprofitable areas are, a detailed analysis of the business must be performed, including revenues, cost of sales and allocatable operating expenses by identifiable departments, business units (divisions, branches, etc.) and product lines and major individual products. A Corporate Treadmill Test analysis as described in

Section II will highlight underperforming areas of the business at a macro level. The steps outlined in this section will provide a more targeted micro analysis of the problem areas within the business.

In addition to evaluating profitability for the various areas, it is important to examine performance in relation to the assets employed in each area. It is very possible to find that an area that is profitable is using an excessive amount of the company's capital to fund its assets, such as inventory, receivables and equipment. Alternatively, a lower profit area might employ a proportionately lower amount of assets. With this information, you will be in a better position to identify turnaround strategies that could include eliminating or curtailing unprofitable or asset-intensive areas, or expanding profitable or asset-efficient areas.

The concept of Financial Health is extensive, and requires an examination of a business from several financial vantage points. There is no one formula or conclusion that will result in a simple answer. Just as when you go to your doctor for your annual physical, there are many areas that need to be examined, probed and tested, and your observations and judgments of all of these factors taken together will indicate whether your patient is financially healthy. This Financial Health review should be done regularly for all businesses, whether they have been through a turnaround or not.

Major components of financial health

1. Profitability
2. Asset efficiency
3. Financial efficiency
4. Product and department efficiency
5. Future capital needs
6. Corporate Treadmill Test

Profitability

Profitability is made up of several components. Analysis and understanding of these components will provide valuable tools for how to make a business healthier.

The major components of profit are:

- Sales (or revenues)
- Cost of sales
- Gross margin
- Operating expenses
- Interest
- Taxes

When comparing the profitability of one business against another, or assessing how to improve the profitability of a business, you need to look closely at all of these components of profit.

If you were to compare two competing businesses, Company B's sales might be higher than those of Company A, but its profits might be lower. This could be because A's cost of sales, operating expenses, interest or taxes might be lower than B's. If this were the case, you would need to analyze and identify the exact cause(s) for the lower costs and search for ways to lower B's cost structure or taxes. A's management, on the other hand, might be trying to ascertain why B's sales level is higher, and what A can do to increase its sales.

Without an analysis of the detailed components of profits, many wrong assumptions or conclusions can be made. For example, you might assume that Company A is worth more than Company B because its profits are higher. If, however, further investigation indicates that B's profits were reduced because of a strike at one of its supplier's plants, which forced B to temporarily order its materials from another and more expensive supplier—you may find that when a normal supply situation returns, B's profits might exceed A's.

48

Another critical element of profitability is non-cash items that are included in the profit determination. The most common non-cash item is depreciation, which reduces a company's profits but does not reduce its cash resources. A company with significant depreciation might appear less profitable, but might in fact be producing more cash. A company that has invested large amounts into state-of-the-art machinery might reflect lower profits (due to higher depreciation) than its competitor with older and fully depreciated equipment—but its actual business might be much stronger due to higher cash flow and newer and more efficient equipment.

Interest and taxes are also very important and significant components of profitability—and their impact must be evaluated to truly understand profitability. Every company has differing costs of capital in the form of interest rates on borrowed money. One company might have borrowed at fixed rates of 11 percent, and another at floating prime rates plus 2 percent. The resulting costs will be very different, depending on what the prime rates are, or are expected to be in the future. With regard to taxes, all companies have different tax structures. One company might have a tax loss that it can carry forward to set-off against future profits. Another company might be paying full tax rates. The impact of a company's tax situation must be studied and factored into any assessment of profitability, or value.

Figure 6[7] sets out historical Income Statements for two fictional Companies, A and B, showing the components of Net Profit discussed above (see figure 11 on page 66 for projected

[7] Assumptions for A and B, respectfully, are: Interest rates - 8%, 10%; Line of credit advances-accounts receivables, year one 70%, 75%, year two 70%, 70% -inventory, year one 40%, 45%, year two 40%, 40%; Term loan advance rates-land and buildings, year one 0%, 65%, year two 0%, 65% -machinery and equipment, year one 40%, 70%, year two 40%, 70%; Term loan amortization rate-land and buildings, 15 years, 18 years -machinery and equipment, 5 years, 8 years; Days cost of sales in accounts payable - 75, 35; Days sales in account receivables - 80, 45; Inventory turnover - 3x, 6x; Tax rate - year one 35%, 37%, year two 38%, 37%; Depreciation -land and buildings 20 years, 15 years, -machinery and equipment 7 years, 8 years; Dividend rate - 15%, 8%; Sales growth rate - 5%, 25%,

Figure 6: INCOME STATEMENTS

	Company A		Company B	
Sales	$9,978,675	100.0%	$12,234,555	100.0%
Cost of Sales	7,345,899	72.6%	9,396,138	76.8%
Gross Margin	2,632,776	26.4%	2,838,417	23.2%
Expenses				
Rent	0	0.0%	269,160	2.2%
Depreciation	571,429	5.7%	243,750	2.0%
SG & A	888,102	8.9%	819,715	6.7%
Labor	518,891	5.2%	709,604	5.8%
Other	99,787	1.0%	244,691	2.0%
	2,078,208	20.8%	2,286,921	18.7%
Net income before				
interest and taxes	554,568	5.6%	551,496	4.5%
Interest	(295,234)	-3.0%	(352,109)	-2.9%
	259,333	2.6%	199,387	1.6%
Taxes	90,767	0.9%	73,773	0.6%
Net income after				
interest and taxes	**$168,567**	**1.7%**	**$125,614**	**1.0%**

Income Statements for the forthcoming year). From these statements, it can be clearly seen how many components affect profitability, and therefore how important it is to understand the reasons and dynamics of every component. Answers you might look for include why their gross margin percentages differ, why A's operating expenses are 20.8 percent of sales vs. B's 18.7 percent, why B's labor cost is 5.8 percent vs. A's 5.2 percent, why A's tax rate is so much lower, etc.

Asset efficiency

When examining asset efficiency, you are assessing how well the business uses its assets financially. That is, the measurement of the amount of profit a business produces in relation to the assets employed in the business[8].

[8] This analysis is a macro-analysis, and should be done in conjunction with, or in addition to, the individual asset efficiency ratios of inventory turnover, days sales in receivables, liquidity ratios, etc.

> This takes the analysis from a one-dimensional to a two-dimensional concept

Not only should you be concerned with profits, you should now be interested in the amount of assets (and ultimately, capital) used to earn the profits. The key tool to measure asset efficiency is the previously mentioned ratio known as Return On Assets Managed (ROAM), described in Part 1: Section II and calculated as follows:

$$\frac{\text{Net profit before Depreciation, Interest \& Taxes (EBDIT)}}{\text{Total Assets, before Accumulated Depreciation}} \times 100$$

Both the numerator and denominator in this calculation are calculated without the impact of depreciation. This is because depreciation is a non-cash book entry that can distort the calculation. Without this adjustment, businesses with substantially depreciated equipment may generate a mis-leadingly high ROAM.

ROAM CALCULATION

	A	B
Projected Net Profit		
Before Interest and Taxes (Fig. 11)	828,077	$803,807
Add: Depreciation	600,714	296,875
Earnings Before Depreciation, Interest and Taxes (EBDIT) [x]	**$1,428,791**	**$1,100,682**
Total Assets (Fig.7)	7,554,746	5,182,187
Add: Accumulated Depreciation	3,500,000	850,000
Gross Assets [y]	**$11,054,746**	**$6,032,187**
ROAM [x/y x 100]	12.9%	18.2%

51

The ROAM calculation on page 51 shows that B's projected performance is expected to be significantly superior to A's. Even though A's Net Profit Before Interest and Taxes is higher, B's ROAM is still higher because B's assets employed are so much lower than A's. This highlights the importance of both dimensions of business performance, i.e., profits in relation to assets employed.

When managers become aware of how important this two-dimensional measure of performance really is, they begin to evaluate business decisions differently. For example, assume two competing companies both plan to pursue a new product line: The first company builds a plant to manufacture the product; the other arranges for a subcontractor to manufacture the product, at a higher cost than its competitor's cost of manufacture. Applying traditional analysis, one might conclude that first company will have a competitive advantage. However, if you consider the assets employed by both companies, it is very likely that the second company, even with its lower profit margins, might generate a higher return on assets. It is for this important reason that managers must think in two dimensions.

Two components of ROAM

Profitability x Asset Turnover = ROAM

or

$$\frac{EBDIT}{Sales} \quad x \quad \frac{Sales}{Gross\ Assets} \quad = \quad \frac{EBDIT}{Gross\ Assets}$$

The ROAM calculation, itself, is also two dimensional, i.e., there are two different and very significant components of the calculation. The first calculation (EBDIT/Sales) is a profitability measurement that determines the profitability of the

Figure 7
BALANCE SHEETS

	Company A	Company B
Current Assets:		
Cash	$469,006	$1,007,794
Accounts Receivable	2,187,107	1,508,370
Inventories	2,448,633	1,566,023
	5,104,746	4,082,187
Fixed Assets:		
Land & Buildings	3,000,000	0
Machinery & Equipment	2,950,000	1,950,000
	5,950,000	1,950,000
Accumulated Depreciation	(3,500,000)	(850,000)
	2,450,000	1,100,000
Total Assets	**$7,554,746**	**$5,182,187**
Current Liabilities:		
Accounts Payable	$1,509,431	$901,000
Accrued Expenses	301,886	180,200
	1,811,318	1,081,199
Interest-Bearing Debt		
Line of Credit	2,510,428	1,835,988
Term Loan	1,180,000	1,365,000
	3,690,428	3,200,988
Shareholders' Equity:		
Capital Stock	1,000,000	500,000
Retained Earnings	1,053,000	400,000
	2,053,000	900,000
Total Liabilities & Equity	**$7,554,746**	**$5,182,187**

business as a percentage of sales. The second calculation (Sales/Gross Assets) is an asset management measurement that determines the business' asset turnover in relation to sales.

When comparing the ROAMs of two businesses or product lines within the same business, the comparison of these two calculations can provide additional insights, as can be seen by performing this analysis on companies A and B.

Profitability	x	Asset Turnover	=	ROAM
A. $\dfrac{1,428,791}{10,477,609}$	x	$\dfrac{10,477,609}{11,054,746}$	=	12.9%
or 13.6%	x	.95	=	12.9%
B. $\dfrac{1,100.682}{15,293,194}$	x	$\dfrac{15,293,194}{6,032,187}$	=	18.2%
or 7.2%	x	2.54	=	18.2%

It can be seen that A's projected Profitability measurement is significantly higher than B's (13.6 percent vs. 7.2 percent). However, B is projecting to more than make up for the reduced profitability with Asset Turnover (2.54 vs. .95 times), resulting in the overall higher ROAM. This analysis indicates

---

Example: Importance of components of ROAM

A retail client who carried two major product categories informed me that Category A generated low gross margins and was their loss-leader to generate volume for Category B. When we calculated the GM/ROI for both categories, the client was surprised to discover that Category A scored better because its inventory turnover was substantially higher than B's. With this information, the client realized that A was a money-maker—for which a loss-leader strategy no longer was appropriate.

that A should be focusing on improving Asset Turnover and B on Profitability.

Understanding the significance of these two components of ROAM is extremely important to the performance of a business. Two businesses could generate identical ROAMs for very different reasons. This analysis is especially important when comparing the performance of different product lines[9].

Financial efficiency

So far we have measured and evaluated profitability in relation to the assets employed. We now evaluate the impact of financing techniques on the ultimate return to shareholders. Is it better for the Assets Managed to be financed by shareholder funds or by outside interest-bearing debt?

In general, there are three broad sources of financing for a business:

1. Non-interest-bearing debt (accounts payable, accruals, etc.)

2. Interest-bearing debt (bank loans, etc., including leases)

3. Shareholders' equity

Every business has differing proportions of these three components. Obviously, the more non-interest-bearing debt, the higher the return to shareholders. This is true as long as non-interest-bearing debt is not carried to an extreme, where suppliers are stretched to the point where they become reluctant to do business with the company, or they raise prices to compensate for payment terms beyond their normal terms. The proportion and amounts of these three sources of funds are largely dependent on the type of business and its assets. (See Part 1: Section II, for a discussion of how this impacts a business, its capital structure, and its cash flow.)

---

[9] As indicated in Part 2: Section II, GM/ROI rather than ROAM is used to compare product lines. The concept is similar except the numerator is gross profit (rather than EBDIT), and the denominator is inventory (rather than gross assets).

Figure 8 sets out in graphical format the components of the balance sheets of A and B. This demonstrates the different proportions of the three sources of funds: Both companies are making use of similar proportions of non-interest-bearing funds (24 percent to 22 percent); however, B is utilizing a significantly higher percentage of debt (64 percent vs. 49 percent). This means B is a more highly leveraged Company than A.

The proportions of these three sources of funds can have a significant impact on the Return On Shareholders' Equity (ROE), which is considered by many analysts to be an

Calculating ROE

$$\frac{\text{Net Income After Taxes (NIAT)}^*}{\text{Shareholders' Equity}}$$

Components of ROE

Net Return on Assets	x	Leverage		
$\dfrac{\text{NIAT}}{\text{Total Assets}}$	x	$\dfrac{\text{Total Assets}}{\text{Shareholders' Equity}}$		
A.	$\dfrac{333,038}{7,554,746}$	x	$\dfrac{7,544,746}{2,053,000}$	=	16.22%
	4.41%		3.7		
B.	$\dfrac{271,349}{5,182,187}$	x	$\dfrac{5,182,187}{900,000}$	=	30.15%
	5.24%		5.8		

* NIAT is calculated from projected EBDIT, Depreciation, Interest and Taxes as follows: NIAT = (EBDIT - Depn - Interest) x (I - Tax Rate)

Figure 8

FUNDING SOURCES

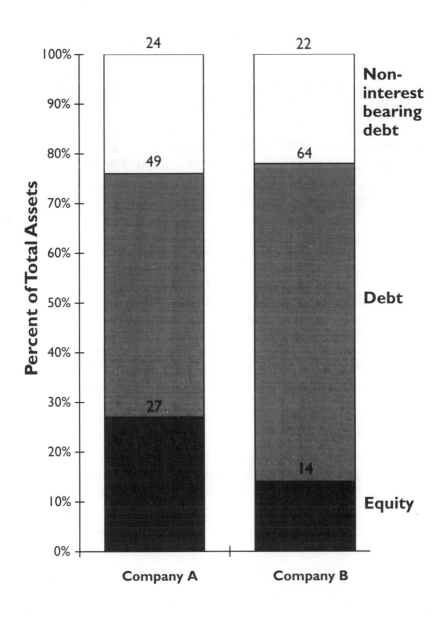

important measure of a business' ability to create value for its shareholders.

The Components of ROE demonstrate the power of leverage: Even though both companies are projecting similar profitability (4.41 percent vs. 5.24 percent), B's significantly higher leverage factor (5.8 vs. 3.7) results in an ROE of almost two times A (30.15 percent vs. 16.22 percent). Without taking into account the risks of leverage, provided a company's ROAM exceeds the cost of its interest-bearing debt, the return on its shareholders' equity (ROE) will be enhanced by an increase in assets financed by debt. To demonstrate an extreme example, a business that has shareholders' equity of $1,000, and debt of $999,000 bearing interest at 10 percent, will generate an ROE of more than 600 percent if the company's ROAM is 11 percent[10].

Impact of extreme leverage

Assets Managed	**$1,000,000**
ROAM @ 11%	110,000
Less: Interest of $999,000 @ 10%	(99,900)
Net Income Before Taxes	10,100
Taxes @ 40%	4,040
Net Income After Taxes	**$6,060** (a)
Shareholders' Equity	**$1,000** (b)
Return on Shareholders' Equity	**606%** [a/b x 100]

In practice, almost infinite leverage of this extreme is highly unlikely, due to lenders' desires to see a more balanced scale of debt and equity. However, the concept of infinite leverage fueled the Leveraged Buyout (LBO) era of the 1980s, whereby entrepreneurs could buy businesses with as little as 10 percent of the total capital needs in the form of shareholder equity. As long as the acquired company's ROAM exceeded the cost of

---

[10] Without taking depreciation or other non-cash charges into account.

funds (generally provided by high-yield or *junk* bonds), the entrepreneur made money. A key ingredient of many LBOs was the acquirer's intention to sell off assets, which would have the effect of reducing assets managed—thus making it easier by reducing the denominator in the calculation, to achieve an acceptable ROAM. Most LBOs failed either because the businesses could not earn enough ROAM to service their costs of funds and other cash outflows, or because the assets managed could not be reduced as planned.

Lenders in the 1990s are now requiring substantially higher percentages of shareholder funds to total capital. This is having the impact of reducing purchase prices for businesses, because acquirers can not afford to pay the lofty prices of the 1980s—and still earn comparable returns on their funds, without a corresponding reduction in total capital (and debt).

Another secondary reason for the attractiveness of debt as a financing source in the United States stems from the fact that interest payments are tax deductible, and dividends are not, which results in double taxation for distributions to corporate shareholders (except for S Corporations, which offer significant tax advantages—but also require specific criteria for qualification).

Product and departmental efficiency

So far, you have examined the business from a *macro* point of view. Before you can finalize the financial assessment of the business, you need to examine its profits, and asset efficiency for all departments, and product lines. From this you will learn where the business truly earns and loses its money, and you should then be able to make informed decisions about which areas of the business to promote, and which areas to eliminate.

Using Company A in the example above, we need to examine A's financial data from two additional points of view. Firstly, we need to analyze the data by branch, department and cost center. To do this effectively, we have to develop methods for allocating overheads and cost centers to productive departments. Thereafter, we need to analyze the data by product line for the company as a whole, and then to the extent possible, we need to analyze the data by product line for each productive branch or department.

Figure 9 sets out the historical Profit and Loss by Branch for Company A. This statement gives us a lot of important information as follows:

- While the Company as a whole is earning an average Gross Margin of 26 percent (Line 3), Branch 1 (30 percent), Branch 3 (28 percent) and Branch 4 (34 percent) are earning above the average margin, while Branch 2 (19 percent) is significantly below the average margin. This would necessitate an investigation into the difference in margins. For example, if the branches operate in different cities, you may find that margins vary widely between cities. The mix of products, and their related margins would be relevant too (this will be identified from the Profit and Loss by Product Statement).

- Branch operating expenses (Line 10) are all reasonably consistent between 13 percent and 15 percent—except for Branch 3 (28 percent), which might be primarily due to its lower sales level.

- All branches (except Branch 3) are contributing profit before Corporate Allocations (Line 11). However, Branch 1 (18 percent) and Branch 4 (19 percent) are generating very healthy percentage contributions, while Branch 2 is marginally contributing (6 percent).

- The concept of allocating Corporate costs to productive branches is a much debated issue. For accounting purposes, it is sometimes considered important that an appropriate amount of overhead

Figure 9: COMPANY A PROFIT AND LOSS BY BRANCH

Line		Total		Branch I		Branch 2		Branch 3		Branch 4		Corp.	Plant[1]
I	Sales	$9,978,675	100%	$1,998,765	100%	$3,501,235	100%	$1,202,444	100%	$3,276,231	100%	$0	
2	Cost of Sales	$7,345,899	74%	1,391,098	70%	2,839,008	81%	867,990	72%	2,147,803	66%	0	
3	Gross Margin	$2,632,776	26%	607,667	30%	662,227	19%	334,454	28%	1,128,428	34%	0	
4	Operating Expenses:												
5	Accommodation	0		0		0		0		0		0	
6	Depreciation	$571,429		64,578		144,567		83,345		$236,496		42,443	
7	SG & A	$888,102		80,566		132,098		161,009		$169,441		344,988	
8	Labor	$518,891		101,223		161,008		82,338		$71,968		102,354	
9	Other	$99,787		5,008		25,665		9,987		$29,129		29,998	
10		$2,078,208	21%	251,375	13%	463,338	13%	336,679	28%	507,033	15%	519,783	
11	Contribution	$554,568	6%	356,292	18%	198,889	6%	(2,225)	-0%	621,395	19%	(519,783)	
12	Corporate Allocation[2]			(66,395)		(124,022)		(37,685)		(171,898)		400,000	
13	Net profit before interest and taxes	554,568		289,897		74,867		(39,910)		449,496		(119,783)	
14	Interest[2]	($295,234)		(44,294)		(82,739)		(25,141)		(114,679)		(28,381)	
15	Net profit before tax	$259,333		245,603		(7,872)		(65,051)		334,817		(148,164)	
16	Assets Managed (Figure 10)	11,054,746		1,438,772		2,687,544		816,632		3,725,029		921,884	1,464,884
17	ROAM[3]	10.2%		29%		13%		10%		23%		-52%	

[1] No revenues reflected for the Plant as it transfers all of its production to the Branches, which transact the sales. No costs reflected for the Plant as the Plant fully recovers its costs in the cost of sales it transfers to Branches. The Plant does have assets managed.

[2] Interest and Corporate Allocation allocated to Branches based on proportion of assets managed.

[3] [(Line 11 + Line 6)/Line 16] × 100

61

expenses incurred in maintaining the Corporate office be allocated to the branches. If this is not done, the branches (and management) can get a distorted view of true branch profitability. The challenge is to decide how much to charge to the branches, and on what basis of allocation.

On line 10, you will notice that total Corporate costs are $519,783. However, on Line 12, you will see that only $400,000 has been allocated to the branches. This is based on the philosophy that branches should only be charged with the amount of Corporate cost that would be saved if that branch were eliminated. If you have four branches and you close one down, there are many Corporate overheads that will not be proportionately reduced, such as the CEO's salary. Many accountants allocate all Corporate costs to productive branches. I prefer to only charge the branches the portion of Corporate costs that would be saved without that branch. This is because if you charge branches a pro-rata share all of the Corporate costs, Branch Managers will not be able to relate those charges to the benefit or impact on their branch, and the desired objective of making the Branch Manager aware of, and accountable for, all costs of running his branch will be lost.

Once you have determined the total amount of Corporate costs that you intend to allocate to the branches[11], you need to formulate a method for allocating that amount to the individual branches. The most commonly used method is to base the allocation on the relative amount of sales for each branch. However, this could be construed to be an

---

[11] In addition to allocating an appropriate amount of corporate costs to the branches, in practice a full analysis and breakdown of corporate costs must be done by department. Then, the costs of departments that support other departments must be allocated accordingly to those departments. This analysis has not been done for purposes of this illustrative example.

unfair system as it penalizes a branch for growing its sales. It is preferable to allocate Corporate costs based on the relative amounts of Assets Managed. This encourages Branch Managers to be more *asset efficient*. The allocations on Line 12 of Figure 9 have been done on the basis of Assets Managed for the four branches. Interest (Line 14) has also been allocated on this basis.

Note that, while allocating corporate overheads to operating divisions may be necessary for accounting purposes, this practice does not facilitate, and often can hinder, the evaluation of division performance from an operating point of view. Managers should be evaluated on factors under their control, and a manager is in no position to impact an expense incurred by the corporate office. For this reason, Return On Assets Managed (ROAM), which is based on *division contribution* (Line 11), is a more effective criteria on which to measure divisional operating performance. The actual ROAMs for each division can then be compared to the target ROAMs determined by a Corporate Treadmill Test analysis (See later in this section and Part 1: Section II) to measure branch performance in relation to company goals.

- When you look at Net Profit Before Interest and Tax (Line 15), you will find that only two of the four branches are now in the black. Branch 2, while it was contributing $74,867 before the Corporate allocation, is in fact losing $7,872 after the corporate and interest allocation.

- Finally, you should examine how well the branches are performing in relation to the assets employed or managed in each branch, i.e., ROAM (See Figure 9 for calculation).

While Branch 4 is producing more net profit ($334,817) than Branch 1 ($245,603), Branch 1 is generating a significantly better ROAM (29 percent vs. 23 percent). This is because Branch 1 has been able to produce nearly two-thirds as much profit as Branch 4, with just over one-third of the Assets Managed.

- Branches 2 and 3 also reveal some illuminating data. While Branch 2 is way ahead on Contribution, because of its significantly higher Assets Managed, its ROAM is almost comparable to Branch 3.

With this information, important management decisions can be made to improve the business. The viability of Branches 2 and 3 should clearly be questioned. Investigations should be made to identify why Branch 2's Gross Margin is so much lower than the other branches, whether Branch Expenses for Branch 3 can be reduced, whether Assets Managed can be reduced and whether sales can be increased. In the case of Branch 4, the focus should be on why its Assets Managed are so much higher than the other branches, and whether they can be reduced. If ways can be found to improve some or all of these areas, the overall performance of the business will improve significantly.

But, before the viability of the business can be established, and that of its individual branches, you need to examine its profitability by product line for each branch, and for the company as a whole. This analysis will highlight the profitability of each product line (and even each individual product), especially in relation to the assets employed (mainly inventory) in each product line. Product lines that are not earning adequate returns on assets employed should be seriously re-evaluated. See Part 1: Section II, including Figure 5 for an example of the profitability by product line analysis.

Future capital needs

Before finalizing a review of a business, there is one more window to peer through. This analysis is the most overlooked

Figure 10
COMPANY A
ASSETS MANAGED

	Total	Branch 1	Branch 2	Branch 3	Branch 4	Corp.	Plant
Cash	469,006					469,006	0
Accounts Receivable	2,187,107	360,873	688,939	196,840	940,456	0	0
Inventories	2,448,633	314,263	582,696	180,701	811,846	0	559,126
Fixed Assets (Net)	2,450,000	314,439	583,021	180,802	812,299	186,480	372,959
	7,554,746	989,574	1,854,656	558,343	2,564,602	655,485	932,085
Add: Accumulated Depreciation¹	3,500,000	449,198	832,888	258,289	1,160,428	266,399	532,799
Assets Managed	**$11,054,746**	**$1,438,772**	**$2,687,544**	**$816,632**	**$3,725,029**	**$921,884**	**$1,464,884**

¹ Accumulated depreciation is added back to avoid accounting (non-cash) items distorting the calculation. If this is not done, business units with older (and more depreciated) assets could misleadingly appear to be more productive than ones with newer assets.

Figure 11:
FORECASTED INCOME STATEMENT
FOR THE NEXT 12 MONTHS

	Company A	Company B
Sales	$10,477,609	$15,293,194
Cost of Sales	(7,492,643)	(11,874,370)
Gross Margin	2,984,966	3,418,824
Expenses:		
Rent	0	296,076
Depreciation	600,714	296,875
SG & A	914,745	963,165
Labor	539,647	780,565
Other	101,782	278,336
	2,156,889	2,615,017
Net profit before interest & taxes	828,077	803,807
Interest	(290,919)	(373,094)
	537,158	430,713
Taxes	(204,120)	(159,364)
Net profit after interest & taxes	**$333,038**	**$271,349**

and probably the most important area of a business to examine. Not only do you need to know how profitable a business is, or how profitable it is in relation to assets employed, it is vital to know how much capital it is going to need in the future—and whether future profits will be sufficient to generate an acceptable return on existing and future capital. To do this, we must forecast the Income Statement and Balance Sheet into the future, and examine the changes that will take place.

Figure 11 sets out the forecasted Income Statements for A and B for the next 12 months, while Figure 12 and Figure 13 set out for A and B, respectively, their projected Balance Sheets in one year from the current time, and the relative changes from the current Balance Sheet. From these statements, you can

Figure 12:
COMPANY A
BALANCE SHEET

	Now	One year later	Change
Cash	$469,006	$164,836	$304,169
Accounts Receivable	2,187,107	2,296,462	(109,355)
Inventories	2,448,633	2,497,548	(48,915)
	5,104,746	4,958,846	
Fixed Assets:			
Land & Building	3,000,000	3,300,000	(300,000)
Machinery & Equipment	2,950,000	3,050,000	(100,000)
	5,950,000	6,350,000	
Accumulated Depreciation	(3,500,000)	(4,100,714)	600,714
	2,450,000	2,249,286	
Total Assets	**$7,554,746**	**$7,208,132**	
Current Liabilities:			
Accounts Payable	$1,509,431	$1,289,584	(219,847)
Accrued Expenses	301,886	257,917	(43,969)
	1,811,318	1,547,501	
Interest-Bearing Debt			
Line of Credit	2,510,428	2,606,543	96,115
Term Loan	1,180,000	976,000	(204,000)
	3,690,428	3,582,543	0
Shareholders' Equity:			
Capital Stock	1,000,000	1,000,000	0
Retained Earnings	1,053,000	1,078,088	25,088
	2,053,000	2,078,088	
Total Liabilities & Equity	**$7,554,746**	**$7,208,132**	

determine A and B's Statements of Changes in Cash Position, which are set out in Figure 14.

With this information, you can begin to get a complete picture of the two companies' Financial Health. It can be seen from the projected Income Statements, Balance Sheets and Statements of Changes in Cash Position, that A's cash is

Figure 13
COMPANY B
BALANCE SHEET

	Now	One year later	Change
Cash	$1.007,794	$1,011,202	($3,407)
Accounts Receivable	1,508,370	1,885,462	(377,092)
Inventories	1,566,023	1,979,062	(413,039)
	4,082,187	4,875,725	
Fixed Assets:			
Land & Building	0	0	0
Machinery & Equipment	1,950,000	2,375,000	(425,000)
	1,950,000	2,375,000	
Accumulated Depreciation	(850,000)	(1,146,875)	296,875
	1,100,000	1,228,125	
Total Assets	**$5,182,187**	**$6,103,850**	
Current Liabilities:			
Accounts Payable	$901,000	$1,138,638	237,639
Accrued Expenses	180,200	227,728	47,528
	1,081,199	1,366,366	
Interest-Bearing Debt			
Line of Credit	1,835,988	2,111,448	275,461
Term Loan	1,365,000	1,454,688	89,688
	3,200,988	3,566,136	
Shareholders' Equity:			
Capital Stock	500,000	500,000	0
Retained Earnings	400,000	671,349	271,349
	900.000	1,171,349	
Total Liabilities & Equity	**$5,182,187**	**$6,103,850**	

projected to decrease by $304,169, whereas B reflects an increase of $3,407.

- While both companies are profitable, A's higher non-cash depreciation results in A's Cash From Operations being substantially higher.

68

Figure 14
STATEMENT OF CHANGES IN CASH POSITION

	Company A	Company B
Net Income after Tax	$333,038	$271,349
Add: Non-cash charges		
Depreciation	600,714	296,875
Cash from Operations	933,753	568,224
Invested in:		
Accounts Receivable	(109,355)	(377,092)
Inventories	(48,915)	(413,039)
Land & Building	(300,000)	0
Machinery & Equipment	(100,000)	(425,000)
	(558,270)	(1,215,131)
Cash After Investing Activities	375,483	(646,907)
Financing Activities:		
Incr./(Redn.) in Accounts Payables	(219,847)	237,639
Incr./(Redn.) in Accrued Expenses	(43,969)	47,528
Incr./(Redn.) in Line of Credit	96,115	275,461
Incr./(Redn.) in Term Loan	(204,000)	89,688
	(371,702)	650,314
Dividends:	(307,950)	0
Resulting in Increase/		
(Decrease) in Cash	**(304,169)**	**3,407**

- B is planning to invest substantially more working capital into accounts receivable, inventories and fixed assets.

- However, B is expected to receive more outside financing than A.

- Because A's accounts payable are already severely stretched out (75 days of cost of sales in accounts payable), A is projecting a reduction in funding available from suppliers, i.e. a significant portion of the past-due debt must be repaid.

Figure 15
CORPORATE TREADMILL TEST

	A	B
Gross Assets Managed [a]	11,054,746	6,032,187
1. Interest - base assets	295,234	352,109
2. Interest on increased lines of credit		
& term loans to finance growth	(4,315)	20,986
Total interest cost	290,919	373,094
3. Principal - existing term loans	236,000	170,625
4. Additional principal on new term loans		
to finance growth	8,000	37,188
Total principal	244,000	207,813
5. Working capital/capital expenditure growth		
-Accounts receivable	109,355	377,092
-Inventory	48,915	413,039
-Land & Buildings	300,000	0
-Machinery & equipment	100,000	425,000
	558,270	1,215,131
Less: Additional credit		
-Accounts payable	(30,153)	(237,639)
-Accrued expenses	43,969	(47,528)
-Line of credit	(96,115)	(275,461)
-Term loan	(40,000)	(297,500)
	435,972	357,004
6. Amounts required to repay past due debts	250,000	0
7. Dividends	307,950	0
8. Taxes[1]	390,547	157,363
Total expenditures [b]	1,919,387	1,095,273
Target ROAM [b/a] x 100	17.36%	18.16%
Actual ROAM	12.92%	18.25%
(Shortfall)/Surplus	-4.44%	0.09%

[1] Taxes is a circular calculation and =
    (Total expenditures - depreciation - interest) x tax rate

70

Corporate Treadmill Test

With all of the above information, you will be able to perform a Corporate Treadmill Test analysis, to determine 1) how much profit the business must generate in order to achieve Positive Cash Flow, and 2) the ROAM that must be generated by individual divisions (and product lines) to achieve the overall company objective.

The Corporate Treadmill Test reflected in Figure 15 indicates that A is projected to fail the test (by 4.44 percent) and B is projected to pass (by .09 percent). Faced with this information, Company A should revisit all the eight components of The Corporate Treadmill Test to determine whether any of the required or committed expenditures can be reduced, so that the company can pass the test. Without this information, Company A might erroneously conclude that all is well. If it does not adjust its strategy to pass The Corporate Treadmill Test, Company A will begin the journey to corporate cardiac arrest.

In order for Company A to achieve its target ROAM of 17.4 percent, Figure 16 indicates that its branches must achieve ROAMs of at least 28.1 percent. A review of Figure 9 indicates that only Branch 1 (29 percent) meets or exceeds this target. In order to improve the performance of the company as a whole, the ROAMs of Branches 2 (13 percent), 3 (10 percent) and 4 (23 percent) should be major areas of management focus.

Figure 16
COMPANY A
Branch ROAM Target

	EBDIT	Gross Assets	ROAM
Company ROAM target (Fig 15)	1,919,387	11,054,746	17.4%
Corporate/plant	519,783	(2,386,768)	
Branch ROAM target	**2,439,170**	**8,667,977**	**28.1%**

Having completed the analyses of future capital needs and the Corporate Treadmill Test, you should have now developed the knowledge required to truly evaluate the *Financial Health* of your corporate patient. This starts with an examination of the Profit and Loss Statement; relates the profits to the assets employed to earn those profits—and the related efficiency of those assets; evaluates how well the company uses its financial assets; then looks at the specific areas where the company earned its profits; and finally, examines capital and profitability needs for the future.

This may have seemed a very lengthy and laborious exercise. In real life, if done properly, it is usually far more extensive and very time consuming, and you are often faced with the practical problems of getting all the information you need, in an accurate and reliable format.

Regardless of the length and complexity of the exercise, however, you cannot truly evaluate the Financial Health of a business without going through an exercise very similar to the one laid out above. Every analyst will have different methods or techniques that he favors, but the basic approach should be very similar. The process is not exact, and there is no established formula or checklist for analyzing a business. Furthermore, the comparative analysis of a business also depends on many other factors that are non-financial in nature.

In practice, you should always look at a minimum of five years historic information, and compare it to five years of projected information. This ten-year period should be looked at critically, to identify inaccuracies or inconsistencies in every line item. When you look at ten years of numbers alongside each other, inconsistencies or trends will clearly become evident. These must be investigated and explained.

With all of this information at your disposal, you will be in a strong position to make the optimum decisions about the viability and future of all of the respective branches, divisions, product lines and other segments of the business.

ACTION STEPS

> Understand all the components of the financial health of your business

> Always explore ways to improve each component of financial health

> Measure, and look for ways to improve, asset efficiency in every area of the business

> Analyze the impact leverage (debt) is having on your shareholders' Return on Equity (ROE)

> Evaluate whether the business can fund its growth plans....

Part two

How to Make
a Business Succeed

Phase I

VITAL SIGNS

A. INTRODUCTION

From the analysis described in Part 1, a detailed understanding of why the business is underperforming should have been established. In addition, the Corporate Treadmill Test will have determined how much profit the business needs to generate in order to achieve Positive Cash Flow. Lastly, the Financial Health review should reveal the financial performance of the individual components of the business.

With all of this information, the Chief Executive of an underperforming company should have a comprehensive analysis of where his problems lie, and he will probably already be thinking about some remedial strategies. However, before the detailed turnaround strategies can be developed, additional diagnostic information must be obtained. This information will help to highlight the company's strengths and weaknesses, and the extent and severity of its problems. Without this information, it is difficult to commence a turnaround program with confidence.

The initial stages of a turnaround are very important; it is generally a time when the atmosphere between all interested parties is extremely tense. For this reason, it is especially important for management to demonstrate that there is a workable plan to return the business to health. However, without carrying out a detailed diagnostic assessment, management might not have the information necessary to develop a realistic turnaround plan—and runs the risk of losing the confidence and support of its lenders, creditors and other interested parties. There is also a danger that incorrect or inappropriate remedial strategies might be implemented.

Example

In the early stages of a recent engagement my firm was involved in, an attractive offer to sell a product line was received and accepted. At the time, the product line was not considered to be important to the company's future. For several reasons, the sale fell through. However, during the sale negotiations, the company discovered that the division being sold was more profitable than previously believed, and the future prospects for its remaining businesses were less attractive than originally thought. With the benefit of a subsequent diagnostic review, the company realized that the sale of that product line had not been the best strategy available.

The analyses outlined in this chapter will provide a comprehensive foundation of information and knowledge on which a turnaround and workout plan can be developed.

B. Cash projection

Many underperforming businesses are faced with an acute (actual or projected) shortage of cash, resulting in the company's inability to meet its obligations. At all stages in a business' life, having enough cash to meet all obligations is important. For an underperforming business, it is of paramount importance. Without cash to operate, a business cannot survive. Even a profitable company can fail if it does not have the liquid cash resources to meet its obligations.

Profits are important in the **long-run** — cash is **vital** in the **short-run**

An important priority in any turnaround or workout program is a realistic Cash Flow Projection, because it is important to understand and quantify in depth all cash in-flows and out-flows. After completing all the other analyses described in this chapter, you will have the information needed to make changes to improve cash flow.

In extreme circumstances, it may even be necessary to sell or liquidate assets at prices below market value, or even at a loss, to generate needed cash. Without an accurate cash flow projection, management will not be able to reliably assess the extent to which such emergency measures are necessary.

A comprehensive cash flow projection provides management and other interested parties with an indication of the depth of the crisis. It provides an anchor that will enable all parties to understand the status of the business, and it becomes the basis around which the turnaround plan can be developed. It is also helpful in justifying the rationale behind workout proposals to creditors.

Cash priorities in a crisis

· Determine current and projected cash resources and obligations
· Develop strategies to conserve and generate cash

79

Timing

The timing of cash receipts and disbursements is important, and must be built into the cash flow projection.

Examples

A sale of goods on credit does not generate cash. Only when the receivable is collected is there an inflow of cash, which might be as lengthy as 120 days after the invoice was issued. How you finance your receivables is also very important to the timing of cash — if you have financed your receivables with a bank or finance company, the bank might advance you the major portion of the receivable (usually 80 percent) on the generation of the invoice. When you collect the cash, the financed portion goes to the bank, and you only get the remainder (20 percent). It is vital that your projections reflect the specific timing of these and all other cash transactions.

If the Company is scheduling a two-week summer shutdown, the cash flow implications can be significant: Most operating expenses (rent, payroll, etc.) will continue. However, production, and therefore material purchases, will stop, but the cash effect will only be felt 30 to 60 days later, depending on their normal payment cycle. Cash receipts will also be reduced at some point in the future, due to the disrupted shipping and billing during the shutdown.

Be realistic

It is also important to be honest with yourself in preparing a cash flow projection. Don't always assume things will work out well. The sooner you accept the situation for what it is, the earlier you'll begin finding real solutions. Be very realistic, and build in contingency provisions. Also, try to have a knowledgeable person, who is not emotionally involved in the business, critically evaluate your projections.

It is very likely that cash needs will turn out to be significantly greater than projected, due to other business problems that emerge when cash is tight, e.g., being placed on C.O.D. by suppliers, or lower sales through customer nervousness.

Because management credibility is so important in a turnaround, establishing unrealistic projections will only serve to set the business up for failure if it misses its projections. As such, only project results you are confident you can achieve.

Focus on details

A good Cash Flow Projection cannot be an overview analysis; it needs to be very specific. For example, when projecting cash disbursements, a detailed study of balances owing to major suppliers must be performed, and the projection must reflect the timing and amount of the specific periodic payments for these and other expenditures.

To be effective, a crisis Cash Flow Projection must be very detailed for at least three months, and can be less exact thereafter. The first two to three months should show weekly cash receipts, disbursements and balances. Thereafter, this should be done monthly for at least six months. For the subsequent six months, projections can be quarterly, and thereafter annually.

Appendix I, Tables 1 and 2, set out an example of the layout a Cash Flow Projection, which reflects all expected incoming cash receipts and outgoing cash disbursements monthly for the ensuing 12-month period.

Reconcile the projections

In order to know that the projection is comprehensive enough, and does not inadvertently leave out significant categories of cash in-flows or out-flows, it is essential to reconcile the projection to the actual Statement of Changes in Cash (also known as Source and Application of Funds Statement) for prior years, and to the projected Statement of Changes in Cash for the forthcoming fiscal period. This will require you to carefully examine historical and projected movement in all balance sheet accounts, which is the ultimate scorecard of cash. If the Cash Flow Projection cannot be reconciled to the Statement of Changes, something has probably been overlooked in its preparation.

Example

If your cash projection indicates that cash collections over the next three months will exceed revenues billed by $500,000, you should check that the accounts receivable balance is also projected to reduce by the same amount. More importantly, you should factor in that your borrowing availability on receivables will reduce by a percentage of the reduction in the receivables resulting in a significantly lower net cash inflow to the business, or a requirement to pay down your bank line of credit.

The reason why it is so important to reconcile the Cash Flow Projection to the Statement of Changes in Cash is because the Cash Flow Projection is usually derived from multiple sources of information—and there is no *double-entry* method of *balancing* the Cash Flow Projection to anything, to ensure that all items are taken into account. The Statement of Changes in Cash, on the other hand, is derived from the general ledger and will not *balance* if any items are excluded, or incorrectly calculated. Another typical example of this arises with accounts receivable. From your historical daily deposits you can tell your historic cash collections, but unless you reconcile these to your accounts receivable account in your general ledger, you run the risk of basing your projections on numbers that are inaccurate for many possible reasons, e.g., a portion of cash collections may be subsequently refunded to customers for returns; some amounts deposited in your bank account may be unrelated to sales (they could be refunds from your suppliers, or proceeds from an insurance claim), etc.

Whenever doing any projection, and especially a cash projection, stand back from the completed calculations to review the numbers for reasonableness and consistency. Ask yourself (and others) if the numbers make sense and are what common sense would indicate them to be. Always try to cross-verify the numbers to other sources, and check for reasonableness.

Example

If your sales projection shows sales growing from $5 million to $10 million over the next three years, check that your plant either has existing capacity to produce $10 million, or that you have projected sufficient capital expenditures to build or buy adequate production capacity.

The reconciliation to the Statement of Changes in cash can also identify items omitted from the Cash Flow Projection. Items such as capital expenditures or loan principal repayments are often forgotten because they don't flow through the income statement. The Statement of Changes will flag these and other similar items.

An example of how to reconcile the Cash Flow Projection to the Statement of Changes is demonstrated in Appendix I, Table 3.

When you have a realistic cash projection, you then know whether your patient's heart is still beating, or whether you need to immediately start Corporate CPR.

What if?

If your cash flow projection is set up on a computerized spreadsheet, it is always helpful to analyze the cash flow implications under differing assumptions. For example, what will cash flow be if sales decline 10 percent, or if interest rates increase 3 percent?

C. BREAK-EVEN ANALYSIS

Before any significant decisions can be made about the viability of the turnaround, the revenue level at which the company can be expected to break even must be determined. With this information, you will know what it will take to be profitable. If you discover that the break-even point is significantly higher than your current sales level, you will be able to assess the increase in sales (or reduction in expenses) necessary to achieve break-even.

In real life situations, the break-even point is not necessarily a stationary target. It can be changed by many different things, including changes in expenses, margins and cost of funds. Your analysis needs to determine the break-even levels under different scenarios, e.g., how the break-even level will be affected if prices are raised 10 percent.

Break-even formula

Fixed Expenses
Variable Contribution Percentage

This calculation necessitates a detailed analysis of fixed and variable expenses, in relation to sales. Examples of fixed expenses are rent, top management salaries and audit costs. Variable expenses change proportionately with sales, e.g., direct labor, commissions and bad debts. Some expenses are semi-variable in that they are fixed to a certain sales level, and

EXAMPLE

Sales

   100 units @ $10 each $1,000.00

Variable Expenses ($5.50 per unit)   550.00

   Variable Contribution   450.00

      Variable Contribution Percentage (of Sales)   45.00% [A]

Fixed Expenses   495.00 [B]

Net Profit/(Loss)   (45.00)

Break-even sales:

$$\frac{\text{Fixed Expenses [B]}}{\text{Variable Contribution Percentage [A]}} \quad = \quad \frac{\$495}{45\%}$$

$$= \quad \$1,100$$

then change for sales levels beyond that. Often, even direct labor has a fixed element, in that there is usually a sales level below which it does not make sense to continue laying off direct workers. This is because it might be hard to operate without a core group of direct workers, and because the business might be concerned about the availability of such laid-off (trained and experienced) workers when increased business dictates a recall.

> In general, more costs are fixed than most managers realize, i.e., there are very few truly variable costs

When you have accurately analyzed the break-even point, and know the amount of fixed expenses and the variable contribution percentage, your ability to project profits and cash flow will be greatly enhanced. This information is of great value to any business, profitable or not. The break-even analysis allows you to do *what if* analyses (see page 86).

EXAMPLE

What if selling prices are increased 10%, but unit volume declines 15%?

Sales (85 units @ $11 each)	$935.00
Variable Expenses (85 units @ $5.50 each)	<u>467.50</u>
Variable Contribution	467.50
Variable Contribution Percentage (of Sales)	50.00%
Fixed Expenses	<u>495.00</u>
Net Profit/(Loss)	**<u>(27.50)</u>**

Break-even	=	<u>$495</u>
		50%
	=	$990

An accurate determination of fixed costs, variable contribution percentage and break-even point can have a very significant impact on business strategy. Figure 17 reflects the break-even graph for a company calculated in two ways. Graph A allocates a higher proportion to fixed expenses ($300,000), resulting in a higher variable contribution (50 percent). Graph B reflects lower fixed expenses ($200,000) and a lower variable contribution percentage (33 percent). Note that both alternatives result in a break-even point of $600,000. However, at sales levels above or below break-even, they produce very different results. As such, if a company does not understand which graph represents its expense structure, wrong decisions could be made. For example, if the company believes graph B is representative of its situation, it may reject some orders that require significant price discounting that otherwise might be accepted if the company is aware that its variable contribution is 50 percent rather than 33 percent.

Because of the significance of this concept, it is very helpful to have your financial statements reflect fixed expenses separately from variable sales and contribution. With this type of regular presentation, management will become more adept at

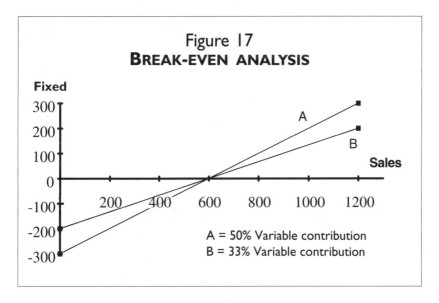

Figure 17
BREAK-EVEN ANALYSIS

A = 50% Variable contribution
B = 33% Variable contribution

understanding the link between fixed/variable expenses, pricing strategies and break-even levels.

Note that the point at which a business breaks even from a profit point of view is not necessarily the same as break-even from a cash point of view. In addition to profit break-even, items that affect cash break-even include depreciation and other non-cash charges, debt payments, working capital changes and capital expenditures. In a turnaround situation, cash break-even is usually more important than profit break-even.

A detailed example of a break-even calculation (including cash break-even) is shown in Appendix II. See also Part 2: Phase III-D for additional discussion of cost strategy.

D. ASSET ANALYSIS

A thorough analysis of the company's assets is important for the following reasons:

- Assets can provide you with the primary source of working capital to fund your turnaround. For example, if your analysis indicates that the company has not been diligent in collecting its receivables, this could (if the debtors are credit-worthy) be good news: A stronger focus on collection of receivables could result in an infusion of cash, until the receivables return to normal terms. The asset analysis could also identify excess or surplus assets not needed for continuing operations, which can be sold to generate cash. Examples of excess or surplus assets include under-utilized machinery, unimproved land, airplane, condo, boat, etc.

- If the turnaround ultimately does not turn out to be successful (i.e., the company cannot be returned to a profitable state), the company's assets will likely be liquidated to satisfy its obligations. It is, therefore, important to know the location, condition and liquidation value of all assets. This analysis will also give insights into the value of the lender's collateral, and how the lender might react to the company's situation.

- Assets can also result in obligations. For example, real estate with environmental contamination may result in significant cost for clean-up.

ASSET ANALYSIS CHECKLIST

· **Receivables**
  - Total amount outstanding, with breakdown by division, product line and customer
  - Analysis of aging
  - Quality and collectibility
  - Large individual accounts or groups of accounts
  - Amounts subject to set-off because of a corresponding payable to that debtor
  - Foreign or government receivables
  - Disputed receivables

- ## Inventory
  - Breakdown by raw materials, work-in-progress, purchased parts and finished goods
  - Breakdown by division, product line and product
  - Turnover by product line and product
  - Obsolete or slow-moving items
  - Overstocked or understocked items
  - Estimated forced and orderly liquidation value[12]

- ## Land and Buildings
  - Description of all properties and improvements
  - Original cost, accumulated depreciation and net book value
  - Condition of improvements and anticipated maintenance requirements
  - Annual maintenance, utility, tax and other costs
  - Environmental status
  - Fair market and liquidation values
  - Extent of current and expected future use of property

- ## Machinery and Equipment
  - Description and location of all machinery and equipment
  - Original cost, accumulated depreciation and net book value for every item and in total
  - Condition, efficiency and effectiveness
  - Current and projected utilization
  - Estimated fair market and liquidation values
  - Projected capital expenditures required for future operations

- ## Other Assets
  Details and likelihood of recovery of:
  - Prepaid expenses or deposits
  - Sundry receivables (e.g., employee loans)

- ## Intangible and Other Assets
  Description and estimated values of:
  - Patents
  - Trademarks
  - Licenses
  - Customer lists
  - Leases

---

[12] *Forced* liquidation value is generally the value that can be generated in a *fire sale*. *Orderly* liquidation value is the proceeds that can be generated by selling divisions, product lines or inventory in the ordinary course of business, within 90 to 120 days.

89

- Tools and dies
- Jigs and fixtures
- Engineering drawings
- Bills of material and costings
- Know-how or trade secrets
- Computer software
- Backlog of committed orders
- Tax losses
- Contractual rights, e.g., distribution rights

For all of the above assets, investigation should be conducted to establish if the assets have been pledged to secure obligations of the company. Unencumbered assets will be more valuable because they may provide the collateral needed to secure additional loans, or at least convince existing lenders to give the company time to work out its problems.

E. OBLIGATIONS ANALYSIS

A detailed understanding of the company's obligations is vital to any turnaround/workout program. An analysis should be carried out to determine the extent and status of all of the company's obligations, which include secured debt, unsecured debt, leases (capital and operating), taxes (withholding and other) and significant contractual obligations.

The satisfaction (or renegotiation) of all obligations is essential for a successful turnaround

---

Unsecured creditors

In order to develop a plan for dealing with unsecured creditors of a distressed business, it is extremely important to have a detailed understanding of the makeup, characteristics and amounts of all creditors. Without this knowledge, you may develop a plan that fails because of facts unknown to you. For example, if you are not aware that a major creditor has a corresponding payable to you that can be set off against your payable to him, a proposal that the creditor accept a reduced payment might embarrass you.

For unsecured creditors, an obligations analysis starts with a review of the company's aged accounts payable schedule, to determine the amount of payables outstanding, and the extent of past due obligations. In most turnaround situations, a handful of major suppliers represent the majority of outstanding payables. It is important to know who these suppliers are, and the status of their accounts payable.

CREDITOR ANALYSIS CHECKLIST

- Major or essential creditors, e.g. utilities, sole source suppliers
- Vendors with whom the company wishes (or needs) to continue doing business, and those it does not
- Payables that are owed less than a nominal amount (usually $500 or $1,000)
- All other payables
- Contingent payables, e.g., warranty claims, pending lawsuits
- Accounts payable that can achieve effective payment through the set-off of a corresponding receivable from that vendor
- Accounts payable that have implemented collection procedures, filed suit against the company or obtained judgments
- Accounts payable with whom the company has entered into payment plans or signed promissory notes payable
- Inter-company accounts
- Unsecured creditors who have obtained guarantees for payment from third parties, e.g. shareholders, affiliated companies
- Creditors who have some form of collateral or liens, e.g., an outside stamper that has possession of the company's dies

With all of this information, you will be able to evaluate how much cash is likely to be needed to take care of past-due obligations to suppliers, and ensure continued sources of supply for ongoing operations.

Accrued liabilities should also be analyzed to determine their effect on cash flow. Most accruals usually carry forward if the company continues on a going-concern basis (e.g., vacation accrual). However, they will involve cash outflow in the event of liquidation of the business. Other accruals (e.g., payroll withholding) could involve cash outflows on a going-concern basis, especially if they are past due.

In addition to accounts payable, a company can also have unsecured obligations to banks, other lenders and bond-holders. These obligations should be analyzed in a manner similar to that outlined for secured creditors below.

Secured creditors

Secured creditors, because of the power afforded by their security interest in your assets, are a very important con-stituent in a turnaround/workout. For this reason, it is essential to have a detailed understanding of the history of the relationship and the terms and conditions of the respective loans. This information will be helpful in developing your plan for secured lenders. For example, if you are not aware that the liquidation value of the lender's collateral is less than the amount of the outstanding loan, a request to the lender to advance more funds may indicate to the lender that you do not understand the intricacies of managing a business in a distressed situation.

SECURED LENDER CHECKLIST

- The amount of secured debt
- Loan renewal or expiration dates
- The form of security for such debt
- Details of interest rates, principal amortization, fees and other costs
- The liquidation value (forced and orderly) of the lender's collateral
- Whether there are any additional guarantees (for example, personal guarantees from shareholders, or guarantees from associated or affiliated companies)
- Whether interest and principal payments are up-to-date, or the extent and timing of payments in arrears
- Whether the company is up-to-date in submitting to the lender all reports required by the loan agreement
- Current *availability* under the line of credit
- Any maximums or *caps* on the line of credit
- Whether the lender's collateral, as determined by formulae contained in the loan agreement, is in excess of the loan outstanding. If the

92

collateral is not in excess, the loan outstanding will be *out-of-formula*, which is generally a serious default of a loan agreement.
- Whether the company has violated any *covenants* in the loan agreement
- Whether the company is in *default* of the loan agreement (see Appendix VII for explanation of covenants and defaults)
- Whether the lender has adequately documented and perfected its secured position
- Whether the lender has inappropriately engaged in any acts that might have caused or contributed to the company's problems

With this information, you will be able to assess the extent of actual or potential problems likely to be experienced with the secured lenders, and whether you might have any cause of action against a lender.

Leases

The analysis of leases and other contracts is also extremely important, for two reasons:

- To establish the details, terms and extent of such obligations

- To be aware of which leases or contracts the company does not need or wish to continue, in the event the company decides to file Chapter 11, in which case it could have (under certain circumstances) the opportunity to reject these contracts (see Part 2: Phase II-K).

EQUIPMENT LEASE CHECKLIST
- The original and remaining length of the lease
- Monthly payments
- Whether payments are up-to-date, or extent of arrear payments
- Residual payment at the end of the lease
- Deposits
- Equipment leased, and condition and value thereof
- Whether the company still needs the equipment
- Whether leases are operating leases or conditional sales contracts

PROPERTY LEASE CHECKLIST

- Description of property
- The original and remaining length of the lease
- Monthly payments
- Percentage rent provisions
- Whether payments are up-to-date, or extent of arrear payments
- Payment escalation provisions
- Deposits
- Details of renewal options
- Whether the company still needs to use the property
- Condition of properties, and anticipated maintenance and improvement expenses

Taxes

Many businesses in distress fall behind in making their various tax and similar payments, e.g., sales tax, FICA, unemployment, workers' compensation, payroll withholding, etc. The consequences of these actions can be very severe, ranging from losing your trading license or insurance coverage to personal liability for withholding payments. As such, falling behind in such payments should be avoided at all costs. To assist this analysis, a schedule should be prepared reflecting all such obligations, clearly identifying amounts in arrears, including interest and penalties due, and the status of negotiations, if any, with taxing authorities.

Contracts

A schedule should be prepared of all significant contracts (including employment contracts) reflecting all material terms and details of the contracts.

F. LIQUIDATION ANALYSIS

The completion of the Asset and Obligations Analyses facilitates the preparation of a Liquidation Analysis. The purpose of this analysis is to determine the cash proceeds that could be generated from the business if it were liquidated. This

94

information is valuable to all parties in a turnaround, but especially relevant in assessing the positions and likely reactions of secured and unsecured creditors.

A secured creditor who would be clearly over-secured in a liquidation of the business (i.e., the net liquidation proceeds from the sale of the collateral securing the lender's loan exceeds the amount of the loan) can generally be expected to react in one of two ways when confronted with a nonperforming loan:

1. If the lender believes that there is a realistic turnaround plan for the business, and has confidence in management, the excess security will often give the lender the confidence to allow the borrower time to rehabilitate its business.

   If the excess collateral is significant, it may even induce the lender to advance additional funds to alleviate the company's short-term cash flow problem.

2. If the lender does not believe in the turnaround plan, or does not have confidence in management, it may well read the excess collateral as an opportunity to *get out while the going is good*, and force a liquidation of the business by calling its loan.

Trade creditors will perform a similar analysis. If they believe liquidation of the business will result in higher net proceeds than management is offering them to support a going-concern turnaround plan, they will not be supportive of the plan. However, their decision might be influenced by a desire to salvage the going-concern business to preserve an important customer. Suppliers, because of the profit margin they earn on sales, can recover a significant portion of a bad debt from the margin on future business.

There are two types of liquidation values, *forced* liquidation and *orderly* liquidation. While there is no precise definition differentiating the two, forced liquidation is generally the value that will be achieved by closing the business down and liquidating all of its assets on a *fire sale* basis. Orderly liquidation, on the other hand, as its name implies, is conducted in a more orderly and planned fashion, whereby assets may be liquidated or sold within a slightly longer time frame.

For example, in liquidating a retail store, there would be the option of discontinuing store operations and conducting an auction sale, or perhaps selling all of the inventory to a liquidator (both of which would generate forced liquidation value). Alternatively, the store might be allowed to continue to operate, while the inventory was sold over a period of time in a *Going Out of Business* sale, which would generate orderly liquidation value.

In a manufacturing or distribution business, orderly liquidation would likely be the net proceeds from the sale of individual divisions or product lines; plus the sale of remaining inventory 1) in the ordinary course for a limited period of time, and 2) in bulk at the end of the period, to brokers or by auction; plus the proceeds from the sale or liquidation of remaining equipment, property and other assets; plus the proceeds from collection of accounts receivable—minus the costs of the dispositions, and the costs to operate the business during the wind-down.

In most circumstances, orderly liquidation will generate significantly more net proceeds than forced liquidation. This often gives management leverage with its creditors, in that management is usually able to achieve orderly liquidation values (through its knowledge of the industry and who likely buyers are), whereas creditors (without management's assistance) can generally only achieve forced liquidation values.

To determine liquidation value, in addition to quantifying the likely proceeds from the liquidation of all assets, the costs of liquidation must also be estimated, as well as the operating costs during the liquidation process.

LIQUIDATION COSTS

- Real estate and other commissions
- Auctioneer costs and commission
- Bankruptcy trustee and professional fees, if a bankruptcy filing is involved
- Advertising
- Termination benefits and payment of vacation pay to discontinued employees
- Income taxes
- Preparation and clean-up of facilities
- Additional staffing
- Miscellaneous expenses

In addition to costs of liquidation, there are consequences of liquidation that may reduce the net liquidation proceeds. These include:

- Actual or potential warranty claims: Many businesses receive warranty claims in the ordinary course of their operations. However, if production is discontinued, the frequency and magnitude of claims may increase because customers realize that they will not be able to make claims in the ordinary course, and they may not be able to receive parts or service in the future.

- Penalties or damage claims resulting from cancellation of orders

While most of these claims will rank as unsecured creditors, many of the claimants will be customers who have accounts payable to the company, giving them the opportunity to use the claims to avoid payment of their bills.

Once the net liquidation proceeds have been determined, they have to be assigned to creditors in order of priority, to determine whether each class of creditor is over- or undersecured. Appendix III provides an example of a forced liquidation calculation.

G. Controls

In order to determine the likelihood of a turnaround, and the reliability of the cash flow projection, the quality of controls over the major assets (primarily cash, receivables, inventory and fixed assets) should be assessed.

Good controls indicate asset protection and preservation. Poor controls result in inefficiency and vanishing assets, in the form of cash shortages, bad debts, inventory shortages and equipment problems. These items have a devastating effect on the success of turnaround efforts. Aside from the impact poor controls will have on the business, they will also serve to undermine the confidence of lenders, creditors, shareholders, potential investors and other interested parties in the turnaround plan. For example, if the accounting system provides information that causes the lender to believe that there is sufficient inventory to secure the line of credit, and this is subsequently discovered to be untrue, the lender's confidence in any information provided by management will be shaken.

Good controls do not necessarily mean complex controls. Often, the simplest controls are the best. For example, many people think a sophisticated computerized inventory system gives good controls. But quite often, taking a physical inventory on a regular basis gives more effective control, provided that discrepancies are investigated and pursued immediately and aggressively. The important aspect of controls is that they must truly give *you* substantial control over the assets for which you are responsible.

There are so many areas of a business that need to be controlled, not all of which are financial. The more complex business in general gets, and the more regulatory requirements that are imposed on business, the harder it gets to identify the areas that need controlling, let alone actually implement the controls. For example, the environmental protection laws are so complex and far-reaching that it is very hard for companies to be aware of all areas of compliance;

immigration laws changed substantially in 1986, imposing many tedious requirements for employers that are very easy to violate unintentionally; COBRA laws impose onerous penalties for relatively minor violations; wrongful dismissal, age and sex discrimination lawsuits are growing rapidly, and are extremely costly and disruptive.

Risk management and control is also an extremely important priority for companies today. Risk management is the controls implemented to minimize losses caused by accidental destruction of property; injuries to employees or others who come into contact with the company, its physical property or products; and liability or other claims from outside parties for the company's actions.

EXAMPLES OF RISK MANAGEMENT CONTROLS

- installing and regularly maintaining fire alarm and protection systems
- appropriate security procedures at the company's premises, including security guards where necessary; appropriate physical protection such as fences, adequate locks, adequate outdoor lighting
- periodically conducting environmental reviews to determine areas of the business that are exposed to environment contamination
- pre-employment physicals of prospective employees before a job offer is made, to avoid the company's having to pay for injuries or illnesses that occurred prior to employment, and to ensure people do not perform functions incompatible with their medical condition
- carrying out regular checks of prospective and current employee driving records, to be aware of employees who are driving on company business while their driving records are below an acceptable standard

Good financial controls are obviously essential and easier to identify and implement.

EXAMPLES OF CASH CONTROLS

- separation of duties relating to cash, and regular reconciliation of all bank accounts, reviewed by a senior manager with enough knowledge about cash matters to identify errors, inconsistencies or misappropriations
- good physical control over cash on hand, blank checks and check signing machines

· clearly defined and implemented policy relating to check signing, required backup documentation and authorization
· careful review and control over imprest cash accounts

EXAMPLES OF INVENTORY AND PRODUCTION CONTROLS

· good physical controls, to prevent damage and pilferage
· regular physical counts (or cycle counts)
· adequate accounting records of inventory and regular reconciliation to physical counts
· appropriate and consistent methods of costing inventory to ensure that products are sold at an acceptable margin and that valuation of inventory is not impacted by costing inconsistencies
· buying procedures to ensure that goods purchased are properly authorized, the best price is obtained, the goods are needed, and the goods are received in the quantity, manner and condition ordered
· production controls to ensure products are manufactured efficiently
· methods to identify and evaluate slow moving, damaged or obsolete inventories

EXAMPLES OF RECEIVABLES CONTROLS

· effective procedures to ensure that all goods shipped are properly invoiced, and correctly charged to the customer's account
· comprehensive policy for granting credit and establishing credit limits
· effective procedures to ensure that accounts stay within credit terms and credit limits
· good and persistent collection efforts, and remedial action for delinquent accounts

EXAMPLES OF ACCOUNTING AND BUDGETING CONTROLS

· timely preparation of comprehensive and accurate monthly and annual financial statements with sufficient detail to show all categories of revenue and expense, broken out by branch or cost center, and departments therein, and by major product lines
· detailed budgets for comparison to monthly financials
· monthly analysis and explanation of all variances between the budget and actual results

Watch very carefully for a control system I call the *prayer system*. This occurs when the company has not implemented effective policy and controls in a certain area, and management prays that the employees do it right. This is a very dangerous and potentially costly approach.

Cross-verification

An excellent way to assess controls, and to get to know the business better, is to check some of the controls yourself. Follow paper trails right through the system, looking for areas of inefficiency or weaknesses in internal controls. Always try to cross-correlate the information you are reviewing, to see if it tallies with other sources of information. For example, during an examination of a business in the construction industry, I was in the process of reviewing the construction profit and loss statements by job. During that month, the company had invoiced its customer for $100,000. I asked the manager how many workers it would take to produce $100,000 worth of work. After receiving his answer, I walked over to the payroll department and asked them to show me the payroll information for that job. From this, I was able to verify that the company had invoiced for work genuinely performed. In most business situations, there is usually a way to cross-verify information and controls. It is a good practice not to accept information and controls at face value—look for ways to achieve independent substantiation.

The existence or non-existence of good controls will have a major bearing on the degree of difficulty of your turnaround strategy. Good controls are not developed overnight—so, if they don't exist, there is usually a great deal of effort needed to implement them. The existence of good controls will increase the reliability of your Cash Flow Projection and will usually make your task a lot easier. Good controls will also build the confidence of lenders and other interested parties in the reliability of information generated by the business.

H. Information systems

Reliable and timely management information is the lifeblood of all management decisions. A good information system, already in place, will assist your turnaround significantly. An inadequate information system will force you to devote valuable time to gathering information, and your decisions, of necessity, will have to be made on less reliable data, thus increasing the risk of failure.

The first priority is to establish whether the company generates enough reliable information for management to know the operational and financial performance of the business, where the problem areas are, and what the historical and future trends are. If this information is not readily available, you will need to find ways to generate enough significant information to make an assessment about the business. This could even include recreating the books and records or making informed estimates.

If adequate current information is not available, and you are forced to rely on intelligent re-creation of records, it is important that you find some kind of reliable *anchor point* on which to base your numbers. For example, if your company has reliable audited financial statements for the last few years, but has very little financial information for the current year-to-date, start by analyzing the two prior years, and try to understand what went on in the business in those years. Was the business profitable? Which departments or products made or lost money? What happened to cash flow? When you understand the two prior years, you will probably be able to extrapolate forward to get an indication of what has taken place in the current year-to-date by adjusting the previous years' numbers by whatever information you have about the current year, such as changes in revenues, margins, expenses, cash flow, etc.

Daily and weekly information

Monthly management information is never adequate. By the time you see the reports, it is too late to do anything about the problem. Daily and weekly reports of important areas are essential tools to provide management with information with which to take effective action to run and improve the business.

EXAMPLES OF DAILY AND WEEKLY REPORTS

- cash receipts, disbursements and balances (reflected in the company's books and recorded at the bank)
- aged accounts receivable and payable (with percentages)
- sales
- inventory levels and inventory turnover
- ratio of gross margins to inventory (GM/ROI) by product
- order backlog
- value and description of purchase orders issued
- purchase price variances
- value of goods received
- value and quantity of goods produced
- value and quantity of goods shipped
- production efficiencies, downtime, re-work, returns, lead-time
- ratio of direct labor to indirect labor
- value of materials scrapped
- manpower levels, wages paid, overtime, vacations, holidays
- revenue per man hour
- updated revenue and profit projections
- availability under bank lines of credit
- compliance with lender covenants
- significant upcoming cash disbursements
- projected cash flow

Integrated systems

While not essential, the best information a business can have is a fully integrated, on-line, database system. This means that all regular users of the system have on-line terminal link-ups to the main computer and can access and request *real time* and customized reports in a *user-friendly* manner. This type of system, if working properly, provides managers with the most up-to-date and relevant information. It also eliminates a significant amount of paper work and duplication of effort that a manual or hybrid manual/computer system necessitates. In addition, it facilitates far greater asset efficiency through the on-line ability to control accounts receivable and inventories. Without integrated information systems, businesses often have unreliable information, because much of the information comes from different and unreconciled sources.

Example

A recent client was confident that his business was profitable because his marketing department provided him with a regular report indicating satisfactory gross margins. However, when I compared the gross margins on those reports to the ones reflected on the statements produced by the accounting department, there were significant differences. On investigation, it was discovered that the marketing department reports were created from salesman reports and did not reflect items such as credits, returns, samples and no-charge goods, all of which served to significantly reduce the gross margin percentage. Because of this erroneous information, the chief executive was not alerted to a significant problem that could have been identified months earlier if the marketing and accounting departments had been using the same database.

104

Communications

Even if the company has the most up-to-date reporting and information system, it will not work effectively if it is not supplemented with a good *communication* system. People in an organization need to talk to each other frequently and productively. Dynamic dialogue (upward and downward) provides the backbone of the mechanism through which the organization functions fluidly, makes improvements, anticipates problems, develops new ideas, and builds camaraderie. Top management must create an environment in which this type of positive communication and dynamic reporting takes place. Management must then make extensive effort to *listen* to what the organization is telling it. If people think management is not listening, they will stop talking. If you notice that they've stopped talking, there are probably problems looming that your staff is not telling you about. Great care must also be taken to ensure that the informal communication system is not used negatively—to promote corporate politics and spread rumors.

I. COST AWARENESS

A review should be conducted to see whether the company has a complete and accurate costing system that provides up-to-date information about the costs of individual products. Many businesses do not truly know their costs. If you do not know your costs, you cannot make intelligent decisions with regard to pricing, volume targets, inventory valuation, break-even, etc.

In the simplest situation, where the company merely buys product from a supplier and resells it in its same form, the product cost will be the price paid to the supplier. Even though it seems simple to identify this, many businesses do not accurately know what they pay for their goods, and how much gross profit they earn when they sell them. This would be easy if the business only purchased one product, and the price paid stayed constant. In practice, however, businesses usually purchase an array of products and prices are not constant. In these situations, the business needs to have a system that tracks costs, and matches those costs to items sold to establish gross profit earned. Very few businesses have this kind of system that works well enough, and most tend to sell for the price they think the market will bear, and *pray* they are earning enough profit.

As hard as it is to know your costs when you are just a middleman, it is significantly harder when you alter or manufacture the product. Under these circumstances, you not only need to know the costs of the individual components making up the finished products, you also need to establish accurately the appropriate amount of labor and overhead to allocate to that particular product. To get this right in anything other than a very simple operation involves a very extensive and accurate costing system.

Many companies have an extensive amount of cost information; the problem often is few know how to appropriately analyze and utilize the data. The same set of data can result in completely divergent decisions, depending on how it is evaluated. In addition, inconsistent or inaccurate accounting for product and inventory costs can wreak havoc on financial statements and the ability to use them to analyze profitability. Having this information in place, and knowing how to use it properly will greatly facilitate the turnaround. If you do not have this information, the turnaround will be significantly harder because you will not have enough data to make key decisions about which products to promote and which to discontinue.

To truly understand its costs, a business needs to be broken down into cost centers, with standard costs and budgets for each cost center and product line. With this information, not only can you price your products more effectively, you will also be able to more accurately pinpoint and develop improvements in efficiency. See Part 2: Phase I-C and Phase III-D for further discussion of costing.

J. Management and employees

The ultimate success or failure of a company is directly related to the competence and strength of its management and employees. Building an effective and cohesive team is a long, slow process of trial and error. (No matter how long you interview a candidate, or how many references you check, hiring is basically a gamble, and you cannot accurately evaluate someone's performance until he or she has been in the job six to 12 months.)

One of your hardest tasks at this stage is to assess the strengths of the key management personnel. If you recently have been appointed CEO of a distressed business, you might not know them well enough to make a decision with confidence. A useful technique is to formulate characteristics and attributes of managers you do know well and consider to be very competent and successful. Then, try to find out enough information about the managers you are evaluating, to assess how they rank in relation to the managers you consider successful.

In general, when evaluating a management team, it will usually be safe to assume that some or all of them are not what you need. If they were, the business would likely not have problems. Most managers have one or more subordinates that are not performing to their satisfaction but, for one reason or another, have not taken any action to remove them. These reasons often include a belief that the subordinate is trying hard, or perhaps needs more time, or that his poor performance is caused by external circumstances. Even worse, a manager may believe he is dependent on this person. Whatever the reasons, management must identify the competent managers and other employees. Anybody who does not fit this description could well hinder the turnaround process. If a competent team is already in place, you've saved yourself a lot of time and work, and you can adapt your turnaround strategy accordingly.

QUALITIES TO LOOK FOR IN MANAGERS

Leadership
- evidence of leadership traits throughout his/her life; e.g., President of High School class, rank in military service, organized charitable activities, led the thrust to develop a new product at previous employer, etc.
- willing to make tough decisions without concern about corporate political consequences; focuses on doing good rather than looking good
- willing to lead from the front, and sets an example of hard and diligent work

Strategic Thinker
- evidence that the manager makes moves that are calculated to achieve a pre-planned and strategic goal, rather than just going along with the flow

People Skills
- good communication skills
- ability to motivate subordinates to achieve their maximum potential
- **not** soft on people. A good manager has to know when to draw the line between sensitivity to employees and being tough and hard-nosed. Consensus management doesn't always work and the good manager knows when to *lay down the law*. You must see evidence of this skill; otherwise, the manager will always be of limited value.

Independent and Creative Mind
- willing to explore the unknown
- ability to think for him/herself
- demonstrated track record of original and creative idea generation

Action oriented
- decisive
- ability to make things *happen*
- makes problems go away rather than multiply
- significant history of successes
- fast learner

Maturity
- experience in dealing with *ups* **and** *downs*
- a realism about what it takes to achieve business success
- able to withstand and learn from constructive criticism

108

To perform this analysis, a complete organization chart should be prepared detailing functions, reporting channels, personnel names, headcounts and salary/wage levels. The résumés, qualifications, and capabilities of all existing personnel should be carefully reviewed to ensure only appropriately qualified and absolutely necessary personnel are retained. This should be approached from a *zero-based budget* point of view, i.e., if I were starting this business today, what functions and how many people would I really need?

K. Goodwill and leverage

Company's Standing

It is very important to determine the company's *standing* with four groups: Customers, employees, suppliers/creditors and lenders. Standing, for purposes of this analysis, is defined as how these groups perceive the company and its management, i.e., is there an adequate level of trust, respect, confidence and support? Once you know this, you can determine who can be depended upon, how much support you will get, how much they are prepared to sacrifice, and who is going to put your *back to the wall*.

An awareness of your standing with these groups will have a major impact on your turnaround. For example, if you know everybody is sympathetic, and have confidence in the company's ability to revive itself, you can usually *buy* a fair amount of time. If, on the other hand, your standing is low, you might find your customers courting your competitors, your employees polishing their résumés, your suppliers placing you on C.O.D., or your lenders calling your loan.

Your standing with lenders and creditors will clearly be impacted by the status of your obligations to them (See Part 2: Phase I-E). Your standing with employees and customers will largely depend on how you have treated them in the past.

Leverage

Once you have determined the company's standing with each group, you also need to determine its Leverage Level with the four groups. What factors can you bring into play to apply pressure on a group? What offsets do you have to neutralize pressure applied on you? For example, if you are negotiating with a lender who has been negligent in filing the paperwork to perfect its security interest (i.e., there is serious question as to whether it is truly a secured creditor), you obviously can afford to be more aggressive.

Fall-back Positions

A key concept of leverage is to determine the fall-back positions you have. When you are in negotiations with creditors or lenders, if you don't have fall-back positions, your negotiating strength is severely hampered. For example, if you are negotiating extended payment terms with a supplier, and you know there is no alternate supplier, you cannot afford to push him as hard.

Surveys

To determine the standing of a business with its customers and employees, a survey questionnaire (possibly with anonymous replies) could be used, requesting comments on a range of topics including product quality, service and complaints. You should also inquire how your company is perceived in relation to your competitors. The responses will be very helpful in determining your standing. Alternatively, you could rely on the more informal approach of individual meetings or telephone conversations with representative groups of employees, customers and even suppliers.

Employee Morale

A motivated workforce is always helpful in achieving a successful turnaround. An interesting question in determining the company's goodwill standing with its employees is whether low morale is a signal of serious problems in the company.

> "Surprisingly, low morale can exist in a relatively successful company; even more surprising is that in a company close to failure, morale can be high."[13]

Despite the importance of a motivated workforce, focusing on keeping employees happy sometimes cannot be your highest priority in the early stages of a crisis. If you have a high *standing* with your employees, and they are committed to the survival of the company, they will likely understand that you have bigger problems to deal with, and that your maximum energy is focused on saving the company, for the benefit of everybody. However, be sure not to rely on your standing with employees for too long; as soon as the crisis is reasonably stabilized, take time to let your employees know that you appreciate their understanding, and try to get things back to normal for them as soon as possible.

L. PRODUCT FRANCHISE

A company's *franchise* was defined in Part 1: Section I (Reasons for Business Failure). The Chief Executive of an underperforming business must critically evaluate the strength of his company's product franchise. A good Product Franchise is one of the most valuable assets a company can have, and one of the hardest to create if you don't have one.

If you decide to use the customer questionnaire or survey approach, you will probably be able to establish the strengths and weaknesses of your products. Not only will you need to determine product acceptance, you will need to ascertain the quality of the service you provide to support your product.

---

[13] Bibeault, Donald B., *Corporate Turnaround: How Managers Turn Losers into Winners.* New York: McGraw Hill (1982), page 70.

The answers to these questions will give you a very good idea of how difficult your remedial action is going to be. If your product has quality or other problems, you will need to budget on significant engineering, design, tooling and other costs. If service is a problem, you'll need to analyze and eliminate the reasons for the service problems.

M. Market analysis

A detailed analysis should be performed of all the markets in which the company operates. The objective of this analysis is to determine the demographics of the market and the company's relative strengths and weaknesses in the marketplace.

Market analysis is a combination of analyzing:

- the size of the total market by product and region
- market demographics, i.e., is the market growing, declining or stable?
- the company's shares of the respective markets, and historical and future trends
- who the competitors are in each product and region, and their market shares
- strengths and weaknesses of the company in relation to its competitors

Obtaining competitive information is not always easy, and requires significant depth of experience in these areas. If the company's in-house marketing personnel are not strong enough to provide this information, you may need to consider bringing in a suitably qualified and experienced consultant. Without this information, you will not be able to develop an effective strategy for the company that will allow it to focus on its marketing strengths, and take advantage of competitor weaknesses.

Example

Before completing a comprehensive market analysis, a small manufacturer decided to diversify into a market dominated by one industry giant. It soon discovered that the market share leader had no intention of allowing a new entrant to get established. The large company dropped prices significantly whenever it competed against the smaller one, and eliminated all profitability in that line. The company quickly concluded that its position in the marketplace was such that it was not cost effective to compete in that way, and it changed its strategy to manufacture under private label for other competitors.

N. REVENUE ANALYSIS

To effectively evaluate the condition of a corporation in a crisis, a full analysis of its revenue base should be carried out. This involves a review of historic revenues (preferably going back five years), to use as a gauge to predict future revenues.

This review should break out the revenues by the following categories:

- branch or department
- major product lines
- major customers
- geographic regions

With this information, you should then be able to identify trends and concentrations. Trends would tell you whether revenues in all of the categories outlined above are increasing, decreasing or erratic. Concentrations would indicate whether the company is excessively reliant on any one region, product line or customer. If concentrations are discovered, further investigation should be conducted to gain an in-depth analysis of that area.

Example

When we reviewed the revenue of one of our clients, analysis reflected that a major aerospace corporation represented more than 50 percent of total revenue. Further research indicated that this customer's revenues and profits were declining, due to military cutbacks in aerospace expenditures. In anticipation of a trend towards further declines in defence spending, a strategy was then developed to diversify into other industries (primarily medical equipment), whereby the company's skills could be converted to similar applications.

It is also important to analyze historical changes in the backlog of orders, including seasonal and cyclical trends, to assist in determining indications for the future.

O. Margins and industry conditions

Within an industry, there are some companies that generate higher profit margins than others, caused by lower costs, better quality, better service or more *added value* given to the customer. Some industries generate higher profit margins than others. This is caused by factors such as extent of competition, ease of entry and level of technology.

If the company is not earning acceptable margins, you need to establish whether it is an industry-wide problem, or whether it relates specifically to the company. These problems could be caused by not buying at optimum prices, not giving the sales force appropriate incentives to sell for the best price, loss of inventory due to spoilage or theft, poor physical controls or obsolescence, or the lack of an adequate information system that identifies margins by individual product, product lines and by customer.

In certain circumstances, if your company's margins are below industry averages, this might give you an opportunity to enhance margins and profitability through the implementation of a *Margin Management* program. Margin Management is the systematic tracking of margins by product, comparing actual margins to target margins, and rewarding salespeople and managers for improvement in margins through an incentive system. (See Part 2: Phase III-B for further discussion on Margin Management.)

Some companies choose to earn lower margins than their competitors, with the objective of making up the lost margin percentage through higher sales volume, e.g., discount stores. The wisdom and effectiveness of this strategy must be evaluated on a case-by-case basis.

At different stages in the economic cycles, industries experience different fortunes and problems, which have a significant impact on the health of the individual companies within the industry. If the industry is in an uptrend, it is a lot easier for individual companies to grow. However, growing industries have their downsides too—they often attract new entrants who can make life very difficult for established companies, because they may use lower pricing as a technique for penetrating the industry. Also, a high-growth industry often becomes overheated, businesses grow too quickly, and can experience cash problems. An industry on the downtrend, on the other hand, presents many problems: The market shrinks, margins get squeezed as competitors fight to retain market share and lenders get nervous as revenues and profits drop. However, a downmarket also presents some very attractive opportunities: Aggressive companies get the opportunity to buy up weaker competitors, and consolidate their industry positions, often at bargain-basement prices. This situation can present some of the greatest opportunities to build a really strong business. This situation is clearly demonstrated by the severe stress experienced by retailers in the early 1990s.

If your company is in a growth industry with good margins, or if the company earns a margin higher than industry averages, your turnaround strategy will be a lot easier. Conversely, a declining industry or low margins could make revival much tougher.

P. Negotiating skills

In all business situations, but especially in a turnaround situation, the negotiating skills of the Chief Executive, his management team and his outside advisers (lawyers, consultants, accountants, etc.) are very important to a successful conclusion. You are always negotiating for something, and to succeed, you've got to win a lot more than you lose.

In order to evaluate the company's ability to work its way out of a crisis, you need to realistically assess whether the management team has the skills to negotiate the often emotionally tense agreements that must be struck with lenders, investors, suppliers, employees and customers. This is even more important if the company's standing with any of these parties is low.

In circumstances where management does not have the ability to successfully negotiate with the various parties, or where relations between the parties have deteriorated to a level where no rational negotiations can take place, it is advisable for management to retain an intermediary to represent it in these negotiations. Such intermediaries could include an experienced attorney or turnaround consultant. I have been involved in several turnarounds where management's relations with lenders have been strained to the point of a serious lack of mutual trust. In these situations, management's ability to successfully negotiate an acceptable agreement with the lender was substantially reduced.

116

SUMMARY OF
NEGOTIATING STRATEGIES

- Create a trusting atmosphere
- Let your opponent speak first
- Say what you have to say clearly and succinctly, and then keep quiet
- Have issues you're willing to let your opponent win
- Lock in your opponent's concessions early/delay making your concessions
- Be patient . . . wait for opportunities
- Find things to dislike about your opponents proposals
- Don't be afraid to act stupid
- Don't get too clever
- Leave theatrics to your opponent
- Negotiate one slice at a time
- Negotiate in ranges
- Play it cool

An integral part of negotiating skills is knowing how hard to push for positions you want. I have seen many attractive deals die because one of the parties insisted on concessions that were not reasonable under the stressed circumstances of a workout. Because workout deals usually involve concessions that are unpalatable to all parties, if one party tries to impose too many concessions, the deal is very likely to collapse.

An expansion of these negotiating strategies for a turnaround situation is covered in Appendix V.

ACTION STEPS

› Take the time to accurately project cash flow over the next 12 months, with in-depth detail for the forthcoming three months

› Use a conservative approach to projecting cash flow: Assume things will work out worse than you might project under healthier circumstances; build in cushions to provide for unforeseen contingencies

› Critically evaluate the cash flow projections to ensure they are accurate and reasonable in light of the business' circumstances

› Perform a break-even analysis so that you will know what revenues will be needed to achieve a break-even on a cash and profit basis

› Analyze and understand the significance of all of the company's assets and obligations

› Perform a liquidation analysis, so that you are aware of the consequences of liquidation for lenders, unsecured creditors and shareholders

› Critically evaluate whether the business has the controls necessary for management to protect and preserve the assets and operations during the turnaround process

› Determine whether the company generates sufficient, accurate, timely and relevant information to assist management in designing and implementing a turnaround plan

› Determine whether the company has an accurate knowledge of the costs of its products

› Evaluate the strengths and competence of management and employees at all levels

Continued from the previous page

› Research the company's standing and leverage level with customers, employees, suppliers/creditors and lenders

› Measure the strength of the company's Product Franchise

› Analyze all the markets the company operates within

› Understand the sources, make-up and characteristics of the company's revenues

› Review the company's margins in relation to its industry

› Critically evaluate management's negotiating skills

Phase II

CORPORATE CPR

A. INTRODUCTION

Corporate CPR refers to the short-term *turnaround* strategies to keep the business *alive* in a *life-threatening* situation, until longer-term strategies that will result in a healthier business can be developed. It is a crisis management time, and requires very creative and, sometimes, aggressive (and often unpopular) actions.

By now, you should have established the extent and severity of the company's problems. You should also have developed a thorough knowledge of the company's cash projection, its break-even levels and other areas of strength, weaknesses, including profitability or lack thereof in all of the various divisions, departments and products. With this information, you will be able to start developing the remedial steps to generate enough cash to survive the crisis.

B. Cash Generation

As described in Part 2: Phase I, cash flow is the most important ingredient of your turnaround. Without adequate cash to meet current obligations (payroll, suppliers, debt retirement and interest, etc.) you cannot continue to function. Every effort must be devoted to finding sources of cash, and to finding ways to stop the business from absorbing cash. There are several ways to generate cash in a crisis. Some can be implemented quickly; others take longer.

Cash flow buys you time to restructure the business. It is little value in a crisis to make profits that are tied up in receivables or inventory. It might even make great sense to sell an asset at a significant loss if it generates the immediate cash you need to stay alive, until more concrete restructuring can be undertaken.

Cash management and control

The first step in a crisis is to ensure that effective controls over cash are in place, and that cash management techniques are efficient. Obtain a list of all bank accounts and authorized signatories, and determine:

- if there are unnecessary balances in accounts
- if there are means by which cash deposits from remote locations can be cleared faster, e.g., by using lock box or other cash management techniques
- if there are means by which the clearing of cash disbursements can be slowed up, e.g., by writing checks on a remote bank

Management should also ensure that controls are in place so that only authorized disbursements can be incurred. Only essential expenditures should be incurred, and cash projections should be continually updated to ensure that a disbursement does not cause the company to run out of cash.

Extending vendor terms

Obtaining additional credit terms from suppliers is the fastest source of cash flow. The company can approach its major suppliers and negotiate an extension of its normal payment terms, by explaining that the company is experiencing cash flow difficulties, which it hopes to overcome through a turn-around program. For example, if your normal terms are net 30 days, you might be able to negotiate payment of, say, six equal monthly installments. Additional terms (e.g., interest, collateral) will depend on your goodwill/leverage level. Usually, the supplier will want to place you on C.O.D. for future purchases. In some cases, suppliers may even want you to prepay (Cash in Advance or C.I.A.) when you place the order. This usually applies if the products are not standard products and are peculiar to your company. In such cases, the supplier does not want to be in a position of being stranded with unique goods produced but not paid for. In extreme cases, suppliers may, for emotional reasons, refuse to supply you even on a C.O.D. or prepay basis.

Note that this approach does not actually result in cash inflow; it merely reduces the cash outflow. If, however, suppliers will continue to supply you on open credit, this will result in cash inflow when you sell the goods, *and* collect the cash.

Generally, for a short-term extension of vendor terms, it is preferable to approach only a few of your larger suppliers, who have more of a stake in your continued operations, and are, therefore, more likely to be flexible. The logistics of negotiating with many smaller, less predictable suppliers are usually not worth the effort. Before deciding which suppliers to approach, analyze their credit terms, your past payment pattern and credit history with that supplier, how much leeway the supplier has given in the past, how important the supplier is to the business and whether you have alternative sources of supply.

In contrast to direct negotiations with vendors, it is often surprising how far creditors can be stretched by just discontinuing payments until creditors call up and request payment. In a crisis, this can buy you very valuable time.

Creditor compromises

In extreme situations (where the company is unable to meet its obligations, and cannot generate sufficient funds from other sources), it is possible to convince the company's suppliers and other creditors to accept a compromise payment of less than the full amount owing to them—which payment might even be payable over an extended period of time. This strategy obviously has many legal implications, and should never be attempted without the guidance of an experienced bankruptcy lawyer. Nevertheless, there are situations where creditors may accept this type of proposal. The most common reason for this is because they believe that such a compromise is necessary to avoid causing the total failure of the business (in which they might not collect anything), and/or where they believe that the compromise will raise their chances of continuing to trade profitably with the company in the future. An almost universal disadvantage of creditor compromises is the loss of supplier credit. With the specter of a compromise proposal, most suppliers will place the company on C.O.D., or they will at least severely restrict credit facilities.

If you do decide to negotiate a compromise with creditors, it is a good idea to employ the services of professional intermediaries, e.g., Turnaround Consultant, or Credit Managers Associations, who can mediate the negotiations with creditors, and give them additional confidence in the situation's successful resolution.

Many underperforming or distressed businesses, while they would like to honor their obligations to the creditors in full, are often not in a position to do so. By the time the reality of their situation is acknowledged, their balance sheets are often depleted to a point where the business is not able to generate enough cash flow to sustain the ongoing business *and* retire past due obligations in full. Most businesses emerging from a turnaround find it difficult enough to sustain current operations; and bearing the additional burden of past due obligations is often unachievable. For this reason, creditor compromises of less than 100 cents on the dollar are often inevitable for some distressed businesses. While this is rarely an appealing alternative for unsecured creditors, it is often a pragmatic one: If the company unrealistically strives for a 100 percent payout to past-due creditors, its good intentions may result in the company's bankruptcy, which may prove to be a significantly less attractive alternative for creditors.

Certain businesses could be seriously hurt by the proposal of a compromise to creditors. An example of this would be a retail department store chain. These businesses are very dependent on vendor credit, and even a hint of trouble could cause vendors to withdraw or reduce their credit limits. Aside from the obvious cash flow implications of C.O.D. for a department store chain, the administration logistics of paying C.O.D. to the hundreds of vendors could make continued operations very difficult. To avoid being placed on C.O.D. by such vendors, the company would have to prove that its business plan was sound and viable, and that its capital structure is adequate to fund the company through the turnaround. This is one of the major reasons why retail chains in Chapter 11 arrange large Debtor-In-Possession credit lines prior to their bankruptcy filing—which indicate to vendors that the company will have the funds to pay them. Businesses also need to consider how their customers may react to news about the workout.

In the current economic climate, most creditors are taking a realistic approach to working with their customers who cannot pay their bills. Our firm has been successful in negotiating numerous out-of-court restructurings of unsecured obligations for clients.

Factors affecting creditor's decision

- Whether they believe that the debtor's management is honest, sincere and capable of managing the company through the turnaround

- Whether the restructuring plan is realistic, achievable and fair to all parties

- Whether they could generate more proceeds (and sooner) if the company were liquidated

- Whether they believe that the company has made any significant preferential payments to its lenders, shareholders, employees, creditors or any other parties; if there are significant preference payments, unsecured creditors may believe that bankruptcy might afford a greater opportunity to recover such payments

- Whether it is important to them to maintain the company as an ongoing customer

---

Generally, some form of *currency* is necessary to induce creditors to accept a delayed and/or reduced payout. Currency, in this situation, is defined as an infusion of cash to enhance the company's balance sheet, and fund any downpayments to creditors under a workout plan. In cases where new equity is being contributed (whether by existing or new shareholders), creditors are usually more at ease because the resulting healthier balance sheet improves their chances of receiving the payout. Currency to fund a workout can also be generated by the sale or liquidation of surplus or underperforming assets. Restructuring plans that include a reasonable initial first down payment for creditors have a greater chance of being approved, and generally some form of currency will be needed to fund such payment.

In structuring a creditor compromise plan, be aware that any *forgiveness* of debt might qualify as taxable income. Unless the company has a net operating loss for tax purposes of a sufficient amount, the company may have to expend cash to pay income taxes on the forgiveness, even though such forgiveness would not result in any immediate cash inflow. You may be able to delay this event by making the forgiveness effective only when the final installment payment is made. Experienced tax counsel should always be consulted.

In all turnaround and workout situations, it is always preferable to be honest and responsive to your creditors. Even if you can't pay, suppliers feel better if you're up-front with them and you're not stringing them along. Tell them you're having difficulties, and don't make commitments unless you know you can keep them.

Creditor compromises can be structured in several different ways, which are outlined in Part 2: Phase II-L.

Additional loans

Another source of funds is lenders (banks, finance companies, etc.). Generally, only existing lenders who already have a substantial outstanding loan to the company will consider lending new money in a cash crisis. If the company is already in serious trouble, the lender will probably have switched the loan to the *workout* department, who are professionals trained to deal with floundering loans. These bankers are very different from your usual friendly account officer—they are not interested in building a relationship, and unlike your loan officer, have no interest in proving that lending you the money in the first place was a good credit decision. Their primary concern is getting the lender's money back, or as much of it as is obtainable, in as quick a time as possible. In most circumstances, it is a lot harder to get new money from the workout department, as opposed to regular loan departments. On the other hand, workout bankers are usually more realistic about the situation than regular bankers, and may be more amenable to negotiating an acceptable compromise.

A lender is unlikely to advance new funds in a crisis if it does not have confidence in management or its turnaround plan, especially if the bank believes it can fully extricate itself from its loan by liquidating its collateral. In fact, in these circumstances, if the lender believes that it can recover all its funds by foreclosing, you may be in a very precarious position, because the lender could desert you just when you need it most. As a result, it is a good idea (if you can arrange it without violating any laws or your loan agreement) to avoid paying the lender down below the level where it could exit the loan intact. For example, if you could sell a property that would result in the lender being paid down to below the value of its collateral, either delay doing it, or renegotiate your arrangement with the lender prior to the transaction, to avoid your act of good faith becoming your *undoing*. I have seen many businesses work very hard to pay down their bank loan in a crisis, only to have the bank *pull the plug* when they were paid down to a comfortable level. In a crisis, sometimes the more you owe your lender, the better. Contrary to what might be expected, your large loan gives you more negotiating power than the bank would like you to believe.

A lender's decision to advance new funds to an underperforming company will be substantially dependent on its confidence in management, which might be impacted by the following:

- How well the lender has been kept informed of the problems
- How early the lender was notified

Factors affecting lender's decision to advance new funds

- If it has confidence in management's ability to turn the company around

- If the lender truly believes the crisis to be temporary and not life-threatening

- If the lender is so deeply involved that it feels that it has more to lose by not *bailing* the company out (as demonstrated in the banks' bailout loan to Donald Trump in 1990)

- If the company or its shareholders can put up enough collateral or guarantees to secure the additional loan. (Lenders tend to view the value of collateral very conservatively in a crisis. They will generally only lend a percentage of *forced liquidation* value, which is often way below book or market value.)

- How many other problems or crises there have been in the past, and how well were they dealt with

- Whether there have been incidences of false information

- Whether the lender feels it has been told the full story

Rather than advancing new funds to a distressed company, many lenders are looking for ways to exit the relationship. Even if it is apparent that the company is turning around, the lender may still want to be paid out. This is due to a phenomenon known as *lender fatigue*. When a lending institution has been through a bad experience with a borrower, it often leaves a bad taste that is very hard to reverse. While the lender may have little choice to remain in the credit for a while, as soon as the company is *bankable* again, it might (sometimes strongly) encourage the borrower to look for another lender.

A lender who is not prepared to advance more funds may be willing, however, to accept slower or delayed principal (and, in some situations, interest) repayments. This can ease your cash flow significantly.

An effective, but expensive, alternative avenue for a troubled company to use for borrowing money is by means of *factoring* its accounts receivable. Factoring companies will advance funds against quality receivables, and generate immediate cash for you (unless your receivables are already securing your existing bank loan).

There are lenders that specialize in financing troubled companies. In some cases, they will lend to businesses that are underperforming or losing money, provided they believe management has developed a viable plan to restore the company to healthy profitability, and if the loan can be strongly supported by collateral. In such cases, the lender will generally lend a percentage of forced liquidation value of receivables, inventory and machinery and equipment. Pricing of such loans can be expensive, sometimes as high as 6 percent over the prime rate, depending on the company's condition and the size of the loan. Some lenders prefer the borrower to file Chapter 11 before making the loan, to give them a *super-priority* secured position approved by the court. (See the bibliography for references to books that provide lists of lenders who do lend to underperforming businesses.)

Debtor-in-possession financing

When a lender lends to a company that is already in Chapter 11, this is known as Debtor-in-Possession financing. To obtain such financing, the company needs to provide the lender (whether it is the existing or a new lender) with some sort of additional collateral to secure the new loan. These lenders usually require high collateral-to-loan ratios and expect substantial fees for the transaction. Terms and conditions are generally very demanding. A Chapter 11 company can usually only achieve additional funds from Debtor-in-Possession financing if it has unencumbered assets that it can put up as collateral. If the company's existing lender does not have a security interest in all of the company's assets, it may be willing to advance new funds to the Debtor-in-Possession if it provides the lender an opportunity to enhance its overall security, or achieve other benefits, like tidying up its documentation or security filings. Often, the existing lender will be persuaded by the threat of a new lender obtaining a priority secured position in the company's good assets (See Part 2: Section II-K for discussion about Chapter 11.)

Liquidation of inventories

Within two to three months, it is usually possible to liquidate some inventory, provided your pricing strategy is realistic, and salespeople or other employees are given an incentive to move the inventory. In order to know which items to focus on in the liquidation, an analysis of the inventory should be done by product line and individual product—to review turnover levels, margins and stock levels.

In certain industries, there are brokers or dealers that specialize in buying distressed inventories. While they will usually pay a lower price, they will often buy in large quantities—providing you with the opportunity to generate cash faster. Care should be taken to ensure that items are sold for a *reasonable* value, to avoid the possibility of the sale being challenged in a subsequent bankruptcy. Wherever possible, get liquidation value appraisals to justify transactions, or alternatively get bids from several buyers.

Collection of receivables

Making an aggressive attempt to collect receivables faster than normal will result in some short-term cash generation. A concerted and well-planned effort to collect receivables usually generates good results. Collectors should be given individual targets that are monitored daily, weekly and monthly. In general, people pay the suppliers that ask for their money—and don't relent! Detailed records must be kept of collection efforts, customer commitments and dates for next contacts. Special efforts should be devoted to collecting very old or disputed receivables; some cases might require help from attorneys or collection agencies.

There is often a temptation to offer a discount to customers to induce them to pay earlier. This is fine if they are not in arrears; if they are in arrears, this practice might cause you problems when the customer realizes that the longer he delays payment, the bigger his discount is likely to be. It is a good idea to incorporate an incentive program for collectors, to encourage them to accelerate the rate of collection.

Inventories, Just-in-Time

Arrangements can often be made with suppliers whereby they hold inventory for you on their floor and only deliver to you when you need the inventory. This enables you to significantly reduce your inventory and improve your cash flow. The supplier will probably like this approach because it reduces his outstanding receivable from you, and also reduces his risk of loss if your company cannot meet all of its obligations. You may even be able to sell some of your existing surplus inventories back to your supplier, on the understanding that you can buy it back when you need it.

Consignment inventories

Some suppliers might be persuaded to give you inventory on consignment (i.e., you don't pay for it until you sell or use it). When you are in a cash crisis, there might be an added advantage to the supplier because he retains ownership of the inventory in the event you file Chapter 11, resulting in him not becoming an unsecured creditor. In such situations, consignment inventories should be physically separated and clearly identified from other inventory, and the supplier may need to take certain legal steps to protect its position as the owner of the inventory. Before entering into a consignment arrangement, ensure that your lender is aware of, and has consented to, the transaction.

Deposits, cash-in-advance

In some situations, it is possible to get your customers to pay for (partially or in full), or buy, products from you when you receive the order or while they are still in process in your plant. This could be done where the customer really needs the product, and doesn't have the ability to easily and quickly source it from another supplier. In such circumstances, you could either ask the customer for an advance payment or you could actually sell the product in process, with an additional payment for the labor involved when it is completed. This latter approach is also advantageous to the customer in the event you are forced into Chapter 11—because the work-in-process belongs to the customer, and won't be tied up in the court proceedings (although in certain circumstances, the Bankruptcy Court can undo such transactions).

Example

In a recent situation, a client of my firm, a distributor of a high-tech product, had substantial orders for a product that could only be manufactured (at that time) by one supplier. The manufacturer was in financial difficulty, and did not have enough funds to purchase the parts to complete the orders that were in progress. The distributor was willing to advance funds to the manufacturer, but its lawyers advised against it: In the event of the manufacturer's

132

bankruptcy, it would become an unsecured creditor, and it would not be able to take possession of the products still in progress in the plant. Instead, the distributor purchased the manufacturer's work-in-progress, and entered into an agreement for the manufacturer to complete the work-in-progress and convert the items into finished goods.

It is also possible for lenders or investors to finance your orders from customers, by buying the purchase contracts from you at a discount or for a fee. The materials and work-in-progress then belong to the investor or lender.

Sale, leaseback

Many businesses own assets, ownership of which is not essential for the continued operation of the company (e.g., land and buildings, machinery, vehicles). If a business owns such assets, they can often be sold to investors, and leased back to the company.

This process might take a while to find a buyer, negotiate and document the transaction. The disadvantage is the investor will usually insist on a very long lease, and the cost to you will often be higher than if you weren't forced to conclude the transaction.

Any investor that purchases an asset from your company, with the intention of leasing it back, will thoroughly evaluate the financial condition of the company to assess its credit worthiness. The resulting probability of completion and cost of the leaseback will be a function of the investor's assessment of quality of the asset and credit risk.

Surplus assets

Purely surplus assets (e.g., raw land, excess inventories or equipment, investments, etc.) can also be liquidated, obviously without being leased back. There are also often opportunities to sell or license intangible assets such as patents, trademarks, customer lists and technology.

Other assets

Most businesses have funds tied up in other assets, which could include the cash surrender value of life insurance policies, loans to shareholders or employees. To the extent possible, these assets should be realized or collected.

Barter

Barter is one of the oldest forms of trading known to man. While not common in today's economic environment, there are companies that facilitate barter transactions. So if it is hard for you to liquidate inventories for cash, it may be possible to trade your surplus inventories (or other assets or services) for other goods or services that you need (which could include airline tickets, advertising space, etc.). This will save you having to buy these items for valuable cash.

Strategic alliance

In a situation where you have a significant backlog of orders, but do not have the cash to purchase the materials to manufacture the products, you could make an arrangement with another manufacturer to make the products, invoice the customer and pay you a commission or finder's fee. This would ultimately have the affect of turning your company into a marketing rather than a manufacturing organization. This would only work if the manufacturer did not become your competitor and try to squeeze you out of the chain.

Investors

Bringing in new partners in the form of venture capital or other investors is a welcome and possible option, but the investors have to be sold on the turnaround prospects, and management's capabilities to achieve the turnaround. There are numerous individuals, venture capital firms and funds that specialize in turnarounds. (See the bibliography for references to books that list such investors.)

In a turnaround situation, it is usually easier to attract investors that have some motive to invest beyond purely financial incentives (often referred to as strategic investors).

The most logical investor to look for in this category is someone who is also looking for employment as well as part ownership of a business. There are many *out-placed* senior executives, who either have cash to invest or who can attract the support of other financial investors, who may be very interested in investing, in return for a senior management position and a sizeable equity stake. Other possible investors include suppliers, customers, employees or even unions (who might like to see the company survive so they can maintain employment levels); competitors (who may want access to your technology, customers, product lines—of course, you'd have to think long and hard before taking this route); and companies that could benefit from the association with your company, such as an overseas supplier of a related product line that would like to *piggy-back* its product onto your distribution channels. One of our clients was recently considering moving its business to a new facility. The owner of that facility was responsive to making a significant equity investment into our client. While not stated openly, the ability to sign up a tenant with a long-term lease was obviously a substantial inducement for the equity investment.

A major reason investors are often reluctant to invest in troubled companies is their concern over what will happen to their investment if the turnaround is unsuccessful and bankruptcy results. Because shareholders rank behind creditors in a liquidation, investors may wish to invest in the form of a loan (e.g., a debenture). If their loan can be secured by any unencumbered assets, they will likely be a lot more comfortable because their position might rank ahead of unsecured creditors in a bankruptcy. In such situations, should the investors also desire *upside* if the turnaround is successful, the debenture or loan can have *conversion rights*, entitling the holder to convert the loan to equity.

The cost of new equity funds for an underperforming or distressed business can be extremely high. Traditional venture capital investors in profitable businesses require potential annual returns of as high as 25 percent to 40 percent. In a turnaround situation, investors are often seeking returns significantly in excess of these amounts. Because of this, if the company is seeking significant amounts of capital, the result can be significant ownership dilution for existing shareholders, often extending to the loss of ownership control.

Because of the negatives described above, many underperforming companies initially reject offers for new equity funds, because of the perceived excessive cost. This decision should be carefully weighed against the alterative options available. If the equity funds are essential to the survival of the company, the cost of rejection of the funds may ultimately turn out to be greater. The owners of an underperforming business often delay making this decision, in the hope that some more attractive alternative becomes available. This delay can make the workout more difficult to achieve and raise the cost of the equity funds even further. As such, while not easy to do, shareholders should evaluate the situation quickly and carefully—and if new equity funds are going to be needed, action should be taken sooner rather than later.

In the event the loss of control becomes unavoidable for existing shareholders, this blow can be softened if the existing shareholders negotiate the right to buy back (or earn back, through performance) control of the business.

C. STABILIZE CREDITOR RELATIONSHIPS

While finding sources of cash is a very high priority at this time, stabilizing relations with secured and unsecured creditors must also be given very close attention. During the Vital Signs check, you will have performed an Obligations Analysis (see Part 2: Phase I-E) to achieve a detailed understanding of the amounts owing to secured and unsecured creditors, how much is past due, what defaults exist and what security is in place.

With this information, you should identify which creditors are likely to create problems for the company, immediately develop a strategy to identify the creditors' needs and concerns, and find ways to satisfy them without giving them preferential treatment. Your objective at all times is to develop enough credibility with creditors to be able to convince them to work with you while you develop a plan to take care of your obligations. If you cannot do this, you run the risk of creditors taking legal or commercial action that could be severely detrimental to the company.

If the company is under significant pressure from trade creditors to make payments that it cannot afford, consideration should be given (in consultation with your attorney and financial advisers) to sending a letter to all past-due creditors to inform them of the company's situation. In most circumstances, this letter should not be sent to essential or sole-source suppliers, and every effort should be made to keep them current; the consequences of default with these creditors could be devastating. Further, this message should be delivered in person to large or important creditors. See Appendix VIII for a sample of an initial letter to creditors.

In the event creditors take a hostile approach to your request for time to develop a workout plan, be prepared to show them a liquidation analysis of the business (See Appendix III) which will usually reflect that liquidation is not a viable strategy for unsecured creditors (who rarely get 100 cents on the dollar on liquidation of a seriously distressed business). This analysis may convince creditors that giving you time to develop a workout plan will be in their best interests. Of course, if liquidation would result in full or substantial payment to all creditors, such analysis may not be helpful in your negotiations.

For additional insights on dealing with unsecured creditors in a turnaround situation, see Part 2: Phase II-L for a discussion of the alternatives to Chapter 11.

In addition, a carefully thought-out strategy for communicating with secured lenders should be developed. In most cases, an open and honest approach should be adopted, whereby the lender is informed of the exact status of the business, the likely consequences and management's remedial strategy. Lenders should also be advised in advance of your strategy for dealing with unsecured creditors. In most workouts, lender support and cooperation is essential for success, and it is very important to maintain regular and forthright communications with your lender.

Most businesses in decline tend to communicate less with their lenders. This worries lenders, who start to doubt management's grasp of the problems or, even worse, its integrity. The lender may react by probing deeper and asking for more information. Management often responds negatively to the lender's apparent mistrust and hardened attitude.

A successful turnaround or workout can only be achieved if communication channels remain open. Both sides must forget the past. Often, responsive communications can only be achieved by bringing new players onto the scene for both sides; rarely can distrustful parties change gears overnight. In the lender's case, there may be a change of loan officers, or the credit may be handed over to the workout department. The company may hire a new Chief Operating Officer or Chief Financial Officer, or may use an attorney or outside crisis manager/consultant to be in the front lines of communications with the lender. Restoration of credibility is essential to the process.

The lender must immediately be brought up to date on the company's situation. A report must cover:

- Up-to-date financial information
- An accurate collateral analysis
- Reasons for the company's decline
- A preliminary outline of a turnaround or workout plan, tailored to the company's circumstances and the lender's likely reactions
- A liquidation analysis

The lender must be clearly and unequivocally reassured that the company recognizes its problems and is committed to change, which will include open, frank and responsive communications. In contrast to previous communications with the lender, the company should present a realistic assessment, and demonstrate to the lender its new-found realism and recognition of its situation. A too-optimistic benchmark will just set the company up for failure in the future. Further, if the lender is fully aware of the problems, it is likely to have a more somber view of the value of its collateral on liquidation and be more receptive to a turnaround or workout plan. Of course, this can be a double-edged sword if the negative news convinces the lender that there is no hope for the company.

If management's intentions seem genuine and honest, and the plan appears realistic, its lender will likely ask for more detailed projections. If the lender is skeptical of management or the plan, it is unlikely to be cooperative and may proceed with foreclosure or other legal action. However, in today's climate, with so many problem loans, banks are more likely to prefer the cooperative route.

In negotiating the turnaround/workout plan with the lender, the company should be careful not to agree to impossible terms, conditions or covenants. The agreement should acknowledge and provide for any losses likely to be incurred during the turnaround phase. The lender must also agree to take actions necessary to fulfill the plan. For example, if receivables are to be factored to raise cash, the lender must agree to release its lien on the receivables. The plan should be flexible enough to provide some leeway for uncertainty of future events. If, for example, the plan calls for a building to be sold in month three, a grace period should be negotiated so that there is no default if the sale occurs in month four. The plan must include regular and frequent reporting so the bank can assess the plan's progress, and the value of its collateral.

D. Solutions, not blame

One of the most important requirements for a successful turnaround is for management to stay calm. This is often easier said than done, but a panicky management team will upset employees, creditors, lenders and customers—and will definitely hamper the recovery.

One very important point to remember: In a crisis situation, everyone is thinking about protecting his or her own interests, and there is very little real sympathy or concern for anybody else's feelings. For example, a banker that had vigorously pursued the company's business for many years might now see the company as a potential contributor to the ruination of his career; his bedside manner might disappear quickly.

As a result, it is essential for management to be unemotional, and to put all their efforts into protecting the company's position. It is a very good idea for the CEO to call a meeting of key management and announce the switching to a *crisis mode* of operations. Acknowledge that the business is experiencing problems and explain the procedures you are implementing to deal with the situation. Express your determination to solve the problems, but avoid any promises or commitments about the outcome. Above all, stress your need for the support and contribution of all managers and employees of the company.

No scapegoats

Another essential requirement is for the management team to stick together and keep the lines of communication flowing. In a crisis, many people clam up and rumors are rife. Mutual trust is vital in this situation. If one manager feels that another is going to use the situation to his advantage, or to the detriment of others, mistrust sets in, and everybody starts protecting his rear, rather than searching for the ultimate solution. The Chief Executive and his Board of Directors, if there is one, must demonstrate to everyone that they are going to attack the problem—and not the people. In every turn-around situation, there is always a natural tendency to find someone to blame. Everybody feels much better if they can attribute the problem to something specific—and usually somebody specific. The problem with this is you start a witch hunt, and the spotlight gets focused on people rather than the problem. In practice, it is my experience that the real problem within the business is usually extremely complicated and pervasive, and finding someone or something to pin the blame on provides a false sense of comfort. In fact, a great deal of brainstorming is required to find the ultimate solution, and this process can be totally disrupted if there is any attempt to find a scapegoat. As a result, in a crisis, you should make every effort to show people *you are looking for a solution, not blame.* In this mode, everybody feels more comfortable and more open to finding solutions. Remember, however, that action speaks louder than words! I have seen a lot of top managers in a crisis tell staff that they shouldn't be defensive, because they are not being attacked personally—and then proceed to rip them to shreds for their (alleged) transgressions. It's not what you say, it's how you behave! If your staff sense they can trust you, they'll open up and produce for you.

141

Build on ideas

The ideas and solutions that are going to work for your business are not necessarily readily available. It is rare that a textbook or expert is going to provide all the answers. The appropriate strategy has to be *squeezed* out over a period of time through constant brainstorming and re-evaluation. Key managers and employees should be called upon to assist in the process of searching for ways to improve the business. Never ridicule somebody for an idea, no matter how ridiculous it seems at the time. You'll only discourage that person (and others) from ever verbalizing another idea. Also, bear in mind that the seeds of some of the best ideas come from suggestions that initially seem absurd. When brainstorming is appropriately applied, you will find many good ideas germinating from suggestions made by employees, despite the fact that the initial suggestion might not be well thought out. Even if only two out of ten ideas are really good, you will find it worthwhile to sit through the other eight so that you can determine which are the *gems*. If you create an atmosphere in which creative and free thinking is encouraged (and recognized and rewarded), you will benefit from the fruits of the ideas that are generated.

Unleash people power

If you create an atmosphere in your company where cost saving and profit enhancement is encouraged and rewarded, you'll be surprised by the ideas that your own employees can generate. I have always been very impressed with the energy and power that is created by brainstorming. The collective energies of a group of people, properly stimulated and unleashed, far exceeds the sum of the individual energies. The process, once started, becomes self-generating—because people enjoy being part of such an exciting and stimulating process, and they thrive on the satisfaction of being an integral part of *change-in-the-making*. It is really not that difficult to achieve, and the rewards can be significant. Just let people know that the company needs **their** help, that their contribution and ideas are appreciated, that all of their ideas will be respected—even the (apparently) absurd ones, and that you expect that many of their ideas will ultimately sow the seed for some of the breakthroughs you are looking for.

Breakthroughs are vital. More of the same won't do in a turnaround!

Lateral thinking

To find the really good solutions, you and your team need to find new approaches, methods and concepts. Don't always look at the problem head on—try to turn it upside-down, inside-out or back-to-front. Many times we get locked into traditional thinking that prevents us from seeing the most simple solution in another plane. Everything can be improved, and new methods can always be found. If you let people slip into complacency, they will become comfortable with the status quo. The really efficient organization institutionalizes and rewards the constant pursuit of improvement. To facilitate this, I recommend a new incentive system recently evolved, known as *Gainsharing*. With Gainsharing, bonuses are paid on improvements in efficiency, rather than just profits. Of course, the problem lies in how to develop a reliable measurement of efficiency.

Some people refer to lateral thinking as a *paradigm shift*, i.e., a change in the fundamental way of thinking. Often, a business is blind to a huge opportunity unless it can make the paradigm shift. An example of this is digital watches—which were developed by the Swiss. However, because of historical biases and beliefs, the Swiss did not believe there was a significant market for these watches. Casio, Seiko, and other Japanese companies soon proved them wrong!

Examples

A retail chain utilized a central warehouse to distribute products to its stores. After an examination of its financial status, it became apparent that its central warehouse was one of its largest costs. While centralized distribution was fundamental to company thinking, the cost analysis forced it to look for ways to do things differently. It negotiated arrangements with wholesalers to supply directly to the stores, which eliminated the cost of the central warehouse, reduced inventories, and also gave the stores greater control over the buying, selection and re-ordering, and improved store morale and performance.

To take the concept of lateral thinking one step further, imagine instead that an analysis had indicated that this retail chain's warehouse was very efficient, and that the stores were the weak link. A creative solution might then have been to sell off the stores as independent franchises, and convert the original business into just a wholesaler that would provide wholesaling services to not only the franchised stores, but also to similar competitive retailers in the area. Rather than being a mediocre retailer, this company might be able to leverage its true skills to become a highly effective wholesaler.

In another situation, a distributor to the retail mass merchandise industry found it could not achieve profitability in its traditional business. It concluded that its primary expertise was distribution logistics and merchandising know-how—and it successfully changed its business focus to sell those services to manufacturers and retailers.

A steel service center client was experiencing difficulty meeting its delivery schedules. The client realized that the delays were due to their two overhead cranes being substantially occupied loading and unloading trucks, rather than facilitating movement of steel during processing. This observation triggered an analysis of the cost/benefit of installing another crane, which appeared to be the only solution. At a production meeting, management mentioned this analysis to one of the foremen, who immediately made a suggestion that would solve the problem without any capital expenditure. His suggestion, which was implemented, was to perform the major part of the processing function during the second shift, when the cranes would not be used for loading and unloading trucks, which only occurred during the first shift. This solution was an excellent example of lateral thinking.

A regional operator of gas stations was experiencing a significant decline in its revenues and profits due to poor general economic conditions and extensive competition. Because the operator perceived his business as a supplier of gasoline, his initial (unsuccessful) efforts were focused on finding ways to sell more gas. In a brainstorming session, the idea evolved that the company's best asset was its superior locations in small towns. As the discussion continued, the group realized that the company, in fact, was a specialty real estate business. After this breakthrough in thinking, ideas flowed as to how to take advantage of the real estate locations, and many ideas were developed in the areas of strategic alliances with other companies who could benefit from being situated in those locations, and also assist the company in selling more gas.

Teamwork and patience

The crisis management team is a unified, unemotional team, dedicated to attacking the problem inch by inch, ready to creatively explore and implement the right solution for its business. The team members also realize that patience is very important in the turnaround process. On a day-to-day basis, progress might seem very slow—on many days, you may even feel you're going backwards. However, if you keep pushing forward in a methodical manner, not allowing setbacks to deter you, you will look back after a period of time, and be amazed at how much you've accomplished.

E. Reduction of expenses

There are few companies that cannot significantly cut operating expenses in a crisis. Most businesses have a layer of excess expenses that can quite easily be identified and eliminated (e.g., country club memberships, company-owned cars, airplanes, condominiums, stadium loges, executive dining rooms, one secretary for every manager, etc.). There are also many other expenses that are not excessive, but can probably be deferred until the cash crisis is over (e.g., trade shows, advertising, training, etc.).

However, it is often easy to mistakenly conclude that a category of expenses is excess when in fact it is very necessary. An example of this would be eliminating or substantially reducing the credit and collections department. In the short term, it could appear to be a quick route to save expenses, but the long-term implications on your receivables and cash flow might be disastrous. Another example is the elimination of most of the employees who have been around for a long time. When it's too late, you may find that you have lost very valuable history of product design, customer or supplier relationships.

A very effective way to eliminate excess expenses is with the use of temporary help. Often, after you have laid people

146

off, you find that one or more of your departments is struggling to keep up with their workload. If you analyze why the departments are behind, you will often find that they are being bogged down by specific and identifiable projects that take time away from their regular work. Many of these projects lend themselves to being done by competent temporaries or consultants. They can be brought in to complete specific tasks within a pre-determined time frame. When the tasks are completed, they leave and you are not faced with the cost and anxiety of separation. If, on the other hand, you recall laid-off employees or you hire new employees, chances are that when they have completed their projects, more work will be found for them to do, and the company commences its cycle of *putting on weight* again. Before hiring the temporary worker, conclude whether the work or project is really necessary. Most companies perform tasks either 1) because they have *always done it that way*, or 2) because nobody has taken the time to find a more efficient way to achieve the objective. Often, a careful analysis will show that the work is really not that necessary. Alternatively, if this task is deemed necessary, before hiring a temporary or new employee, find other tasks that can be simplified, reduced or eliminated, to free up time from existing workers.

Don't rely on belt-tightening, search for structural change

After you have eliminated clearly excess expenditures, continued *belt-tightening* techniques do not achieve significant results. For further reductions to be achieved, it is essential that new and more efficient methods be found in all areas of the business. This is ultimately the real key to improving a business. It's just like going on a crash diet—you will probably eventually put the weight (and more) back. If you ask employees, who are already working hard, to work even harder, they will be able to keep it up for a while, but eventually something will give. If, however, you find a diet that teaches people to eat differently, but without starving themselves or depriving them of their favorite foods, the chances of keeping the weight off permanently are much greater. In a business setting, I call this *structural change*. If the method of operation can be changed so that the function can be performed at a lower cost, but without unacceptable increase in stress or side-effects, such structural change will contribute to a more efficient organization. So, search for structural change. If you encourage your whole organization to pursue structural change with diligence, you will be impressed by the improvements that lower cost or increase profitability and cash flow that can be found. Everybody's life will be made easier.

Upgrading machinery is a very good way to achieve structural change and lower costs. Newer machinery can often pay for itself very quickly, in the form of improved quality, labor savings and faster throughput. Often, minor additions or adjustments to equipment or plant layout can result in significant improvements in efficiency. Such additions can contribute to reduced labor cost, lower scrap rates, fewer quality problems, and increased customer satisfaction.

Voice mail and computer aided design (CAD) systems are examples of technological advances that have enabled businesses to reduce overheads and achieve significant other benefits. Voice mail enables most businesses to eliminate receptionists, and facilitates enhanced communications (although there are some critics). CAD systems eliminate laborious drawing of standard design functions, and provides the ability to make rapid changes to drawings. Creative design of tools and dies can also contribute significantly to efficiency. Machine tools or dies that can convert multiple steps into one step can be very helpful. Achieving this kind of grass roots momentum towards structural change will be the best turnaround strategy you could adopt. Without changes that make functions easier, you will have to rely on continued belt-tightening techniques to reduce overheads.

148

Examples

A construction equipment manufacturer shipped one of its products in batches of 100. As the product came off the paint line, a worker counted 100 units, placed them on a skid and banded the skid. The company noticed that some customers complained that the skids they received contained less than 100 items. Naturally, no customers complained that they received too many items. Plant management developed a simple and low-cost solution: First, they made minor adjustments to the paint line so that completed items would automatically drop off the paint line onto the skid. This eliminated the need for it to be done manually. Then, they purchased an inexpensive electronic counter, and attached it to the end of the paint line. As the items progressed towards the end of the line, they were counted by the counter. When the counter reached 100, a bell rang and a worker involved in some other function walked to the paint line and banded the skid. These two simple ideas resulted in significant labor savings, improved customer relations and eliminated over-shipments to customers.

In another situation, a company's welders were able to show management that an overhead monorail system would make it significantly easier for them to maneuver parts before and after welding. The resulting improvement in efficiency paid for the cost of the monorail in months.

A manufacturing company found that their completed products, after final assembly, travelled more than 100 yards to the shipping department. By moving the shipping area to the end of the production line, they were able to eliminate a fork truck and driver, and significantly improve communications between production and shipping, thus enhancing customer satisfaction.

An entrepreneurial group recently acquired a business whose equipment was 25 years out-of-date. They then set out to achieve a turnaround by motivating their employees to work harder in the hope of reducing costs. They soon learned that such belt-tightening techniques would never overcome the competitive advantage enjoyed by competitors with newer machinery that required one-fifth of the labor cost. Within 18 months of the acquisition, the company filed for bankruptcy.

Lower the river

An expense reduction technique used by some turnaround experts involves lowering the *river* of expenses until the *ship* runs aground. You then let back in a little water and the ship floats comfortably. It's based on the belief that if you don't lower expenses to the point where it becomes severely difficult to operate, you will never know how low you could have gone. There are obviously risks associated with this strategy— a key person who is laid off might not be available or willing to return, and a replacement might be costly and difficult to train.

Black box

The challenge in lowering costs is enhanced and facilitated by understanding what I call the *black box* theory. To manufacture and deliver a product, most businesses go through countless activities. All of these go through the black box we call purchasing, receiving, manufacturing, operations, administration, accounting, sales, shipping, collection and customer service. Because of the complexity and unpredictability of the millions of permutations and combinations of events, and possibility for error, most businesses do not even scratch the surface of understanding what truly takes place in the black box. As a result, they leave most of it to the laws of probability, which is not an acceptable approach for a business that strives to be the best. As such, the leading corporations work hard to study and understand what goes on in their black box, and to develop systems and procedures to take control of these activities, rather than be controlled by them. To truly achieve significant reductions in expenses, it is important to understand the true cost of an activity, function or product.

Example

An equipment rental company engages in renting its equipment in several different market segments, all with varying complexities and complications. In some markets, high product liability and worker compensation claims are experienced; in other markets, excessive bad debts represent a significant problem; and in yet others, inventory shrinkage is abnormally high. For this company to significantly improve its profits, it will have to understand all of these issues. It will then have to develop techniques to manage and reduce these exposures, or redirect its strategy away from these markets.

One of the apparent reasons for Wal-Mart's huge success is its ability to understand and reduce the cost of the logistics of getting product from the manufacturer to the customer. Many of its competitors are still staring at the black box trying to figure out how to get in, let alone begin taking action.

Less is more

Many times, after a staff layoff, the remaining people seem to have more time on their hands and are more efficient. This could indicate that the people who were laid off were not needed for effective operations (and who, in fact, may have reduced operational effectiveness because they were in the way). Ironically, and contrary to what one might expect, the morale of the people who survive a layoff often goes up rather than down (provided the surviving employees feel that the layoff was handled in a manner that does not threaten their continued security and peace of mind). This is because they are usually grateful that they made the *cut*, they take it as a compliment that they were good enough not to be laid off and they are often delighted that management has finally taken action to get rid of the weak passengers that weren't (by their perception) doing their jobs anyway. Obviously, there will always be surviving employees that are upset to see their friends leave, who believe management was wrong and who expect that they might be victims of the next round of cuts. Often, these employees will start polishing their résumés or start looking for another job before they are axed.

However, if you carry on laying people off, you will reach a point where organizational effectiveness is seriously and adversely affected. At this stage, you must stop and consider recalling some of the laid-off people.

Prioritize expenses

In identifying which expenses should be reduced, you should list all operating expenses in order of magnitude, with the largest at the top of the list. Then, starting at the top, identify ways to eliminate or reduce expenses.

Brace yourself

Elimination of expenses can be a very traumatic experience. You have to keep reminding yourself that the survival of the company takes precedence over everything else.

> While compassion is needed, if you are not willing
> or able to make the tough decisions, you may risk the
> viability of the business, and ultimately the liveli-
> hoods of the people you're trying to protect

Reduction in force

Manpower is usually very close to the top of the list of largest operating expenses. It is also usually one of the easiest areas to eliminate excess expenses—quickly and at relatively low cost (not counting emotional cost). As said earlier, eliminating excess expenses often increases efficiency.

An effective approach is to eliminate, say, one person from a group, spread the workload to the remaining people, and perhaps give the remaining people a small increase in wages, or an opportunity to earn a bonus if certain targets are achieved. The overall cost to the company could be significantly lower.

In addition to (or instead of) layoffs, there is always the option of asking employees to take salary or wage reductions. This may require renegotiation of union contracts, which may not be easy. You may prefer to leave this as an absolute last resort, because it is very demotivating for people, who are working their hearts out to manage the crisis, to have to deal with a pay cut. It is often better to lay off one more marginal person so that you can continue to reward the productive people (with the exception of senior management, with whom you can often trade pay cuts for an incentive bonus tied to the successful completion of the turnaround). If you are forced to resort to pay cuts for non-management employees, the blow can be softened significantly if the employees are given stock options or other similar incentives to compensate them for their hard work at less pay.

While pay cuts for unionized workers may not always be feasible, it is always useful to negotiate changes in union work rules, to give you more flexibility in allocating work to union employees. This will enable you to run the business more efficiently because you will be free to redesign products and job allocations without union resistance. In general, the benefits of significantly improved efficiency will outweigh the savings of a pay cut coupled with the associated reduction in morale.

Another option is to reduce worktime for all workers until the crisis passes. For example, establish a four-day work week, close the plant for a period of time or require employees to use up vacation time. This approach is generally fairer in that all employees are treated equally. Also, it gives you a better chance of keeping the workforce intact for the time when production demands pickup. However, if the crisis extends for a long time, this approach will not work, because the better workers will not tolerate the reduction in pay and will start looking elsewhere for jobs.

Before commencing any layoffs, review the organization chart showing all department—and list all employees, their job functions, salaries and length of service. This will give you the starting point to identify areas of excessive or redundant staffing or remuneration.

In general, the people that you need to keep can be separated into two categories. The people who don't fall into one of these two categories are probably not necessary. The two categories that you cannot do without are:

Thinkers and leaders

These are the brains behind the organization, those who do the planning, strategizing and managing of the day-to-day business and crises that arise. No successful turnaround can be achieved without a group of talented, competent, analytical and creative management personnel, who have the ability to assess the company's situation, and find and implement solutions that work. (In order to ensure that you don't lose any of these key employees, it is a good idea to implement a bonus plan for them—to reward them for playing an instrumental role in the turnaround, and for staying the course.)

Front line producers

These are the people who bat for the company every day—the people that produce the output of the company. This category includes not only direct and visible producers (e.g., salespeople, production personnel), but also less visible, but key, support personnel, without whose tireless efforts the visible producers would be unable to effectively do their jobs. This category includes accounting, data processing, payroll, warehousemen, factory helpers, etc.

The third, and not so useful, group essentially gets in between the Thinkers and the Front Line Producers, and often serves to confuse, complicate or slow matters down. This group includes middle management, support personnel or staff functions that either achieve nothing, or work hard at creating work and complications, or people that don't have

---

Failsafe technique
for evaluating employees

Ask yourself, "If I were interviewing this person for a job today, and knowing what I know now about him/her, and considering the financial position the business is in, would I hire him/her?"

---

enough current skills or future potential to be worth keeping. Without compelling reasons to the contrary, members of this group should be eliminated. In practice, it is not too difficult to sort people into these three categories, and make your decisions accordingly.

Incentives

Another option, rather than cutting wages, is increasing the required output of workers, by increasing production rates. Let's assume the required production standard is 100 units a day. If you can raise the standard to 125 units a day, this would *theoretically* allow you to eliminate 20 percent of your workforce. In practice, however, it is extremely hard to get workers to produce at a higher rate when they know the company is in trouble—because they assume (often, quite correctly) that they will be working their way out of a job. However, if you can show the workforce that this will not result in a loss of jobs, and instead will strengthen the company's position through higher revenues at a lower cost, it will often be very well received—especially if you build in an incentive system to reward employees (workers and management) for higher productivity. To convince workers that higher production rates will not result in a loss of jobs, provide them with factual evidence of the existing backlog of orders, or marketing efforts to generate business, so that they can see that there will be enough work to accommodate the higher output, without layoffs.

One of the plants with which I was involved implemented a very successful incentive program that ultimately resulted in the complete turnaround of a significantly underperforming business. The incentive program rewarded direct and indirect workers for production in excess of standard production rates. The plan worked very well for two major reasons: First, most workers worked hard to achieve the additional standard hours and earn the extra money. Second, because the incentive was paid monthly, the workers very soon became accustomed to receiving the incentive checks, and began to build them into their spending budgets—meaning that they had to continue working hard to maintain their lifestyle. Additional advantages to the company included:

- Additional production hours without benefit costs
- Significantly improved throughput, and responsiveness to customers
- Higher morale
- Other spinoff improvement in efficiencies discovered by workers in the pursuit of faster production

In contrast to this, if the company's crisis results in part from a reduction in orders, a major problem you may face is a significant decline in worker productivity. In a recent turnaround on which my firm worked, the productivity of the distressed company's workforce dropped as much as 40 percent, because the workers made sure that they stretched the backlog of orders long enough to protect their jobs. Management was reluctant to implement further layoffs because they wanted to retain the skilled workers in the event orders increased. Such situations should be monitored very carefully. If the decline in orders continues for more than a few weeks, serious consideration should be given to proceeding with the layoffs to avoid the plant becoming accustomed to operating at substantially lower productivity levels.

In a turnaround, it is always a good idea to set up incentive plans for all levels of employees to get everybody focused on the goal of saving the company. The incentive plan should be designed to steer people toward improvement in areas that are problems, such as quality, efficiency, delivery and service. Individual incentives are really only effective where individual workers can have a direct and measurable impact on output. Where productivity is more reliant on interdependent work between a group of workers, individual incentives will not work well. In such cases, group plans (e.g., profit sharing plans) should be explored.

There is always a downside with incentive plans, for the following reasons:

- They rarely work well for both parties: They usually work better for either the employee or the company—resulting in dissatisfaction for one of them.
- To be effective, they need to be well thought out, and fairly and consistently implemented. This is not always an easy task.
- Employees are usually very creative in making the system work for them—and often spend a lot of energy thinking about the incentive plan, rather than doing their jobs.

Despite the disadvantages, incentive plans are often very helpful in a turnaround situation.

Cross training

To facilitate the efficient reduction of workforce, it is important to cross-train workers, so that they know how to perform the functions of other workers. If workers are not cross-trained, you will have less flexibility in reducing manpower because you may have to retain a worker who is the only person able to perform a function, even if that function does not take a lot of time.

Burning bridges

When terminating staff, be sure to take legal advice on the proper approach and procedure. This will help you avoid costly and unpleasant charges by former employees against the company. Also, it is essential to complete the layoff in the most humane, sensitive and fair manner possible. Being laid off is very traumatic, and people deeply appreciate it if the company goes out of its way to ease the blow. Furthermore, I have found that it never pays to burn any bridges. People with whom you sever relationships in business have an uncanny habit of popping up again sometime in the future.

Unsaid messages to surviving employees

In a major layoff, the message you send to the surviving employees will be very important. Many thoughts and concerns will be going through their minds, and the way in which you carry out the layoff will either alleviate or aggravate their fears. The first thought they are likely to have is, "If this can happen to those guys, how do I know I'm not next?" If you don't allay this fear, the better employees could well be thinking that they'd rather *jump ship* before the inevitable firing squad takes aim at them. It would be easy for you if you could make an announcement reassuring all remaining employees that there will be no further layoffs. But this may not be wise because you never know for sure whether you'll need to take such action, and the worst action you could take is to go back on your word. It is often advisable to make an announcement that you deeply regret having taken the action you were forced to take in the financial best interests of the company; you don't anticipate any further layoffs, but that you cannot give absolute assurances of this; you recognize the need to create an environment in which people can feel secure and get back to thinking about work, rather than their job security—and to achieve this, any people that are subject to further layoffs will receive a significantly expanded severance package, which will give them the financial security of not having to worry about immediately finding a job. This approach obviously may cost the company more, but the payback of a relaxed, secure and trusting work force may be well worth the cost.

Employee trust

The concept of a trusting workforce is always very important to a company—but especially so in a layoff situation. Anything you can do to establish the integrity and dependability of the company will be a great help to re-establish the trust that is always in question in a layoff. If a company loses the trust of its employees, it has very serious problems. As a result, layoffs or manpower reductions should be a very infrequent and unusual occurrence in a company's life. Provided that it is done in a fair and considerate manner, the infrequent layoff may not seriously jeopardize the employees' trust in the company. If, however, layoffs start to be seen as normal and frequent, the employees will become insecure, and the company will lose the unquestioned loyalty and commitment of its workforce. Some companies have accepted lower profits to retain their no-layoff record. Every CEO in a turnaround situation must consider the trade-off between the advantages of lower expenses in the short-term, and the disadvantages of the negative effect of layoffs on the company and employees.

Benefits

An area that often can be cut in a crisis is company-paid benefits. The most expensive benefit today is group medical and dental insurance. Look for opportunities to cut, or share more of the cost with employees (for example, switching group insurance to an HMO, or increasing the deductible). Usually, when a company is in a crisis, employees expect some sort of benefit reduction—and the reaction, while not enthusiastic, is usually not as negative as a pay cut.

Purchasing

For most companies, purchasing materials and other supplies represents one of the largest expenditures. There are almost always significant opportunities for savings from better purchasing.

Items purchased should be listed in order of dollar magnitude (highest at top of the list). Usually the top 20 items will comprise 70 percent to 80 percent of the dollar value of all items purchased. Bids should be requested from several suppliers for the top value items. It is very rare that prices cannot be reduced. Because of the volume of purchases, a small price saving can have a big impact on the bottom line. Don't be afraid to put pressure on suppliers to reduce prices.

One way for you to really know whether you are getting the best price for the major items you purchase is for you to do a costing exercise on your suppliers' products. If you can determine the breakdown of their costs, you can then evaluate whether you are being charged a fair price, or whether there is room for you to bargain their prices down. For example, if you are purchasing tubular steel, you need to know the best price for which the supplier can purchase steel coil, and what his labor and overhead costs are in converting the coil into tube (including the process of slitting the coil, and then rolling and welding it into tube). With this information, you can determine whether you are paying a fair price, and you should have a reasonably good idea when changes to your supplier's cost have taken place—and whether there is an opportunity for you to negotiate a price adjustment. This type of exercise should be carried out for all major expenditures. Naturally, obtaining some of this information might be easier said than done. Nevertheless, with a little detective work, a reasonable estimate can usually be obtained. You might even be able to get a lot of the information from strategic questioning of your supplier's employees. It also can't do any harm to let the supplier know how well versed you are about his cost structure. The approach recommended in this paragraph is not dissimilar from the steps a savvy car buyer might take before he enters the dealership. If his research has provided him with a reasonable estimate of the dealer's cost, he will be in a better position to negotiate for the best price.

Look for creative ways to cut purchase costs through substitute products (e.g., plastic parts instead of steel), and through alternate channels (e.g., forming a buying co-op, buying excess inventories from competitors, etc.).

Subcontracting

Try to focus your company's efforts in areas where you have primary expertise. Wherever possible, delegate non-primary or short-run items to outside sources who may be better equipped than you to perform these functions. Subcontracting is a very effective way to keep your expenses to the absolute minimum. The ideal situation is to only have a core group of essential people on your payroll: All short-run, seasonal, cyclical and peak-load work should either be subcontracted, or done by temporaries.

Your employees should concentrate their efforts on areas where they are most efficient. Many functions that sidetrack an employee from normal activities could easily be subcontracted. It may appear that you can perform these functions in-house at an economical cost. In reality, this is usually not the case.

Capital investment considerations also affect the subcontracting decision. If you have to acquire a piece of equipment that you can only utilize a small percentage of the time, it will be more cost effective to subcontract that activity to somebody else who has significantly higher volumes in that activity and, therefore, can achieve greater economies of scale. If you already own the machine, but only utilize it a small percentage of the time, consider selling the machine and subcontracting the activity. You can then redeploy the cash proceeds to more productive areas of the business.

Of course, there are non-financial factors that impact the decision not to subcontract, even if it makes financial sense. These include:

- An inability to control quality
- Timing or logistic considerations
- Confidentiality or trade-secret issues

Other significant advantages of subcontracting are:

- You know your exact cost because you receive an invoice. If you make it yourself, cost is a moving target that depends on volume, purchase prices, efficiencies, etc.
- You can often significantly reduce your inventories, provided you can set up a *just-in-time* system with the subcontractor.

Overhead reduction

There are many other overhead expenses that can be eliminated or reduced in a crisis. These include:

- Janitorial services: Employees can all help out for one hour a week
- Express courier services: It's very easy to get into the habit of using these even when the item *absolutely positively* need *not* to reach its destination overnight
- Investigate and implement ways to reduce utility costs
- Apply for reductions or abatements in property taxes
- Property, casualty, product liability, group medical and other insurance: Obtain competitive quotes from at least three brokers. Ask them to look for creative ways to reduce the cost, e.g., self insurance, captives

- Negotiate lower rates with telephone carriers, or switch to discount carrier

- Ask for discounts from all service providers (e.g., utilities, travel agencies, printers, etc.). In so many circumstances, discounts are available on request. In other situations, providers will willingly agree in order to maintain you as a customer

- Reduce travel expenses: New budget hotels are low cost and good basic accommodation. Use budget car rental companies, discount airlines and have breakfast with customers rather than lunch or dinner

- Professional services (auditors, legal, etc.): You can usually negotiate better rates, and wherever possible, seek competitive bids

- Sublease unused parts of your facility to reduce occupancy cost, or relocate to lower cost premises (consider relocation to areas that offer lower wage rates, incentives or rebates). You could even sublet some of your idle plant and machinery to other manufacturers

It is vitally important that you create an atmosphere in which everybody is encouraged to eliminate waste and inefficiency. Consider publishing a monthly newsletter acknowledging individual ideas and awarding prizes for eliminating waste or promoting efficiency. Set the example yourself by always being frugal and budget conscious.

Example

It became evident that one of the major uncontrollable costs of a manufacturing company was workers' compensation claims. To counteract this, a program was implemented whereby every worker who had an injury-free week (with full attendance) received a ticket for a drawing. At the end of the month, all tickets were placed in a hat. The winner of the drawing received a prize, such as a bicycle, camera, etc. Within one year, lost work days due to injury or absence declined from over 300 to less than 40. The savings to the company, in reduced workers' compensation premiums, the elimination of the disruption and lost production related to the injuries, and increased productivity and morale, were substantial.

Expense reduction vs. sales increase

A very important (but not so obvious) concept of a turn-around strategy is that *a dollar of expense saved is equivalent to several dollars of increased revenue*. In other words, you are just as well off if you can reduce expenses by $1.00, than if you increase your sales by several dollars.

The example on page 166 compares two alternative methods to achieve additional cash flow. Alternative 1 assumes that sales can be increased by 10 percent (from $10,000 to $11,000). This results in an additional variable contribution of $400, and an equivalent amount of additional profit contribution (no additional fixed expenses). However, because an additional $225 is invested in additional receivables and inventory, the incremental cash flow generated from Alternative 1 is only $175. Alternative 2, rather than assuming any increase in sales, determines the reduction in fixed expenses that have to be achieved to produce the same $175 cash flow improvement. The conclusion in this example is that a $175 reduction in fixed costs ($3,500—$3,325) achieves the same cash flow result as a $1,000 increase in sales. This indicates that, in this example, a $1.00 reduction in expenses achieves the same cash flow result as a $5.71 increase in sales

	ALTERNATIVE 1			ALTERNATIVE 2
	Base	Addi-tional	Total	Expense Reduction
Sales	$10,000	$1,000	$11,000	$10,000
Variable				
Contribution	4,000	400	4,400	4,000
Fixed Expenses	3,500		3,500	3,325
Profit				
Contribution	500	400	900	675
Working Capital				
Investment[14]		(225)	(225)	0
Net Cash Flow	**$500**	**$175**	**$675**	**$675**

[14] Estimated working capital investment for additional $1,000 in sales assumed to be:
Inventory - Cost of sales ($600) divided by inventory
turnover of, say, six times p.a. $100
Receivables - Additional sales of $1,000 at 1.5 months
outstanding, i.e., $1,000 x 1.5/12   125
                                                                                  $225

($1,000/$175). Generally in a turnaround, greater benefits can be yielded by the diligent attention to reducing fixed expenses.

F. ELIMINATE NONPROFITABLE DIVISIONS, PRODUCTS OR CUSTOMERS

Most businesses (especially those in a crisis) have losing divisions, product lines or departments. Management often has an emotional investment in turning these losers into winners. It almost always takes more time and money than expected. The analysis performed in Part 1: Sections II and III should have highlighted any such divisions or product lines that are not providing an adequate return on the assets employed.

Losing divisions, aside from being cash drains, usually take up a disproportionate amount of
management time, with the result that the productive divisions might not receive the attention they
deserve, thus not achieving their maximum profit
potential

Management usually justifies keeping the division because
it would cost more to eliminate it. Often this is true in the very
short-term, but it's amazing how good it feels to ultimately be
rid of those drains.

Management often believes the turnaround is just around
the corner. However, the goal just keeps slipping out of its
hands, and the timetable keeps getting pushed back. As a
result, always assume a losing division will continue losing,
unless you have compelling reasons to believe it will change
in the near term.

Example

In one situation in which I was involved, management was very enthusiastically building a new
division that it was convinced would provide the
super profits that the existing core division was not
generating. As the division rapidly grew and built a
substantial backlog of orders, several very plausible
explanations were presented as to why the division
was on the *verge* of being exceptionally profitable.
Later, when the profits still didn't materialize, management concluded that a change in the method of
accounting for work-in-progress would rectify the
situation. The board of directors finally made the
decision to overrule division management and close
the division down when one of the division

managers announced that the *real problem* with the division was that corporate headquarters did not understand that this type of business *just wasn't that profitable*. A lot of unnecessary cost and expense could have been saved if everybody could have acknowledged the mistake a lot sooner.

Other often overlooked opportunities for improved profitability and cash flow are the elimination of nonprofitable products and customers. Again, emotional attachments usually make it hard for management to detach itself enough to evaluate rationally. It is very important for businesses to continually evaluate profitability by product line and by customer.

In determining which divisions or product lines should be eliminated, not only those that are actually losing money should be considered. Those that are not earning an adequate Return On Assets (as determined by the Treadmill Test, see Part 1: Section II) should also be closely examined to see if they should be eliminated.

Unless there are compelling reasons to the contrary, underperforming divisions and product lines should also be sold or liquidated.

Profitability should always be evaluated in relation to the assets the company needs to employ to maintain those divisions, products or customers. When this exercise is carried out, you will often find that the profit being earned from a particular product line is not sufficient in relation to the amount of assets the company has to tie up (e.g., inventory, receivables, trucks, etc.). In these situations, ways should be explored to improve such profitability or asset management. If this can't be done, consideration should be given to eliminating the division, product or customer, unless there are other strategic reasons for not doing so.

Consolidation of profit or cost centers

If it does not make sense to eliminate product lines or divisions, consider consolidating two (or more) areas that can function under one overhead structure instead of two.

Example

One of our clients had its management and sales office in one city, and manufacturing and order entry in another (probably because the company president didn't want to move to the less-than-desirable plant location). This resulted in significant duplication of effort and expenses (aside from inefficiency and communications problems). After a new CEO was installed, a decision was made to move the sales and management office to the plant, resulting in substantial overhead reductions.

Unprofitable areas can generate cash

An often overlooked and very important advantage of closing a losing division or product line is the working capital that will be freed by the division as it winds down. Even though it might have generated an operating loss, as you liquidate receivables and inventories you can achieve a positive cash flow because you are not replacing them with new inventory or receivables. In addition, cash flow improves due to elimination of the division's operating loss.

Focus

Another important reason to eliminate underperforming divisions, branches or product lines is to attain a clear and dedicated focus. In today's fiercely competitive world, it is hard enough to be the best at one activity—and when a person or business attempts to be the best at more than one, their energies and focus becomes diluted. Because it is so vital to long-term success to be a leader in your field, such dilution is likely to reduce the chances of being the very best. For example, it is rare for a company to be outstanding at manufacturing and marketing. The skills and mindset required for these two areas are so different. This applies very aptly in the personal computer area, where many of the manufacturers have opted to market through resellers because they know their own limitations in marketing. With our own clients we have seen, time and time again, a single-division thriving business evolve into a three- or four-division underperforming problem. Gerber Products Co., the large manufacturer of baby food products, appears to have utilized a tight focus to significantly improve its business.

"It has tried diversifying into other baby items—day-care centers, clothes, toys—and failed each time.... Refocusing on baby food has doubled Gerber's return on equity, averaging 14.5% in the 1980s, to an average of over 29% since 1990."

Forbes, October 12, 1992

Downsizing of multiple division or product businesses has several advantages:

- The business can focus its attention on what it does best.

- The effectiveness of management can be improved by scaling the business down to a size within its capabilities to manage. Management that appears to be incapable of running a multiple-division business might be competent in a single- division operation.

- Cash flow can be improved significantly, as described above, by the liquidation of assets and the elimination of operating losses.

A recent client operated a very profitable single-store retail business. An equity investor offered to inject the funds to support an acquisition strategy. Within a year, the business had expanded to three stores within the same city—but was losing significant amounts. The owner of the business soon realized that the skills and systems required to run a chain (even a small chain) were very different from those needed for a single store. Six months later, the client had liquidated two of the three stores, and returned to a very profitable single-store business. This client is now a true believer in the benefits of *focus*.

Even diversified companies are apparently discovering the importance of focus.

> "Sears plans to dispose of its Dean Witter brokerage unit, most of its Coldwell Banker real estate division and 20% of its Allstate insurance business, increasing the company's focus on retailing, where it is struggling."
>
> *The Wall Street Journal*, September 30, 1992

G. STRENGTHEN MANAGEMENT TEAM

While Corporate CPR usually involves a concerted effort to reduce manpower, one expense you cannot afford to cut in a crisis is *Key Management*. Key management are those who help the CEO make decisions, and manage staff, and to whom responsibility for important areas can be delegated. Often, in the pursuit of expense reduction during a crisis, management will conclude that it cannot afford the personnel in certain functions. If this function is a *key* management or control position, you might discover after the fact that you couldn't afford **not** to have that person. In fact, because a substantial part of the CEO's time in a crisis will be devoted to managing the crisis (i.e., dealing with lenders, creditors, investors, etc.), the need to have competent management who can function with minimal direction is even greater than under normal circumstances.

Hire the best

There is often a tendency to promote someone from within to fill a key management position, because it is usually cheaper and it's easier than going through the searching, interviewing and hiring process. However, you need to have the best qualified people. You do not have time (or perhaps the knowledge) to train people. You cannot afford to pay the price of the person's mistakes while he or she climbs the learning curve. It is often cheaper to get an experienced and qualified person immediately. The additional salary is usually tenfold saved by the elimination of costly mistakes caused by inexperience. However, even if you are willing to pay top dollar for the best people, there is no guarantee that you will find the right people to help you in your crisis. Truly good people are rarely available, especially when the company is floundering. Finding the right key management is, therefore, your biggest headache. Promoting from within, and hiring from the outside both have their risks and problems. There is no magic formula in this area and you have to make individual judgment calls.

Sometimes, you may feel there is nobody in the organization that has the experience or ability to grow into the required position fast enough. You then decide to hire from the outside, and you risk resistance from some people within. If you hire the right person, he or she can usually gain acceptance within a short period of time. However, regardless of your assessment of the manager's performance, you must back the person until such acceptance is achieved. If people sense you have doubts about the new manager, you might fuel the internal resistance and facilitate the demise of a potentially good employee. Of course, you need to be aware that not all internal resistance to the new employee is ill-intentioned—it is always possible (in fact, very likely) that you hired the *wrong person*. After allowing a reasonable period of time for the manager to settle into the position, be ready to accept this reality, and take appropriate steps to correct it before more damage is done.

Competence

In many turnarounds, a major contributing reason for the crisis is ineffective or non-cooperative management. This is often the case in an acquisition situation. To carry out a successful turnaround, you must know that you have a competent team that can be depended on. This usually requires you to weed out the *ineffective* managers and the *con artists*.

Ineffective managers fill a position and either never get anything done, or whatever is done is actually carried out by subordinates, with little or no input from themselves. These managers can be eliminated immediately. There is often a major spin-off benefit resulting from unleashing the potential of previously stifled subordinates. Ineffective managers often have all the right qualifications and experience. They often look the part, say all the right things and know what needs to be done. The problem is they just don't get it done! Place a high priority on identifying them and getting rid of them. How are you going to identify them if they look so convincing? Start by critically evaluating everybody that looks convincing. A good percentage of them are ineffective managers. Often, the managers that don't look perfect turn out to be the best managers.

Con artists are those managers who present themselves in a way that does not represent either their true abilities or their real intentions or motives. They are usually very dangerous, as they are constantly working to circumvent or upstage your efforts. Conmen are much more difficult to identify than ineffective managers, because they are often smart enough to avoid giving the signals that would lead you to recognize them. Usually, you will develop a deep-down *gut* feel that the manager is not to be trusted, but the manager will probably have very subtly and effectively convinced you (and perhaps others) that you can't live without him. Whenever you sense this, you must act by checking what the manager is doing behind the scenes. The very fact that you feel you can't do without someone is cause enough for you to investigate. You may find the person to be very loyal and truly (and, hopefully, temporarily) indispensable. On the other hand, you may identify and eliminate some very serious and dangerous undercover espionage.

As a general rule, in an acquisition-type turnaround situation, it will be very unusual if all the management are worth keeping. So, search out the ineffective managers and the con artists. They are there—you just have to find them!

Experience vs. competence

It is always preferable to hire somebody with prior experience in the job function or industry. However, if you have to choose between experience and competence, competence should win most times. In a turnaround, you need managers who can think creatively and get things done. A competent manager can pick up enough industry knowledge in a reasonable period of time; an experienced but incompetent manager can do little to help you.

Loyalty

You will be far better off to have a smaller, more compact management team that you know you can depend on. In crisis management, loyalty is essential. You cannot afford to have anybody on your team who is not totally committed to the cause. They must also be willing to work very hard—without constantly putting you under the pressure of explaining *what's in it for them*.

Focus On strengths

In searching for the right people for your management team, you will quickly find that nobody is perfect. If you form a picture in your mind of the person you would like to fill a position, most times you will be disappointed. Almost nobody has all the qualities we look for. It is usually best to focus on people's strengths rather than their weaknesses—ask yourself *Is the employee good at what he/she's good at*? If there are ten qualities you are looking for, you are better off with somebody who is excellent at seven and terrible at three, as opposed to somebody who is average at all ten. To have an *excellent* business, you need people who are *great* at what they do. If they're weak in a few areas, get someone to cover for them.

Heart in the right place

Another key factor to decide is whether the manager or employee has the interests of the company at heart. Will the person exhibit loyalty, commitment, enthusiasm and a willingness to do what it takes? Not everyone fits this description, but you will find that there are many that do. If you can find people like this, **and** they're *good at what they're good at*—you're going in the right direction. Be careful, however, of people who are willing to totally subjugate their interests to those of the company. They might have some psychological need to commit to something, which could detract from their ability to be an independent, free-thinking manager.

Human resource priorities

Even if all your people are competent and dedicated, they might not possess the types of skills you need for your turnaround. With the appropriate management in place, your task of turning the company around will be significantly easier. The types of managers needed for a successful turnaround, and the related focus of management, can be different from a normal thriving business, as described below:

- **Accounting and finance**
  While important for all companies, accounting becomes even more important in a turnaround situation. This is because accurate accounting information is vital to understand the company's status and develop strategic alternatives. Furthermore, reporting to outsiders (e.g., lenders, suppliers, bankruptcy court) increases substantially in a crisis. In addition, time devoted to negotiations with secured and unsecured creditors is extensive in a turnaround.

- **Operations**
  Operations management takes on more importance in a turnaround, as the company tries to cut expenses and find ways to improve efficiency.

- **Sales and marketing**
  While sales management remains important to help maintain (and, in some cases, build) sales levels during the crisis, marketing often takes a back seat, due to the focus on short-term sales performance, rather than long-term positioning or product recognition. Emphasis should still be placed on ensuring and enhancing customer satisfaction, however.

- **Manufacturing and quality control**
  Strong emphasis should be placed in these areas to find ways to lower costs and enhance productivity.

- **Engineering and product development**
  These areas are not usually high-priority areas in a turnaround. A company in a crisis generally should not be focusing on development. To the extent that it can help in lower costs through redesigning existing operations or products, engineering is important.

- **Personnel and human resources**
  These areas continue to be important in the efforts to maintain morale and commitment of employees. They take on lesser importance in the areas of recruiting, employee development, training and related fields.

H. STRATEGIC TURNAROUND PLAN

Sections B through G above have discussed many options and strategies available under a short-to-medium-term Turnaround Strategy. These must now be formulated into a Turnaround Strategic Plan. You must decide what route you are going to take, and put it into action. For example, if you are going to approach suppliers for extended payment terms, identify which suppliers, decide on negotiating parameters, give responsibility to someone for negotiating the deals and monitor progress. If you are going to effect a layoff, identify who will be laid off, when the layoff will take place, who will be responsible for effecting the layoffs, etc.

Define success

Before developing the Turnaround Strategic Plan, it is important to define what result will be considered a *success*. Success can be very different for the various parties in a turnaround. For example, a liquidation that results in a payout of 100 cents on the dollar will be a great success for unsecured creditors, but might be a dismal failure for employees who lose their jobs, or shareholders who receive no payout and have no ongoing business value. If the CEO or shareholders have personally guaranteed all of the debts of the company, a full payout to guaranteed creditors might be a success for them, if they have substantial personal net worth that would be at risk if the guarantees are called on.

For most owner/chief executives, the likely definition of success will be a future ongoing business that can earn a sustainable profit and service all of its obligations. This is often best achieved through a downsizing of the company, where portions of the operations are sold off or liquidated to take care of debt obligations, with a smaller but more viable ongoing business. If you do not define what success means to you, it will be very hard to develop and implement a Turnaround Strategic Plan that gets you to where you'd like to be. More importantly, it is essential that your success goal is realistic and achievable. Aiming too high can often result in the loss of everything.

Dynamic process

Things change fast in a crisis, and plans made today are out-of-date tomorrow. This is normal and to be expected. Nevertheless, it is essential that formal planning in writing be done. The exercise of writing the plan down is a very good discipline and forces the writer to be clear in his mind what the plan is and how it will work. The written plan also affords key employees the ability to have a clear understanding of the turnaround plan.

The Strategic Plan must include a detailed budget for the next 12 months together with a forecast for the subsequent four years. Budgeting is a very important skill as the budget becomes the benchmark against which you evaluate your performance; a conservative budget can often give you a false sense of accomplishment. In preparing a budget, it is very important to analyze the numbers in relation to historical data, watching especially for cyclical trends. It is helpful to do a graphical presentation of the prior year Profit and Loss statement, by month—and then overlay the forthcoming years' budget. Variances between the budget and the historical results will be clearly evident, and should be investigated. This should also be done for the Balance Sheet and Statement of Changes in Cash—and where possible should be done by branch and by product. (An example of a Strategic Plan for a turnaround is included as Appendix IV.)

The Turnaround Strategic Plan must then be monitored, adjusted and updated every single day. The CEO's function is to keep all resources moving in accordance with the plan, and to make the necessary adjustments and modifications as circumstances dictate. The Strategic Plan, together with up-to-date budgets, should serve as a tool to facilitate everybody pulling together. The whole corporate team needs to start working harmoniously, and with a common purpose and vision. Without this, the turnaround is less likely to work.

Freeze expenditures

One of the most important controls to be implemented in your turnaround plan is a wage, hiring and capital expenditure freeze. After you have implemented a cost-reduction plan, it is essential that there be no new hires or wage increases without the express written approval of the CEO, who should strenuously avoid such moves. Once the process of re-hiring or spending begins, it is very hard to know where to draw the line. Controls should also be implemented to monitor and approve all capital and other expenditures and expenses, to ensure that only absolutely necessary expenditures are incurred. On the other hand, it is also important to have enough qualified and competent personnel to ensure the turnaround is achieved. The strategic plan must provide for the costs of such personnel.

I. CASH FLOW PROJECTION UPDATE AND MONITORING

With the Turnaround Strategic Plan formulated, you now need to do a revised Cash Flow Projection, taking into account all the new strategies you have developed. For example, if you decide to do a sale and leaseback of a building that will be completed on July 1, on that date you will receive a cash injection of the selling price (less brokerage, legal fees and other costs) and on the first of each following month, you will have rent to pay. The cash injection from the sale might be used to lower your bank debt, and hence lower your interest bill. All of these items must be reflected in your Cash Flow Projection. Actual cash in and out flows must then be inserted alongside the projection on a weekly basis. Variances between actual and projected cash flows should be analyzed and investigated. At least once a week, the Cash Flow Projection should be revised and updated to take account of actual cash in and out flows, as well as changes in the Turnaround Strategic Plan.

J. COMMUNICATIONS

It is very important at all stages of the turnaround program that you maintain open and honest communications with all key groups that interact with the company, including employees (and union leaders, if applicable), creditors, lenders and shareholders. Keep them informed of your plans, progress and setbacks. If you try very hard to avoid surprises, they will usually reward you with support and encouragement. There may be selected situations where it is clearly not beneficial to provide information to one or more parties. A hostile creditor, for example, may use the information to your detriment. In such cases, the CEO, in consultation with his attorney and financial adviser, should evaluate and determine an appropriate strategy.

Examples

Boake Sells, the former CEO of Revco D.S., established a *hotline* so that employees could call him directly to voice their concerns or seek explanation or clarification about Revco's strategy. Not only would this make employees at all levels feel they were involved in the turnaround, it might also indicate to them that the CEO cares about their concerns. This apparently had a significant impact on Revco's progress.

A recent client in a crisis kept his employees at all levels informed of developments, good and bad. His door was always open and anybody walking by could hear what was being discussed in meetings. When I asked him why he did this, he said, "When the door is open they don't bother to listen because they know I'm not hiding anything. This way, they can get on with their jobs, instead of speculating or fueling rumors."

In every workout in which I have been involved, I have seen significant benefits for those companies that invested the time and effort in regular and honest communications with all interested parties. Many of the most successful CEOs work hard to memorize the names and personal details of hundreds of employees. The benefits of this strategy are significant.

K. CHAPTER 11

While it is generally preferable that your turnaround strategy be achieved in an out-of-court manner, there are circumstances that force businesses to resort to a Chapter 11 filing.

If the business in a cash crisis cannot reach an acceptable agreement with its secured or unsecured creditors (that will result in the business being able to continue operating), the business may be best served by seeking the temporary protection from creditors and utilizing the reorganization provisions contained in Chapter 11 of the Bankruptcy Reform Act of 1978 (commonly referred to as the Bankruptcy Code), as amended, codified in Title 11 of the United States Code. This is known as filing a *voluntary* petition for reorganization (an *involuntary* petition commencing an involuntary bankruptcy case, under either Chapter 7 or 11 of the Bankruptcy Code, can also be instituted by a requisite number of creditors—generally, three creditors with undisputed unsecured claims totalling at least $5,000.)

Because of the disadvantages of Chapter 11, discussed later in this book, the filing of a voluntary bankruptcy petition should be a last resort for a business. Every effort should be exhausted to reach an accommodation with creditors before seeking protection from the courts. In a recent case in which my firm was involved, relations between the company and the lender had deteriorated to the extent where both parties were ready to fight it out in court. The company's attorneys wisely advised their client that it would be better served finding a compromise position with the bank to avoid having to file Chapter 11. The attorneys convinced the company's management that it might be advantageous to retain the services of an outside turnaround consultant to assist the company in regaining credibility with the bank. The bank agreed to give the company time to work out its problems if the company would hire a consultant that could help the company identify what its problems were, and assist in developing a plan for solving them. In this case, the company was given a valuable opportunity to work out its problems, without the numerous disadvantages of being in Chapter 11.

A business need not be insolvent to file a voluntary petition. It is quite possible for a company that is profitable or has a positive net worth to need to file bankruptcy, if it is illiquid and does not have enough cash to meet its obligations. A bankruptcy petition can also be a valuable tool for a company that is subject to significant litigation. Companies like Johns-Manville and A.H. Robins have been able to use Chapter 11 to stay multiple suits against them, and thus facilitate a more orderly and rational resolution of such litigation.

The major benefit of a Chapter 11 filing to the debtor company is *time*. All creditors are held at bay while the debtor is given time to prepare a plan to take care of its obligations. Chapter 11 automatically *stays* (i.e. restrains) all parties, including creditors, from taking further action against the debtor or its property. Chapter 11 also gives the debtor the opportunity (with certain exceptions) to accept or reject (with certain time limits) leases and other burdensome executory contracts. As a result, a debtor can extricate itself out of lease or other obligations that it will not need for its ongoing operations. For example, Chapter 11 cases have allowed debtors (e.g., Continental Airlines) to successfully reject or renegotiate collective bargaining agreements (subject to certain requirements).

Debtor in possession

In a typical Chapter 11 case, the business continues to operate after the voluntary petition is filed. The existing owners and management usually continue to run the business and are then referred to as the *debtor in possession*. In rare Chapter 11 cases, creditors can be successful in obtaining an order from the bankruptcy judge requiring the United States Trustee to appoint a *trustee*, who will then take over the operation of the business. Trustees can be appointed if there is *cause* (fraud, dishonesty, mismanagement or incompetence) or if the appointment of a trustee is *in the interest of creditors, and equity security holders, and other interests of the estate.*

Post-petition funding

Obtaining funding and credit after the Chapter 11 filing is very important for the business. Credit obtained in the ordinary course of business after the filing is given a priority position over pre-petition creditors. If this is not sufficient to enable the business to obtain new funding or credit, the bankruptcy court can authorize greater protection for post-petition creditors that could even include a *super priority* position, i.e., a lien on encumbered property that is equal or senior to existing liens. This can only be done if there is *adequate protection* of the pre-petition secured creditor's interest.

The Chapter 11 plan

The debtor-in-possession has the exclusive right to submit a plan of reorganization during the first 120 days after the date the Chapter 11 petition is filed. If the debtor files a plan within this 120-day period, the debtor is entitled to an additional 60 days to solicit acceptances of the plan. Thus, no other plan may be filed during the first 180 days of the case. The bankruptcy judge has the power to extend or reduce the 120- or 180-day periods. If the debtor fails to file a plan and obtain creditor acceptance within the specified time periods, any party in interest may file a plan after the *exclusive* period has expired. If a trustee has been appointed, the debtor, a creditor, the creditor's committee and any other party in interest may file a plan.

A Chapter 11 plan may alter the rights of secured creditors, unsecured creditors and shareholders. The Bankruptcy Code allows for the plan to divide *substantially similar* claims into classes, and treat each claim in a particular class in the same manner.

The plan should explain the proposed amount and timing of payments to the various classes of creditors. It may also specify how the payment plan will be achieved. The plan must include a written disclosure statement that provides interested parties with adequate information, to enable them to make an informed decision on whether to accept or reject the plan.

The plan must provide for cash payments in full to holders of *administrative expense* claims, which include claims for professional fees (i.e., compensation for attorneys, accountants, consultants, investment bankers and the trustee), wages and other costs necessary for preserving the estate after the commencement of the case. Unsecured claims for wages and other employee compensation earned within 90 days of the filing up to $2,000 per employee also receive priority treatment. Claims owing for taxes are accorded priority, but may receive deferred cash payments for no longer than six years from the date of *assessment*, provided the total payments have a present value equal to the full allowed amount of the claim.

All of the various *impaired* classes of claims and equity interests vote separately on the Chapter 11 plan (*Impairment* is defined in Section 1124 of the Bankruptcy Code). A class of claims has accepted a plan when more than one-half in number and at least two-thirds in amount of the allowed claims actually voting on the plan approve the plan. If there are dissenting creditors within an accepting class of creditors, the court can only approve the plan if it finds that such holder will receive at least as much as it would if the debtor liquidated under Chapter 7 of the Bankruptcy Code.

For a plan to be confirmed, the bankruptcy court must hold a hearing to give interested parties an opportunity to raise objections to the plan. Subject to certain requirements of the Bankruptcy Code, if every class of claims and interests accepts the plan, the plan will be confirmed by the court. If the plan is not approved by every class, it can only be confirmed if the following requirements are met:

1. At least one *impaired* class of claims accepted the plan.
2. The plan does not discriminate unfairly.
3. The plan is fair and equitable.

If these requirements are met, a class of claims or interests can be forced to accept the plan, even if they voted against it (known as a *cramdown*). For the court to approve the plan, it must find that the plan is *feasible*, i.e., it is unlikely to result in liquidation or additional reorganization unless such events are contemplated in the plan.

Effect of confirmation

After the Chapter 11 plan is confirmed, the debtor's obligations to creditors and other interested parties are governed by the plan, and the debtor is discharged from any other prepetition obligations (subject to some exceptions provided for by the Bankruptcy Code). The plan also binds all other parties, including any entity purchasing property or issuing securities under the plan, and any creditor, equity security holder or general partner of the debtor, regardless of whether such party is impaired or accepts the plan (with certain exclusions). Confirmation of the plan vests all property with the debtor except as provided in the plan, and all property dealt with under the plan is free and clear of all claims and interests except as otherwise provided in the plan.

Preferential or fraudulent payments

The Bankruptcy Code gives the bankruptcy trustee (and a debtor-in-possession) the right to avoid and recover certain transfers (known as *preferences*) of an insolvent debtor if it can be established that the transfer gave a creditor an advantage over other creditors. This applies to transfers made within 90 days before the filing of the bankruptcy petition (a longer period applies for transfers to insiders). This power, and the defenses thereto, are contained in Section 547 of the Bankruptcy Code. The Code also empowers the trustee to invalidate *fraudulent conveyances*, i.e., generally transfers made with the actual intent to hinder, delay or defraud creditors. If the trustee can prove intentional or constructive fraud (defined in Section 548 of the Code), transfers made within one year before bankruptcy can be set aside. Constructive fraud applies if *reasonably equivalent value* was not received by the debtor, **and** the debtor was either insolvent or rendered insolvent, was left with unreasonably small capital or had debts beyond its ability to pay[15].

186

The impact of preferential or fraudulent transfers in a bankruptcy situation is that it gives the debtor the opportunity to recover *property* that it may have previously transferred to other creditors. This can have the result of providing the debtor a much needed source of funds. An example of potentially fraudulent transfers are Leveraged Buyouts (LBOs). Often the acquirer of an LBO target will cause the target to become responsible for the LBO loan, which could include granting the lender a guarantee or a security interest in the target's assets. This weakens the financial condition of the target and, if such leverage renders the target insolvent or unreasonably weakens its capitalization, the rights of other creditors of the target are impaired. The fraudulent transfer laws give those creditors, or a trustee in bankruptcy on their behalf, the right to challenge the validity of the loans, as well as the distributions to selling shareholders. This could have the impact of voiding the lender's security interests in the collateral for the loan.

Disadvantages of Chapter 11

While existing management usually remains in control of the business, substantial loss of its control results because court approval is required for many transactions, which include engaging in new ventures, expending capital, or selling assets. Creditors also have a significantly greater say in the affairs of the company.

If the company's assets are pledged as security for a loan, any cash the company receives after the Chapter 11 filing may be *cash collateral*, which can only be used with the consent of the secured creditor or lender or by approval of the court through a *cash collateral order*. In order for the debtor to be allowed to continue to use the cash or any other secured asset, it must demonstrate that the secured creditor or lender is

[15] Note that some State laws specify longer time periods than Federal law for preferential or fraudulent transfers. Such State law provisions may be utilized by the trustee under Section 544 of the Bankruptcy Code.

When Chapter 11 makes sense

- Where secured creditors refuse to allow the company time to resolve its problem—and commence action to call its loans or seize cash or other collateral

- Where the company has significant contracts that it wishes to break—executory contracts (e.g., leases, employment contracts) can be rejected in bankruptcy

- Where the company has substantial interest-bearing debt, and the value of the collateral of secured lenders is such that they are significantly undersecured. In such circumstances, the company may not have to pay interest on the secured debt

- Where competing interests are too conflicting or complex to resolve on an out-of-court basis, e.g., multiple levels of shareholders, secured lenders and unsecured lenders; numerous lawsuits or judgements pursued by creditors, etc.

- Where the company has made significant preference payments, which can be recovered in bankruptcy

- Where new lenders will only advance the funds if they can be afforded the super-priority lien status bankruptcy can provide

- Where suppliers will only advance credit if they receive the post-petition priority afforded by bankruptcy

- Where it is more advantageous from a tax point of view. There are certain circumstances where bankruptcy provides tax benefits not available in out-of-court workouts.

adequately protected from any deterioration in the value of its collateral. Examples of what adequate protection could constitute include an additional lien on other property, or periodic cash payments to the lien creditor equal to the decrease in value of the creditor's interest in the collateral (e.g., monthly payments equal to the depreciation resulting from the ongoing use of a car). If you do not negotiate a cash collateral arrangement with your lender prior to the bankruptcy filing, it is very possible that the lender may freeze your bank accounts until a court order is issued. For this reason, it is important to make these arrangements prior to the filing.

While the *stigma* of bankruptcy is receding, there is still the strong likelihood that a Chapter 11 filing will negatively impact the company's image and business. It could very well affect customers' willingness to continue buying because of their concern about the longevity of the business. This is especially likely where there is long lead time between order placement and shipment or where customers rely on the company for support and service in the future. Customers in these circumstances might be concerned about their ability to obtain merchandise or service in the event the company discontinues operations. Suppliers will no doubt be extremely concerned and will likely place the company on C.O.D., or even worse, may refuse to supply at all. Competitors will usually use the filing to boost their competitive advantage.

The costs of a Chapter 11 filing can be very substantial. Not only will the debtor be required to pay for its own lawyers, accountants and other professionals (much of it in advance), it will also have to pay for the professionals representing all the various official creditor and equity committees. Because of this, many debtors *cannot afford to go bankrupt*. Bankruptcy is also an extremely time-consuming process. At a time when management needs to be devoting its efforts to running the business, it will be spending much of its time submitting the required reports, meeting with lawyers and other advisers and managing the Chapter 11 process.

Chapter 11 may in fact create a conflict of interest for management or shareholders that may be detrimental to their best interests. Management, as the debtor-in-possession of a Chapter 11 company, must act in a fiduciary capacity in the best interests of the company's shareholders *and* creditors. There are circumstances where the interests of creditors may be in conflict with those of management or shareholders. It is even possible that, in order to execute its fiduciary duty, management may have to sue themselves or their shareholders. An example of this could occur if management or shareholders received preference payments that are recoverable by the debtor's estate.

L. ALTERNATIVES TO CHAPTER 11

There are several viable and effective strategies that achieve many of the benefits that Chapter 11 offers, at a significantly lower cost and without most of the disadvantages of Chapter 11.

Out-of-Court workout

As said earlier, for companies that cannot meet their obligations to their creditors, an *out-of-court workout* may be an option. This involves negotiating a debt restructuring with some or all of the business' creditors, secured and unsecured. Unlike Chapter 11, there are no specific laws or regulations that govern out-of-court workouts.

A workout, by its nature, cannot be achieved if the parties are hostile to each other—and, therefore, must be a *cooperative workout*. Many attempted workouts end up in Chapter 11 or Chapter 7 (liquidation) because the parties could not overcome the hostility between them.

The major advantage of a cooperative workout is the ability of the parties to work together to maximize the value of the company. In a hostile environment, significant value can be

---

How creditors evaluate workout proposals

- The reasonableness of the plan

- Creditors' perception of the fairness of the plan and management's integrity

- Whether the plan proposed to creditors has a value that exceeds that which can be achieved by creditors through alternative means

---

lost while the parties are arguing, or even worse, not talking. In a recent case, a client discontinued an unprofitable product line but waited for several months to begin the collection of the related receivables—because the company, its lenders and creditors could not reach a consensus on a strategy. The ultimate cost to all parties was significant.

Workouts can be achieved with secured and unsecured creditors. However, the more complex and conflicting the needs and interests of creditors, the harder it will be to achieve consensus on a negotiated basis. Further, workouts should not be attempted if there is no reasonable hope of returning the company to viability.

A major benefit of Chapter 11 that is not available in a workout is the *cramdown* provisions in the Bankruptcy Code. These provisions allow the Bankruptcy Court to force dissenting creditors to accept if two-thirds in value and 50 percent in number of the creditors in that class approve the plan. In out-of-court workouts, this often results in a problem called the *hold-out* problem, which occurs when the majority of creditors agree to the workout proposal, but a minority do not. Without the cramdown provisions, the debtor cannot force creditors to accept, and the company can find itself in the awkward position of having some dissenting creditors hold it hostage.

So while the majority of creditors might have agreed to an extended payment period (say, for example, 36 months) dissenting creditors might still proceed with legal action against the company to pursue their claim. The company's only recourse in this situation is negotiation and persuasion—by demonstrating to creditors that their dissent could cause the failure of the company, which might result in a significantly worse outcome for creditors. To successfully negotiate this, be prepared to let hold-out creditors know that you are ready to file Chapter 11 if they pursue their suits, which would *stay* their claims. With the last few holdout creditors, there is always the temptation to partially or totally accede to their demands to avoid jeopardizing the workout. This obviously would result in giving some creditors preferential treatment over others. While the facts and circumstances would dictate whether or not making such payments are illegal, this could open the company to claims of bad faith, misrepresentation or even fraud from other creditors. To be safe, consult an experienced bankruptcy attorney before making any such payments.

One technique that can be used to neutralize the leverage that hold-out creditors may have is to voluntarily grant a security interest in the company's assets (ranking behind secured creditors) to a trustee for unsecured creditors[16]. The effect of this is to eliminate the advantage hold-out creditors can achieve by pursuing their claims, because their claims will now rank behind a security interest for all creditors, including themselves. There is some risk to this strategy for the owners of the company, because the security interest for creditors cannot be removed without an agreement with creditors. In addition, hold-out creditors could still attempt to file an involuntary Chapter 11, in the hope of overturning the security interest as a preference. However, for a company that is in a deadlock with its creditors, and is heading for bankruptcy court in any case, this can be an effective strategy.

[16]   Developed by Brian Bash, Chairman of the bankruptcy department of the Cleveland, Ohio law firm of Kahn, Kleinman, Yanowitz & Arnson.

Another method of counteracting hold-out creditors is a pre-packaged Chapter 11: Here, the company does not file Chapter 11, but as part of its workout process, it obtains consents from creditors in the form required for a Chapter 11 proceeding. If the company is then unable or reluctant to consummate the out-of-court restructuring because of hold-out creditors, but it does obtain enough votes to satisfy the lower voting requirements of Chapter 11 (i.e.., two-thirds in amount and more than one-half in number of allowed claims of such class actually voting on the plan), the company can then file a pre-packaged Chapter 11 and force the dissenting creditors to go along with the plan.

Another area of concern is how the business conducts itself with its vendors. Once a business knows it is probably not going to meet its obligations in the ordinary course, and that it will likely resort to a debt restructuring, it is advisable to avoid accepting new or additional credit from vendors that will result in an increase in their outstanding balances. If a creditor can prove that the company deliberately accepted new or additional credit when it knew it would not be able to pay within negotiated terms, the company, and perhaps management, could be accused of fraudulent intent. In many circumstances, it is better for all parties if the company buys on a C.O.D. basis. This eliminates the possibility of such fraud claims and forces the company to only buy what it needs.

Another problem that is also experienced in workouts is creditors' demands for *override* payments. Even if you are paying on C.O.D., many vendors will require an additional payment toward its old accounts receivable. These payments can be very detrimental for two reasons:

- The override payment will eat into the cash flow to be generated from the eventual sale of that item, and may even result in negative cash flow.
- They set an unhealthy precedent that, if adopted by other creditors, could be very harmful.

As such, override payments should be avoided wherever possible. Note that such payments might qualify as preference payments if the company subsequently files for bankruptcy within a prescribed period and, as such, may be recoverable.

Workouts can include the renegotiation or restructuring of many aspects of the debt, which might include:

- Extended payment period
- Partial forgiveness of principal outstanding
- Adjustment to interest rates
- Deferment of principal payments
- Adjustment to equity conversion privileges

Essential information for creditors

- The company's current financial status, including a liquidation value

- Reasons for the company's problems

- Management's plan to correct the problems

Because management's credibility with secured and unsecured creditors is usually weakened by the company's lack of performance, it is often helpful to use intermediaries to assist in the process. There is a rapidly emerging industry of turnaround consultants and crisis managers who are experienced in facilitating the workout process. In most cases, secured and unsecured creditors welcome the involvement of well-qualified and respected turnaround consultants or crisis managers. Such involvement can often make the difference between success or failure of a workout. Their contribution often extends to adding credibility, giving valuable advice on business and debt restructuring, and assistance in negotiation and implementation of the restructuring.

One of the most significant advantages of out-of-court workouts (as opposed to Chapter 11) to current shareholders of a business, is a substantially higher probability of them retaining all or a portion of the equity ownership of the business. The rules of Chapter 11 do not allow shareholders to retain their ownership unless:

1. Creditors are paid in full, or
2. Creditors who are not paid in full consent, or
3. Shareholders provide *new value* for the equity received.

Another advantage of out-of-court workouts is the ability to keep the company's troubles relatively private. Chapter 11, with its required disclosures and public scrutiny of its affairs in court hearings, affords no potential of privacy. In a workout, information will usually be disclosed to creditors, but will not be readily available to customers or the press, unless provided to them by creditors. The ability to keep one's troubles *within the family* is very valuable.

The workout gives the debtor the option of dealing with creditors individually, or as a group. This can also be advantageous because it is usually easier to negotiate with parties one-on-one, but there are times where you may feel a group meeting will be helpful or more effective. There are also circumstances where it may be appropriate, or where creditors may require it, to form an informal or formal creditors' committee to review the plan and make recommendations to other creditors. If the circumstances of the case are complex, a creditors' committee may be helpful to you, because they will likely be willing to invest more time than other creditors to investigate and understand the facts. The circumstances of each case will dictate whether a creditors' committee is appropriate. Even if you do not form a committee, it is advisable to personally solicit the support of all major creditors. If you are able to indicate to the creditor group at large that your major creditors are supporting the plan, your chances of success will increase significantly.

A concern of sophisticated creditors in a workout stems from the fact that the terms of the workout may be detrimental to creditors in the event of bankruptcy. This can occur in one of two ways:

- Any payments received by creditors as part of the workout plan may qualify as preference payments under a bankruptcy plan, and could be voidable.

- Creditors who agree to reduce their claims as part of a workout will have a proportionately smaller claim in a subsequent bankruptcy.

To avoid this, many creditors will require that any forgiveness of debt only applies and becomes effective when the debtor has completed the payment schedule under the plan.

At the commencement of a workout, a letter should be sent to all past creditors (other than essential creditors) advising:

1. That the company is having cash flow problems.

2. That you are conducting an analysis to identify turnaround and workout strategies that will restore the business to good health.

3. If applicable, that you have retained outside consultants to assist you in this analysis.

4. That you will advise them, by a predetermined date, the outcome of your analysis.

5. If applicable, that during this period you do not intend to make any payments on past-due obligations.

An example of this type of letter to creditors is included as Appendix VIII. This letter should be personally delivered by the CEO or other corporate officer to all major creditors. The letter should generally be personally addressed to the creditor's credit manager.

When the turnaround and workout analysis has been completed, a Creditor Composition Agreement should be drafted by an experienced bankruptcy attorney and sent to all creditors from whom you are seeking participation. This document is the agreement between the company and each of its creditors that agrees to the plan. The agreement should contain information similar to that contained in a typical Chapter 11 Plan of Reorganization and Disclosure Statement. An example of a Creditor Composition Agreement is included as Appendix IX. See also Part 2: Section II-B for additional comments on creditor compromises.

Note that Appendices VIII and IX are provided for informational purposes. In a specific practical situation, such documents should be prepared by experienced financial and legal advisers, and should be tailored to the specific circumstances of that case.

Bulk transfers

Many state laws provide a mechanism via *bulk transfer* laws, under which the major part of the company's materials, supplies, merchandise, inventory and related equipment can be sold (not in the ordinary course of business). The Ohio Uniform Commercial Code (§1306.04) provides that the transfer is ineffective against creditors if the creditor does not receive at least ten days notice. The notice must also state, amongst other things, whether the debts of the transferrer will be paid in full as they fall due.

Essentially, such mechanism provides the opportunity to sell the major assets of a business to a new entity and, if necessary or appropriate, propose in the notice what amounts to a restructuring of the transferrer's debts. Creditors who receive the notice can evaluate the terms of the proposed transfer and decide whether to take appropriate legal action to try to prevent the sale. Their decision process will likely be very similar to those of a creditor receiving a workout proposal. Their major concerns will be:

- Is reasonable consideration being paid for the assets?
- Is the proposal fair?
- Are there other alternatives that might result in a higher value for the creditor?

There are at least three major differences between a bulk transfer and a workout:

- To successfully achieve a workout, consent of creditors must be obtained. In a bulk transfer, creditors' consent is not required, and creditors must take legal action at their own expense within the ten-day period to block the sale.
- The ten-day notice period for a bulk transfer forces creditors to make a decision substantially faster than is usually required in a workout.
- In a bulk transfer, it is significantly harder for existing shareholders to have an ownership interest in the acquiring entity, without contributing equivalent new equity.

Because shareholders rank junior to unsecured creditors, creditors who received less than 100 cents on the dollar will likely argue that any equity existing shareholders receive in the acquiring entity for which they did not pay equivalent value, rightfully belongs to the creditors.

Their decision about whether to pursue their objections will likely be impacted by how they perceive the value of what has been offered to them in the proposal. For example, if a creditor expected to receive 20 cents on the dollar, and the proposal offers him 50 cents on the dollar, he is less likely to take action to prevent shareholders from receiving ownership in the acquiring entity.

Even if shareholders cannot negotiate ownership in the acquiring entity, there are ways whereby they can receive significant benefit from a bulk transfer. These include:

- Where creditors, as part of the transaction, agree to release the personal guarantees of shareholders
- Where the buyer and seller negotiate in good faith a non-compete agreement for existing shareholders, which calls for payments to the shareholders in return for their agreement not to compete against the buyer's company
- Where existing shareholders receive employment contracts from the acquiring entity
- Where existing shareholders might be able to earn *sweat equity* over time, by making a significant contribution of their effort and skills to the new entity

Even these benefits could be challenged by unsecured creditors on the grounds that they confer value to shareholders that may rightfully belong to creditors.

Secured Party sales

A secured party sale is another mechanism to effect the sale of the business to an acquiring entity. It differs from the bulk transfer mechanism in that the assets are foreclosed on by the secured lender, who sells them to the acquirer.

A major difference stems from the fact that unsecured creditors do not have to receive notice of, or approve, the sale. However, the burden of proof is on the secured lender to demonstrate that sale was commercially reasonable.

In practice, most secured lenders are not comfortable participating in a secured party sale, because of the risk of unsecured creditors challenging the commercial reasonableness of the sale. Ironically, a significantly undersecured lender might be more comfortable with a secured party sale, especially if it is agreeing to forgive part of its debt. The rationale behind this is that it will be extremely hard for creditors to challenge the commercial reasonableness if the lender is not receiving full payment. The argument would be, how could unsecured creditors be prejudiced if the lender could not be paid in full? Of course, this argument would not hold up if it could be proven that the lender allowed the sale to take place at prices below fair value.

The same issues about existing shareholders receiving ownership in the acquiring entity or other benefits from the sale apply here, and will be judged in a manner similar to that described above for bulk transfers.

Both bulk transfers and secured party sales, by their natures, invite litigation, because they can create the impression (which may be true or false) that creditors' rights are being prejudiced. As such, it is very important to plan and execute such strategies very carefully and only with expert legal and financial counsel. An out-of-court workout is less susceptible to litigation in that creditor acceptances are sought prior to proceeding with the transaction. However, there is always the possibility of litigation with hold-out creditors.

ACTION STEPS

> Take control of all cash, and bank accounts
> Explore cash management opportunities to increase cash flow
> Consider negotiating extended payment terms from major vendors

> Investigate whether there are any realistic sources for additional loans

> Establish a program to liquidate excess or slow-moving inventories

> Implement more aggressive receivable collection efforts

> Research other opportunities for cash generation or preservation, e.g., just-in-time inventories, consignment inventories, cash in advance or deposits, sale and leaseback, sale of surplus assets, barter and strategic alliances

> Search for potential, and suitable, investors

> Stabilize creditor relationships

> Establish and encourage an atmosphere where creative brainstorming facilitates a continual flow of new ideas

> Scrutinize every area of expenditure and, starting with the largest, search for ways to reduce

> Motivate your employees to pursue new and improved methods through structural change

> Eliminate nonprofitable divisions, products or customers

> Ensure that you have a capable, competent and loyal team

> Define what success means to you, and develop a detailed strategic plan to pursue

> Always maintain open lines of communication with your lenders, vendors, employees and shareholders

> Research and consider the benefits and negatives of Chapter 11, and out-of-court workout techniques

Phase III

RECUPERATION

A. INTRODUCTION

The process of developing, implementing, monitoring and adjusting the Turnaround Strategic Plan is intended to bring the company to a point where it is no longer in a life-threatening situation. From there you can start changing from a crisis management mode to one that will provide a solid base for the future, where the business can return to meeting all of its ongoing obligations, and provide an acceptable return to its shareholders.

The length of time it will take to get a company from the Corporate CPR phase to the Recuperation Phase will depend on the circumstances and the severity of the *illness*. In actual practice, it is usually not possible at the time to identify a clear cut-off point when the company moves into the next phase. Looking back, it is often a lot clearer. Also, many of the strategies undertaken in the Corporate CPR phase are laying the ground work for the Recuperation phase, resulting in an

202

overlap between phases. Conversely, many Recuperation Phase activities might be researched and implemented during the Corporate CPR Phase.

B. ENHANCING PROFITABILITY

In the Corporate CPR Phase, cash flow was of paramount concern. As you move into Recuperation, profitability takes on more importance because, in the long run, it is only profits that will sustain the company, and ensure positive cash flow in the future.

Profitability can be achieved by any combination of:

- increasing revenues
- improving profit margins
- reducing operating expenses
- growth by acquisition

INCREASING REVENUES

Increasing revenues can be achieved by a combination of increasing prices, increasing your share of the available market within existing product lines, entering into new markets or by developing new products.

Raising prices

In today's world of minimal inflation, the option of increasing prices as a route to increasing revenues is often overlooked. In practice, you have to weigh this alternative very carefully. Sometimes, the price increase can be achieved without too much reaction from customers. However, there is always the risk of the price increase having a negative effect. It is possible, though, that even if you raise prices, your unit volume might drop by a lesser percentage than the price increase, resulting in an overall improvement in your profits, and cash flow.

203

Before raising prices, you should research competitor pricing, and how your customers would react to a price increase.

It is often found that businesses sell selected products to certain customers at prices that are not economically viable. This could have resulted from a historical relationship. Raising prices in this situation achieves one of two objectives: If the customer accepts the price increase, the relationship can now become economically attractive for the company. If the customer rejects the increase, the company does not need to waste its efforts and resources on a loss-making relationship.

In most turnaround situations, there are usually many opportunities to raise selected prices without significant adverse reaction. Your research might indicate that there is no room for price increases in your primary products, but there may be opportunities with lower volume products. Most customers are only aware of the prices for the regularly purchased items, and might not even notice or care about increases in items they buy infrequently.

Even if you cannot find opportunities to increase prices, there may still be avenues to increase the net prices of products. This can be done by changing items that don't effect the gross prices, but do change other factors that are less apparent to the customer—but very relevant to your bottom line. Such items include payment terms, early payment discounts, volume discounts, rebates and promotions. Many companies are not aware of how much these items truly cost them; you may find that some of these items can be changed without any significant customer resistance.

Increasing market share

Increased market share may be achieved by more effective penetration of existing markets, or by expanding your territory coverage into new markets. To increase market penetration or territory coverage, you can do one or a combination of the following:

- Most importantly, pay more attention to your customers and their needs: **Make sure everybody in the company knows the customer is number one**. Involve customers in key decisions about products, pricing, advertising, etc. Ask customers how **you can improve, and how you can make them more competitive**. The CEO should set the example by being involved in sales and customer satisfaction.

- Improve the quality, training and effectiveness of your sales force, with the aim of achieving more sales per salesperson. Salespeople are usually very different from clerical or production people, and there is often friction between the sales force and the rest of the organization. What makes sales so different from most other functions in a business is that sales is not conducted in a controlled environment—unlike manufacturing, which is easily controlled with accounting systems and similar controls. With sales, you are always dealing with the *ever-unpredictable* customer, who rarely behaves the way you might expect. Because of this, it is so important that the salesperson—your ambassador—be able to interact with the customer in a way where mutual empathy and trust is established, and where the customer is gently (but firmly) guided into buying your products, not only once—but repeatedly. This type of ability is not present in every salesperson. Also, contrary to popular belief, there is no stereotype: Good salespeople come in all shapes and sizes.

  A type of salesperson to be careful of is one I call *million-dollar Joe*. This type of salesperson is always very close to landing a large order, but somehow never quite gets the purchase order—and usually spends a lot of your time and money in the process. After a while, you start to get suspicious of this guy,

205

but you could really use that order, so you look on the brighter side of things. Eventually, you realize that the order is never forthcoming, and you finally send Joe and his elusive order down the road. Don't' be surprised if Joe shows up very soon thereafter working for your competitor, until the competitor gets tired of waiting for the million-dollar order.

- Increase the number of salespeople. In most businesses, sales do not just happen. You have to be out in the market place staking your claim for every potential order. The more *balls you have in the air*, the higher the ultimate orders. Provided the market is there, more salespeople who are well managed and effective can bring in more business. You obviously need to be selective enough to only pursue orders that you have a high probability of winning.

- Increase or improve your advertising and promotion. This is one of the hardest areas to measure and act on. You have to decide whether increased expenditures in this area will generate enough benefit. If you already have a good *Product Franchise*, your need to spend in this area might be reduced. However, it always pays to have good product literature, and advertising may be necessary to maintain or build on your products' or your company's image. This is one area where you are never going to get any clear-cut answers. Your advertising company will always try to convince you of the benefits of regular reinforcement. Unless you are in a retail business where you might be able to gauge the short-term impact of a particular promotion, it is very hard to measure the longer-term impact and cost/benefit of advertising and promotion.

- Expand into other geographic markets. If there is limited growth potential in your existing territories, consider expanding into other territories. This may involve significant up-front costs, in setting up branches, distribution centers or plants. Alternatively, sales reps can be used to keep the costs down. These costs must be weighed against the projected sales and profit potential from that territory. Careful consideration should be given to the adequacy of capital resources to effectively pursue the expansion. Such geographic expansion options also include exploring export potential to other countries, which often includes more research and complications than local expansion.

- Improve your market intelligence, thereby improving your sales effectiveness with better knowledge. Most businesses do not have a formal competitive information gathering system; management usually depends on the informal information flow to gather its data about competitors. This is analogous to an army moving ahead with an invasion without any reconnaissance or intelligence work. You are at a disadvantage because you have no accurate and up-to-date knowledge of the enemy's position, strength or plans.

  In order for a business to maximize its marketing effectiveness (and, ultimately, its revenues) it should have a formal system for gathering information about competitor activities. This would include information about:

  - customers
  - new products
  - pricing strategies
  - advertising and promotion
  - acquisitions, new facilities
  - manufacturing methods and cost advantages

- sources of supply
- inventory levels
- financial strength

Your marketing department should set up a network of information sources to ensure that you are kept abreast of this information on a regular basis. This data should be regularly updated and, where appropriate, graphed and correlated to other factors. For example, graph a competitor's pricing strategy in relation to factors such as type of product, size of order, customer characteristics and geographic location. From this analysis, you may learn valuable information that could provide you with the ability to predict how that competitor might price the next order. Without this information, your business could miss out on important opportunities or trends.

- Improve effectiveness of distribution channels. There are several different channels including direct distribution through company-owned outlets, distributors, dealers, telemarketing, multi-level marketing, franchises, licensees, mail-order, catalogue sales and independent sales representatives. All of these channels have their advantages and disadvantages—some will work for one business, and others for another. Every CEO must review the existing channels being used by his business, evaluate whether these are the most effective to achieve the company's objectives and explore whether new methods can be used to improve the corporation's marketing effectiveness and sales. For example, some companies have abandoned selling through distributors in favor of selling direct. This gives them greater control over their marketing and higher margins. There are, course, many disadvantages of such a strategy, which include higher selling expenses and reduced market penetration.

Example

Dell Computer of Austin, Texas has used direct selling very effectively to build, in less than eight years, a computer company achieving annual revenues close to $2 billion, despite intense competition and a sluggish economy.

"From its earliest days Dell cut out the middleman, selling its computers direct to consumers via heavy advertising in the computer press and toll-free numbers.... In the face of this stepped-up competition, Dell's (800) lines are ringing off the hooks."

Forbes, October 12, 1992

Non-financial reasons to buy

When a company tries to increase its sales, there is always the temptation to achieve this through lowering unit prices. However, significant results can be achieved if salespeople are trained to promote non-price benefits. AT&T used this approach very effectively in its advertising campaign to compete with discount long-distance telephone carriers: They stressed non-financial factors, such as the audio quality of their lines, and the ability to get assistance from their operators.

Gregg Foster, CEO of Elyria Foundry, Inc. and winner of *Inc. Magazine's* 1992 Turnaround Entrepreneur of the Year, incorporated some of these non-financial factors (see box on next page) as a foundation of the outstanding turnaround of Elyria Foundry, based in Elyria, Ohio. Foster believes that customers

Non-financial reasons to buy

- Quality
- Reliability
- Financial stability
- Fast delivery and turnaround
- Employee empowerment to solve problems
- Depth of inventory

- Integrity
- Service
- Responsiveness
- Technical expertise
- Breadth of inventory selection

will focus on price if you do not demonstrate the value of the non-financial benefits of doing business with you. Before you can educate your customers to think this way, you must create an awareness within your company of the importance of enhancing and promoting non-financial benefits. These non-financial benefits are especially valuable in differentiating your company from its competitors.

Example

If a competitors product is similar to yours but its company is weak financially, your company's financial strength should be emphasized to demonstrate to the customer that he is less likely to experience disruptions in supply by dealing with your company.

To maximize the effectiveness of non-financial benefits, your salespeople should be trained to probe customers to learn which benefits are important to them, and which they fear losing.

Example

If you manufacture a relatively inexpensive part or component that your customer installs into a larger finished product with critical delivery deadlines, your probing may uncover that your customer has a significant concern that late deliveries of your component could delay shipment of his product. With this information, you should promote the reliability of your on-time delivery record.

Customers must feel that you care enough to take the time to understand their business and needs. If customers have grown accustomed to relying on your company to respond to their concerns and take care of their problems, it will be hard for your competitors to make inroads with those customers. Building personal relationships with customers also helps to solidify your position.

New products

Growth in sales by entering new product lines generally involves the expenses of research and development, tooling, training, advertising and promotion. In addition, there is often a great deal of cost associated with the mistakes made while climbing the *learning curve* of a new product.

When a business is not profitable due to a lack of revenue, it is very tempting to venture into new markets or products. It is easy to get enthusiastic about these new prospects. The reality is that it is very hard to penetrate new markets or products successfully. Most times, the venture fails for quite some time. Persistence can often reward you, but the process usually takes longer and costs more than you originally anticipated. New ventures do not work well until they become debugged and grooved—and fit in with every aspect of

211

the organization; it is almost impossible to get it right the first, or even the second, time. Be realistic—don't expect miracles.

Ironically, though, some of the best lessons I have learned have been from failed ventures into new products or markets. Despite the fact that those ventures often did not contribute to any profits, the organization benefited significantly in the form of new production and other ideas that paid for the mistakes of the failed products several times over. As with most experiences in life, we sometimes learn a lot more from *failure* than *success*. When we experience failure, we do a lot of *soul-searching* to analyze the reason for the failure, and search for possible solutions. This fosters the kind of brainstorming and creative problem solving that is so essential in the turn-around process. The lessons that are learned from such failures, and the ideas and strategies that evolve from such experiences, can often be adapted or modified to become the catalyst for strategies to solve problems and create opportunities in other areas of the business.

Example

One of the plants for which I had overall responsibility for was not profitable, primarily due to a lack of volume. The plant operated at about 40 percent of its maximum production capacity, and extensive marketing efforts within its existing product range could not significantly increase the volume. A decision was made that the plant should seek to diversify into a new product range in a different industry that was close enough technologically for the plant to apply the same basic manufacturing skills it used for its existing product line. After an exhaustive search, a salesman succeeded in writing a large order for a product range that the plant had never manufactured before, but appeared to be well within its capabilities. Three months later, the plant was a disaster zone. A few miscalculations had substantially increased the time it took to manufacture the product. With wafer-thin margins, losses mounted quickly. Plant management tried very hard in vain to find ways to get the costs down. While they were focusing their attention on this problem, their existing core business suffered significantly and customers began to complain. Shortly thereafter, we made the decision to abandon the new product line and take a write-off of the remaining costs. Surprisingly, the plant's profitability soon began to increase significantly. When management analyzed the reasons for this improvement, it was discovered that during their search to find ways to lower the cost of the abandoned product, they discovered new methods and equipment that could significantly lower the cost of the core product line. That plant still operates at 40 percent of capacity, but is now very profitable operating just its core business.

The moral of the story is that businesses always need to try new things to grow and develop. In a crisis, the risks should be thought out very carefully and minimized to every extent possible (unless you're making a last-ditch attempt). If the venture fails, try to at least get some spin-off benefit.

In general, during a turnaround process, one of the most effective routes for growth is the increasing of market share in existing markets, through more effective customer satisfaction, sales and marketing, and lower prices, where appropriate. This presents the lowest risk approach—but again is not easy. Your competitors will not sit back idly while you take away their customers. Another reasonably low-risk option for growth is through limited product extension—gradually adding products that are extensions of, or complementary to, your existing product lines.

Private label

For businesses that have excess production capacity, an effective way to increase sales is to manufacture for your competitors under a private labelling arrangement. This works especially well if the product line is not a core product for the competitor, and if the competitor does not compete directly against you.

Example

A recent client manufactured a certain product range exclusively for commercial applications. To expand his sales, he would have dearly loved to pursue the residential market. Because of the difficulty in establishing an effective distribution system, a decision was made to approach one of the major companies already in the residential market. We discovered that this product line, while of significant volume in relation to my client's business, represented a very small percentage of the larger company's volume and, more importantly, that they were having substantial production problems in their plant. It soon became obvious to both parties that a private label manufacturing arrangement was the answer to both companies' problems.

Licensing and franchising

For businesses unable to market their products in some regions or territories, revenue and income can be increased by allowing somebody else to manufacture and market your product in that region under license from you. You will then be able to earn royalties from sales in that region. Franchising is a form of licensing that has allowed many relatively small businesses to compete nationally and internationally.

Positioning

An important part of increasing revenues is a concept known as *positioning* of your products; that is, how the marketplace perceives your products. This involves examining and improving, if necessary, every phase of the product—from research and development, to manufacturing, quality control, packaging, advertising, promotion and customer service. For example, new packaging might allow you to market a product as a premium-priced item, rather than at discount pricing.

The sales manager

Whatever strategy you adopt to increase revenues, for the strategy to work and achieve your desired objective, it is essential that you have an effective sales force, led by a truly competent Sales Manager. The choice of a Sales Manager is always an important decision. He will be the person who will be implementing your sales and marketing plan, and will have a significant impact on how the marketplace perceives your company and—more importantly—whether they will reward your company with their purchase orders.

The qualities and experience needed to be a truly competent Sales Manager are extensive. These obviously include leadership and management skills, sales experience and product knowledge. These are all very important and necessary. However, there are three essential qualities to look for in a Sales Manager (see box below)

Essential qualities for a sales manager

- street smarts
- empathy
- profit orientation

A *street smart* Sales Manager knows the *ins* and *outs* of business and the industry in which he operates. He knows when to be tough and when to be charming. He is an outstanding ambassador for the company, but is also very comfortable in the *trenches*. He is always aware of his competitors' strengths and weaknesses. He also has *empathy* for his sales force and his customers. Empathy is a very important ingredient in successfully being able to influence and direct circumstances in your favor. Having empathy means understanding how the other person truly feels in a situation—what his fears and concerns are, and what is important to him. If you have this kind of empathy for someone, there will be a feeling of mutual understanding that can foster a close bond. This is the kind of atmosphere and relationship needed for a Sales Manager to motivate his sales force, and to close deals with his customers. The competent Sales Manager will also be *profit oriented*. Many salespeople focus on sales rather than profits. Only profitable sales are good for the company, and a Sales Manager with a profit orientation will steer the whole company to pursue profitable business. If you have the right Sales Manager, he will build and train a sales force that will give the company the best chance of increasing revenues and profits.

It is important to note that the skills required for a successful manager are different from those of a successful salesperson. Many companies make the mistake of unsuccessfully promoting their best salesperson to sales manager. Being a good salesperson does not guarantee success as a sales manager, where the primary skills required are managerial.

Costs of growth

There is at least one caveat to achieving a turnaround through revenue growth. Growth in a turnaround situation often exacerbates the very problem you are trying to solve, i.e., a shortage of cash. To build revenues, you usually need to invest funds into inventory, equipment, additional facilities and receivables. These investments all require cash, which is usually a scarce commodity in a crisis. Furthermore, as often happens, being on C.O.D. with suppliers means you have to pay for everything up front, long before you can convert it to cash. This makes it extremely difficult for a turnaround company to grow its way out of the crisis, unless new funds are available from other sources.

An additional problem that can result from revenue growth is the potential for increased uncollectible receivables. Revenue growth usually means taking on new customers whose credit-worthiness is unknown to you. These customers clearly represent a greater credit risk than your existing customers with whose payment patterns you are familiar.

IMPROVING PROFIT MARGINS

Profit margins are directly tied to the concepts of *Value Added*, and *Production Efficiencies*. Commodity products (e.g., sugar) sell at the market price because they are homogeneous: Nobody gets a premium because there is no Value Added. The price is determined purely by supply and demand. The only thing that can affect profit margins of a commodity product is Production Efficiencies; i.e., if you can find a way to produce (or buy) the product more efficiently and for a lower cost than your competitor, you will earn a higher profit margin. You may also be able to earn a higher margin due to better service or availability.

Value added

For non-commodity products, Value Added and Production Efficiencies can affect profit margins. For example, a Maytag washer and dryer can command a higher price than a no-name competitor because of the perceived Added Value of Maytag's low failure rate (a very good positioning strategy).

The concept of Added Value is as much *perception* as it is *reality*. In other words, it is not enough that your product is superior, it is vital that the customer *believes* it to be superior.

Items that create value added

- quality
- service
- availability
- support
- sizzle (prestige, status, etc.)

If a company can find ways to increase its Value Added, and communicate the Value Added to its customers, it should be able to earn a higher margin. The company should be sure that the expense involved in increased Value Added will be more than offset by higher profits from better margins. If not, the Value Added approach would not be worth it, and you would be better off concentrating your efforts on Production Efficiencies.

Oil companies try to *differentiate* their commodity product by promoting the additives that apparently improve the performance of the petroleum. Whether the value added is reality or perception, they are sometimes able to increase their margins through a differentiation technique.

Production efficiencies

A business should always strive for ways to reduce the costs of producing its product. The company that can produce a product at a lower cost than its competitor will be able to earn a higher margin. Wal-Mart, now the largest retailer in the world, is causing huge headaches for its competitors because it has apparently been able to significantly reduce the cost of delivering its product to its customers. This has enabled it to develop a reputation of consistently being able to provide customers with everyday low prices.

Production efficiencies can be achieved by better purchasing, materials management, improved work flows and

218

logistics, more efficient machinery and engineering or design changes to reduce the cost of the product.

Margin management

Profits can often be improved by a margin management program that gives management the ability to monitor and manage gross margins for all products.

This type of system will help to reduce situations where salespeople take the easy route to receiving an order, by giving additional discounts. First, the reduced margin will be flagged on the Margin Management report. Further, additional price discounts will have a progressively negative impact on salesperson commissions. In addition, a Margin Management program will provide incentives for management and salespeople to change the mix of sales to promote higher margin products.

Components of a margin management program

- an information system that provides daily, weekly and monthly information about margins by product, product line, division and customer
- target margins for all products
- an incentive system for management and salespeople that progressively rewards them for higher margins

---

REDUCING OPERATING EXPENSES

Techniques for reducing Operating Expenses were covered extensively in the CPR Phase. The following are some additional tips:

Keep expenses down

As you move into Recuperation, and as things start to improve and the pressure eases, there is a very strong temptation to start increasing operating expenses: Everybody has been operating with very tight budgets for a long time, and all of a sudden, there is a swell of requests for additional manpower and other expenses.

In the Corporate CPR Phase, you were forced to learn how to operate *lean and mean*. After being overweight, it feels very good to shed the excess weight. However, now that you are skinny and have been watching your diet for so long, you feel it's okay to treat yourself to the occasional piece of *cheesecake*. Pretty soon, if you don't watch it carefully, you are back to your old weight and, often, more! In Recuperation, it is normal to put back a few *pounds* to facilitate growth, but it should be a conscious, controlled and monitored decision. Those expenses can creep back fast, if you don't watch them very closely.

Look for sacred cows

It is quite natural when your company has improved significantly, and is *out of the woods*, for you to be less self-critical, and to do less soul-searching for ways to improve your business. To avoid this trap, it is helpful to have somebody outside your company challenge you periodically to justify all of your expenses. If you do this diligently, you will find that many areas you always considered sacred can be discarded. Keep thinking and searching. Look at the business from different vantage points. If you're not continually finding areas to cut, you're not looking critically enough. Every activity, project, product and division should be continually re-evaluated to ensure they can be justified by the Corporate Treadmill Test (see Part 1: Section II).

Measure, measure

What gets measured gets improved!

Measuring performance gives people benchmarks and focus towards improving. Always look for ways to measure performance and efficiency, and encourage people to find ways to improve. For example, ask your accounts payable department to place on the department door a sheet of paper that reflects the number of invoices processed each day. Watch their pride and satisfaction increase as they receive favorable comments from other departments about their improvements. Opportunities for improvement through measurement exist in most areas of the business. One area that is hard to measure, though, is salesmen's performance—the salesman that makes the most calls does not necessarily achieve the highest sales. Quality is far more important than quantity. Many good salespeople vehemently resist being compelled to constantly report their efforts. This is one area where you may find too much measurement to be counter-productive.

Important production improvement goals

1. The distance materials travel from incoming truck to outgoing truck.

2. The number of times materials is handled during its time in the plant.

3. The average length of time material is in the plant

When you have this information, plant management should be focused on ways to improve these statistics. Without much effort, most plants can achieve significant improvements in these measurements. The resulting reduction of production costs can be substantial. Every reduction of these statistics results in a smoother and more efficient production flow—because these improvements can only be achieved by better plant layouts, changes in manufacturing methods and just-in-time inventories. All of these changes contribute substantially to the lowering of costs.

Efficiency doesn't just happen by itself. It must be *squeezed* out at every level, through measurement and improvement

---

Critical efficiency factors

Important benchmarks to measure in a plant are downtime, rework, scrap, returns, leadtime, on-time delivery, overtime, efficiency, ratio of direct labor to indirect labor, set-up times and inventory turnover.

Statistical Process Control (SPC) is a measurement system that has been adopted by many successful companies to track and improve their performance, quality and error rates. This process often starts with their suppliers, to make sure there is strict control over raw material and other purchased items.

Improvements in performance in these *critical efficiency factors* can result in significant reductions in cost, and in improved workflow. The permutations and combinations of activities in a plant are too numerous to manage by the "seat of your pants." These complexities create huge opportunities to find ways to do things better. Once you start measuring the critical efficiency factors, you will provide the stimulus for grass roots discovery of ways to improve scores. These efficiency breakthroughs are not something that is created by MBAs at the corporate head office—it is only on the shop floor that this can happen. Measurement is the starting point.

- Worker *downtime* is one of the most costly inefficiencies: If a worker is ready to work, but is unable to do so because of unavailable parts, equipment problems, etc., not only does that worker become indirect labor for that time period, the company also suffers because of the lost production, and related disruption in workflow. Because of this, it is essential to measure downtime, hold supervisors accountable and develop systems to reduce it.

- *Rework* is also extremely costly: Valuable time is lost, materials may be scrapped and workflow is disrupted. To help reduce rework, workers should check their output at every step of the production process. Moreover, workers should be required to perform the rework on their own time.

- *Scrap* can result from inefficient design, inferior materials or from errors in manufacturing. A goal should be established to continually reduce scrap. If parts are to be scrapped, they should be identified as early as possible in the production process, so that further labor is not invested in parts that are ultimately going to be scrapped. Again, training workers to inspect their own work at every step of the production process will facilitate this.

- *Returns* indicate customer dissatisfaction of some sort. This could result from manufacturing defects, marketing related problems, overshipments to customers or from customer dissatisfaction with the product. The costs, in lost customer goodwill, increased handling and potential scrap, can be substantial.

- *Leadtime* is a throughput measurement, tracking the length of time it takes from the date an order is received to the date it is shipped. Reducing leadtime can result in enhanced profits through faster shipments, and cost savings (and customer satisfaction) due to inventory reductions, and the efficiency achieved from the techniques employed to speed up throughput. To reduce leadtime, the production process should be studied to identify *bottlenecks*, i.e., steps in the production flow that slow up production. Bottlenecks could be caused by many factors including inadequate equipment capacity, shortages in materials. Once bottlenecks are identified, methods should be sought to reduce the problem, e.g., sub-contract part of the production, improve just-in-time arrangements with suppliers, etc.

- *On-time delivery* measures the company's track record in meeting delivery commitments to customers. Poor performance in this area could indicate inefficiency in the production process.

- *Overtime* is sometimes unavoidable. However, it is expensive because workers are usually paid premium rates. While it often cannot be eliminated, overtime should be monitored and controlled.

- *A Direct Labor Hour* is a measure of output, rather than a period of time: If the standard production rate is ten units an hour and a worker produces 60 units in an eight-hour day, he will have produced six standard hours [60/10], and have achieved *efficiency* of 75 percent [6/8]. The other two hours will be considered *indirect labor*, which will be added to all of the other truly indirect hours (maintenance, janitors, helpers, fork-lift drivers, etc.). The ratio of *direct labor to indirect labor* is very important in that it encompasses the key elements of efficiency and minimizing indirect labor (both real indirect and inefficient direct labor). Direct labor is productivity; indirect labor is overhead. Maximization of this ratio will produce significant results.

- Time spent by workers on *setup* is indirect labor, which reduces time available for direct labor. Improving setup time is an important part of reducing costs and increasing responsiveness. With shorter setup times, a business can be more efficient with shorter-run orders. Techniques should be sought (e.g., quick-change dies) to reduce setup time.

- *Inventory Turnover* is an asset management measurement. There are several ways to calculate this. The traditional way is:

$$\frac{\text{Cost of Sales}}{\text{Inventory}}$$

While this is of some value, a more informative measure is GM/ROI, calculated by:

$$\frac{\text{Gross Margin Dollars}}{\text{Inventory}}$$

As discussed in Part 1: Section II, this ratio provides a tool to compare the inventory turnover by product line. As also stated in that section, this is one of the most important measurements, because it links the two essential elements of profit to asset turnover for each product line. This measurement improves as you generate more gross margin with as little inventory as possible, and it takes account of the symbiotic relationship between the two elements.

While these are all important measurements, there are many more to identify and track. Look for the *critical efficiency factors* in your business, measure **and improve** them.

225

Improvement through measurement really works: Utilizing many of the above measurements, a plant for which I was responsible, which had annual sales volume of $8 million, achieved a turnaround from losses of $1 million to profits of a similar amount in less than 18 months, without any increase in sales.

GROWTH BY ACQUISITION

Revenues and profitability can also be increased by acquisition, but the risks of taking on the additional headaches and burden of a new acquisition during the Recuperation phase should be evaluated very carefully. A strategic acquisition of a company that complements your company or offers an opportunity for marketing or production synergies may make sense if it gives the company a greater chance for survival, provided the company has the resources to pursue it.

(See Part 2: Phase III-C for additional comments on this subject, and Appendix VI for acquisition strategies in a turnaround situation.)

C. INDUSTRY CONSOLIDATION

Many businesses (and industries) in the United States are operating with significant excess capacity. Many of our clients have found their plants operating at 25 percent to 40 percent of production capacity, a level at which most businesses have difficulty thriving. With sluggish economic growth, mature businesses are unlikely to be able to achieve sufficient sales growth to fully utilize their capacity. In these situations, an industry consolidation strategy may be appropriate, whereby stronger companies buy up weaker ones, or where comparably-sized competitors merge.

Example

One of our recent clients was a $10 million manufacturer in a very mature industry. For several years, it tried in vain to increase sales to generate production beyond 25 percent of capacity. After a conclusion was reached that sales growth was not realistic, a strategy was developed to merge with another $10 million competitor in a similar situation. These two companies, which were collectively losing nearly $1 million per annum, have now merged and are earning significant profits. The shareholders of my client are very happy to own a smaller share of a now profitable company.

Another form of industry consolidation is vertical integration. Here, an underperforming business may merge with, or acquire, one of its suppliers or customers—or even better, one of its competitor's customers.

Example

A job-shop manufacturing client with significant excess capacity could barely achieve enough sales volume to break even. We developed a strategy to pursue a merger with one of the companies that my client had unsuccessfully quoted significant business to. The strategy had two significant advantages: First, the relationship would significantly increase production volume, and second, the job-shop would be able to acquire a proprietary product line manufactured by the merger partner, thereby making the job-shop less dependent on a continual bid process.

Industry consolidation strategies will likely become more and more prevalent as businesses search for ways to utilize capacity more effectively.

D. COST STRATEGY

Pricing strategies

In checking your Vital Signs, you should have established how accurately the company knows its operating costs. If you established that there is a low level of Cost Awareness, an immediate Corporate CPR strategy would be to develop a high level of cost awareness. Knowing your costs, and knowing how to interpret them, can have a very significant impact on your ability to be more competitive. An accurate and perceptive knowledge of your costs will also tell you whether you should make a product yourself, or whether you should buy it from somebody else.

As described in Part 2: Phase I, accurately identifying product costs requires a detailed study of the work involved in, and related cost of, every step in the production process. You need to determine the exact amount of materials used, labor required and supplies consumed.

If that was the end of it, your task wouldn't be too tough, because with such processes as material analysis, time and motion studies, these items are reasonably easy to quantify. But now comes the hard part—deciding what to do with the more abstract element of costs, including the costs of research and development, engineering, tooling, setting up machinery, factory overhead costs (supervision, heating, depreciation of equipment, etc.), as well as general operating costs (administrative, sales and general management).

Variable costing

Accountants like to use what is known as the *Full Absorption* method of costing, whereby a business allocates to the cost of the product not only the *Direct Costs* that are expended in producing that product (material, labor, supplies, etc.), but also a portion of all other *Indirect Costs*. That is, general costs that cannot be directly related to the cost of individual products (rent, heating, etc.). This method, while giving a lot of comfort to the accountant, is very stifling for the business. This is because it does not tell you the most important thing you need to know—what funds will actually have to be expended to make one more unit. This concept is known as Marginal Cost. To illustrate, consider a situation in which you have orders to produce 1,000 units for the month (which represents a reasonably normal order level, but is only about 60 percent of your production capacity) and you are asked to give a very competitive quote on an additional 100 units.

Key question: How low can you drop your price, to get the order?

Let's assume your costs to produce the first 1,000 units are as follows:

Materials	$ 50,000
Labor	25,000
Supplies, etc.	10,000
Production Overheads	<u>65,000</u>
	$150,000

So, based on your present orders, you are planning to expend $150,000 to produce 1,000 units. Your accountant would tell you (based on the full absorption costing method) that your standard unit cost is $150 ($150,000 ÷ 1,000 units). Even though your normal markup is 25 percent, you tell your sales department to markup the cost with a very small profit margin of, say 15 percent (i.e., selling price of $172.50) because you really want the order. A few days later, the Sales Manager

229

tells you the order was awarded to your competitor for a price of $143.75. You respond by telling him that if your competitor wants to sell below his cost, that's his choice!

Let's look at the situation as the competitor might see it.

	Costs to Produce 1,000 units	Marginal Costs additional 100 units	Total Costs 1,100 units
Materials	$50,000.00	$5,000.00	$55,000.00
Labor	25,000.00	2,500.00	27,500.00
Supplies	10,000.00	1,000.00	11,000.00
Production Overhead	65,000.00	3,000.00	68,000.00
Total Cost	**$150,000.00**	**$11,500.00**	**$161,500.00**
Unit Cost	**$150.00**	**$115.00**	**$146.82**

The competitor's accountant tells him that his average unit cost drops from $150 for 1,000 units to $146.82 for 1,100 units. But, more importantly, the accountant tells him that even though the average unit cost is $146.82, he will only have to expend $115 per unit to produce the additional 100 units (Marginal Cost). The competitor then marks up his real cost by a healthy 25 percent to arrive at his selling price of $143.75. He gets the order, and generates $28.75 per unit ($2,875 in total) contribution towards his overheads and profits.

Did the competitor sell below his cost? Yes, if you consider his cost to be full absorption cost; no, if you look at his *real* incremental cost!

Why is Marginal Cost lower than the Full Absorption Cost? Because many Operating and Production Costs (such as rent) do not increase as your production increases. You have to pay the rent whether you produce the additional 100 units or not. Why burden the cost of the 100 units with a portion of the rent? You don't need to spend any *incremental* funds on rent to produce the additional units. Therefore, rent is not part of your real cost to produce those units.

There are two very important caveats when applying this costing approach:

- It can only be used if you clearly have excess production capacity. If the production of the additional 100 units prevents you from being able to produce part of the first 1,000 units (for which you are earning your normal Full Absorption profit margin), the cost of the additional 100 units goes up by the profit lost from the units not produced (including the cost of goodwill lost from irate customers who didn't receive their goods).

- It can only be used to price incremental business, i.e., additional business you would not have gotten in any case. If you used this pricing approach to price the first 1,000 units, your profit and loss would look like this:

Revenue - 1,000 units @ $143.75	$143,750
Total Operating and Production Costs	150,000
Net Loss	**$6,250**

So, it can be clearly seen that a high level of cost awareness is essential to the decision making required to achieve the maximum profit potential of the business. It also is very important to realize that Marginal Costing does not mean you have to *leave money on the table*. Just because your heightened cost awareness tells you that you can make the additional units at a lower cost, you do not have to lower your price. This should only be done if competitive forces are such that the lower price is needed to get the order. It's great to know your cost—but use it for your benefit, not your customers'!

One more word of caution. Don't tell your salespeople what your Marginal Cost is (or how it is calculated) because, if you do, you're likely to find this pricing technique suddenly become *essential* for every order.

Activity-based costing

With the drive to accurately pinpoint the true costs of every product, Activity-Based Costing has been recently developed. This approach attempts to identify and allocate all costs related to a particular product. Whereas, under Full Absorption Costing, the cost of the engineering department might be allocated to all products on the basis of sales or assets employed, under Activity-Based Costing, engineering would be allocated based on the complexity of the products and the amount of engineering time involved for each product. Under Activity-Based Costing, all activities in the business are analyzed in detail to determine their impact on the cost of a product. While this is an expensive and time-consuming process, the ultimate result for the business is accurate knowledge of the true costs to produce a product. Without this knowledge, there is a risk that products will be sold at insufficient margins, or even at a loss.

E. QUALITY ASSURANCE

Mistakes are very costly to the company, both financially and to its image. This applies to errors in production, as well as administrative and other foul-ups.

Error rates are greatly reduced when procedures and controls become *consistent*. Almost every facet of the business can benefit from grooved procedures. Although it is a long, slow and tedious process, controls and consistent procedures must be built into every function. There is no substitute for an inch-by-inch approach to ensuring every base is covered. Create an atmosphere that encourages *continuous improvement*.

Many people think Quality Assurance applies only to a manufacturing situation. However, it is vital that Quality

Assurance permeate every part of the company. A goal of *zero defects* might be somewhat out of reach, but it's a very worthwhile target for which to aim.

Everybody's an inspector

The checking and measuring of quality should be built into every job and procedure in the company. If people know the *buck stops with them*, they will make sure the quality is there, and inspectors will be become redundant. If people feel that they are an integral part of the process, and their contribution is respected and appreciated, their pride in their work will zoom, and they will become their own best critics. They will feel that there is a part of them in everything the company does, whether producing a product or providing a service, and their pride of ownership will make them the best *inspection department* you could find (at the lowest cost).

Quality assurance should not be relegated to an inspection department

---

In order to maintain quality levels on an ongoing basis, it is important for as many employees as possible (at all levels) to have some customer contact, so they are always aware of whom they are serving.

Payback

There is a current trend in business to believe that improving quality cures all ills of a business. While the pursuit of improved quality is an essential and important part of the success of all companies, quality alone will not result in a healthy company if there are fundamental other weaknesses or problems, e.g., an inadequate distribution network. Further, investing funds into improved quality will only make economic sense if customers are willing to pay for the improved quality. Many companies have invested huge amounts into improved quality, only to find that customers were not prepared to pay for the additional quality.

F. FINANCING

In the Corporate CPR phase, obtaining sufficient cash to keep the business *afloat* is a primary concern. This may even necessitate obtaining funds from a variety of sources with terms, conditions and costs that are not favorable to the company. As the business regains strength, becomes profitable and begins its emergence out of a turnaround situation, it becomes important to set in place favorable and cost-efficient financing that will facilitate the company's rehabilitation and growth.

In addition to bank financing, other financing options also become available at this point. These include venture capital, private placements of debt and equity instruments, government-assisted financing for expansion of equipment or facilities and public offerings of debt and equity. These and other alternative forms of financing offer significant benefits and some disadvantages to the emerging business. They are usually complicated and time-consuming to implement, and require the advice of experts in the fields of investment banking, law and accounting.

Banks (and other similar lenders) still remain the most viable and achievable funding source at this stage of the company's development. Dealing with banks is an art form that requires a lot of experience and skill. Every bank has its own agenda of what it is interested in, and under what terms, conditions and cost. The industry you are in also has a significant bearing on a bank's level of interest. At certain times, some industries are very attractive to banks, and they pursue them aggressively; at other times, for one reason or another, they won't *touch* that industry, e.g. real estate. If your industry is *in*, your efforts will be a lot easier. Knowing how to deal with banks, and understanding the refinancing process, will be very helpful to you.

Because of the concept known as lender fatigue, described earlier in this book, the existing lender is often reluctant to finance a company emerging from a turnaround, even if most of its problems do appear to be corrected. As such, most emerging companies would be well served to start building relationships with other lenders during the turnaround process, so that they will have alternative sources of finance should their existing lender elect to withdraw.

Explaining the past

Most prospective lenders will approach a turnaround company with a great deal of skepticism. You will be *guilty* until proven *innocent*. As a result, take extra care to ensure that you are fully prepared before you approach any lenders. All of the information in the box below must be professionally and comprehensively prepared in presentation format. Obtaining the help of an outside consultant who is experienced in this area will be very helpful. In general, it is rare that a lender will believe that the same management team that got the company into trouble can lead it out. As such, be prepared to

---

What a prospective lender will want to know

- the cause and extent of the company's past problems

- how those problems have been dealt with and why they will not recur

- the company's plan for future success

- why the plan is realistic and achievable

- the assumptions, facts and circumstances on which the plan has been based

- whether management has the expertise and experience to achieve the plan

---

demonstrate that you have identified and corrected management deficiencies. Always try to have at least a few new and well-qualified faces in the line-up to support this.

Cash flow lending

Most lenders today finance emerging businesses through their asset-based lending department. Every lender will tell you that it is cash flow that is most important to them, but they all focus very heavily on the fall-back of collateral security, i.e., the assets they will be able to liquidate if you default on the loan. They do scrutinize your projections of cash flow very carefully, and will not lend without adequate cash flow. But even if your cash flow projection is great, inadequate asset-backing could jeopardize the loan. In short, they'll lend on cash flow, if the assets are there to fully collateralize the cash flow. As a result, most loans to emerging middle-market companies (medium-sized, in banking terminology) are based on formulas calculated as varying percentages on the different classes of assets you have. For example, you can usually borrow 75 percent to 85 percent of *eligible* accounts receivable, 30 percent to 50 percent of *eligible* inventories, and 60 percent to 80 percent of the *liquidation* value of fixed assets.

These terms *eligible* and *liquidation* value may not seem important at first, but after a while, they take on a major significance. Eligible accounts receivable usually excludes all amounts more than 90 days outstanding, all accounts where more than 10 percent of the account is more than 90 days outstanding, accounts receivable to the extent the company also has a corresponding payable to the debtor that could be *contra'd*, all government or foreign receivables, and often excludes any receivable that the lender, in its *sole discretion*, does not want to finance. Eligible inventories could exclude items that the lender, in its sole discretion, feels are obsolete, slow moving or otherwise unmerchantable. *Liquidation* values of fixed assets are based on independent appraisals of such assets. If you read the fine print of most standard loan agreements, you will find that the lender has a lot of powers, and can take a lot of action in its sole discretion. This puts you in a weak position if the relationship turns sour and the lender decides to flex its muscles. To protect yourself, always try to negotiate at the minimum that such discretionary powers be based on the lender's sole and *reasonable* discretion.

(See Appendix VII for an outline of the process and mechanics of refinancing debt in a turnaround situation.)

G. MANAGEMENT APPROACH

Forget the past

To achieve a successful turnaround, it is important that the CEO and the management team be ready to accept the reality of the situation—and develop and implement a plan that makes sense for the future, regardless of what happened in the past. In a turnaround, many ideas, projects, products or people that seemed so important in the past might have to be abandoned, because the company does not have the finances to support them. To reach this state of mind is not easy for many CEOs, who do not like to admit failure. The issue, however, is not failure—it is saving the company! Without understanding this, management will have difficulty achieving success in a turnaround.

Management style

How you manage is probably the most important factor in a successful turnaround. If you create the right environment that stimulates a team approach to solving the problem, half the battle will already have been won. In the Recuperation Phase, your style as a CEO will probably need to change somewhat. During the Corporate CPR Phase, you may be forced to be more autocratic. The crisis conditions do not always allow time for debate. In Recuperation, you need to

237

start building more of an *interactive* management style, because the long-term survival of the company will strongly depend on the effectiveness of the management team, not just the skills of the CEO. Interactive management only works with a loyal and competent management team, and usually does not work until you have identified and eliminated all of the *Ineffective* and *Con artist* managers.

Even after you have graduated to interactive management, there are always a few employees who somehow make you feel *you work for them* rather than *they work for you*. You may feel that you can't make them happy, and that you are spending a lot of time and energy trying to achieve this elusive goal. You will find that it is often impossible, and that the best approach is to put the *shoe on the other foot*—in other words, find a way to let him or her know that you're the one who needs to be kept happy—or else!

Role of the CEO

As we approach the beginning of the 21st century, the role of the Chief Executive Officer is very different from what it was 20 or 30 years ago. In the 1950s through the 1970s, change happened at a much slower pace than today, and the average CEO worked his way up the ladder over a long career that culminated in the top job in his late 50s or 60s. Now change is much faster: The world is rapidly becoming one marketplace, competition is expanding at breakneck speed, communications are instantaneous and the demands placed on the corporate leader are far greater. Instead of years of competent and loyal experience being the main prerequisite for the job, a whole new set of skills, qualifications and characteristics are needed.

The most important role for the Chief Executive is to establish the *vision* for the corporation. Where is the company headed? What opportunities will it pursue? How will it get there? What level of risk is it comfortable with? The CEO must then communicate the vision to everybody connected with the business, including employees, shareholders and lenders. The message must be simple and clear; people cannot understand a brilliant but complicated plan.

The CEOs message must be inspirational. He must lead the organization to new heights; he must build and constantly reinforce the company's soul, and personality, and he must instill confidence in the company's mission. To achieve this, his personal integrity, ethics and honor must be evident to everybody with whom he deals. People must know that he can be depended on, but that he is tough enough to make the hard decisions.

The effective CEO must also be able to translate vision into reality. Efficiently harnessing and marshalling all available resources is an essential skill. Smooth and effortless execution of the plan is key. Selecting, training and delegating to the right people is fundamental to success. He is the conductor that leads all of these resources to play in harmony.

The Chief Executive, while he must be seen at all times to be human, cannot allow himself the luxury of showing the *troops* that he is losing hope. He has a responsibility to keep thinking positively (but always realistically) and demonstrating that there is a way out. An experienced CEO never shows panic, because he has learned that even the most desperate situations have a way of easing in time. Often in a crisis, there is a temptation to take a very short-term view—whereas, if you learn to *fasten your seat belt*, and *ride out the storm*, you can usually look back and laugh at those numerous situations in your past that appeared life threatening.

A CEO without vision is at best a manager—he can not be a leader that will withstand all obstacles, capitalize on opportunities and create many new opportunities. In all phases of a company's life, from inception through to maturity, and especially during a crisis, the skills and abilities of the Chief Executive Officer are one of the most significant factors in corporate success.

If, after serious reflection, you conclude that the above five paragraphs don't describe you, you will save yourself untold stress by pursuing one of the following paths:

- Hire somebody that does fit this description to run your business for you.
  - If this person is appropriately qualified, don't interfere with the way he runs the business.
  - If the person is not appropriately qualified, don't hire him.
- Alternatively, retain an experienced and competent investment banker to sell the business for you.

H. MOTIVATION

The key to continued health of the corporate patient is the motivation and morale of its work force. If people are motivated, they can achieve great heights. Most people normally operate at an efficiency level well below their maximum potential. The manager's most important role in a business is finding the way to unleash each person's latent abilities, talents, and enthusiasm.

Contributors to employee motivation

1. Self-Esteem
2. Growth Potential
3. Fair and Consistent Treatment

Self-esteem

Nothing is more important to an individual's motivation than how good he/she feels about him/herself. Our moods, energy and creativity are totally dependent on our level of self-esteem. If you treat employees as *incompetents*, it will be hard for them to perform in any other way. On the other hand, if you show you respect them and their skills, they'll feel like a million dollars, and it will be evident in their performance.

People should always be considered the company's major asset. Management usually does not tolerate disrespect for the company's physical assets, and it is just as important that disrespect for your *people assets* not be tolerated. Employees will quickly sense your concern for the individual's self-esteem and respect, and they will reward you with a very motivated attitude. A major part of this concept of self-esteem is the fact that, in a company, nobody is more important than anybody else. The President may have more responsibility than the receptionist or the truck driver (and is usually paid more for bearing that responsibility), but everybody is equally important in the chain that defines the company's image and determines its potential. The receptionist who *answers the phone with a smile*, or the driver who is courteous to the customer are vital links in the chain, and should be treated with equal respect.

Some time ago, an administrative staff member came to me and told me that she found her office depressing and would really like it to be painted. She added that she guessed this might apply to several other people, too. I suggested that she check with the other people, and then get quotes from three painters. She came back a few days later with three written quotations, and asked me which one she should choose. I told her to choose the one she thought would give us the best value. A few days later, she came back to tell me the painter had completed the job, and asked if I would review his work before the accounting department released the check. I told her that she should review his work, authorize the release of the check if she was satisfied with the work, and after the painter had left with his check, I would review the job *she* had done. After my review, I congratulated her on a job well done, and she beamed with pride.

This experience highlighted two very important lessons:

- At a very small risk to me (how badly could she have gone wrong?), I was able to show her that I trusted her judgment. This *unleashed* her latent abilities and contributed to raising her level of performance way above normal levels.

- Managers often perceive that an employee who is a responsible, decision-making adult at home, becomes an irresponsible child when he or she walks into the workplace. The secretary that I mentioned is a mother of two children, and would not hesitate to paint a few rooms in her house. However, being given this responsibility at work became a major motivational event. This is, therefore, a simple and easy tool at management's disposal.

An important contributor to, or detractor from, self-esteem is how the employee perceives your feelings about him/her. An example will illustrate what I mean here. Should the CEO care if an employee occasionally shows up to work a few minutes late, as long as they get the job done? If you walk through the offices and an employee is reading the morning paper (or two employees are chatting over a cup of coffee), should you reprimand them? The key here is to show people that you value their *output*, rather than their *input*. Along the same lines, don't be impressed by people just because they work hard at working long hours, or who never have time for a vacation. If they know that you are interested in *real* work, they will not waste time pretending to work. In such an environment, an employee who arrives at work late because he/she has to take care of personal matters, will usually more than make up for the lost time. (Of course, this can be done to excess, and can become a problem.)

It is always useful to remember that most employees can usually tell when managers are only pretending to care about self-esteem. As a general rule, subordinates understand their bosses' motives better than bosses understand those of their employees. You can usually *pull the wool* over your boss's eyes, but you can seldom fool your subordinates. They see the real you—under all circumstances; your boss sees you on your best behavior.

Growth potential

The ability to grow within an organization is often very motivating: Most people want to improve themselves and, if you can show them that hard and dedicated work will get them ahead in the organization, the pain or the drudgery of the hard work is lessened by their anticipation of the rewards it might bring. The secret is to encourage them to be thinking about the rewards of tomorrow, rather than the pain of today.

You and your employees can achieve great satisfaction and reward from encouraging and nurturing people to grow, develop and advance. In almost every organization, there are *diamonds in the rough*—people who have the potential to be highly competent or effective, but who have been suppressed by their boss, or for some other reason have not unleashed their full abilities. When you let these people know that you respect their contribution and skills, and that you will give them the opportunity to advance if they perform well, many people will amaze you (and, often, themselves) with what they can do.

This approach has an inherent risk: When a person has advanced to the peak of his potential, take care not to promote him beyond his level of competence. Acting otherwise activates what is known as the Peter Principle—which states that employees tend to rise to the level of their own incompetence. You would then be faced with the choice of demoting (or re-assigning) him or losing him. This is a very painful situation for both parties and should be avoided at all costs.

243

It is also important to be aware that pushing an employee toward further growth is not right for everybody, and is not always necessary for the company. If people are happy and motivated where they are, there is no need to push them. You will only make them feel pressured, and you may push somebody out of a job he's an expert in, into one he knows (and cares) little about. *If it ain't broke, don't fix it!*

In general, though, you will find that an organization that has a growth mentality—where individual as well as corporate growth is encouraged—will develop a vibrance and momentum that makes growth an exciting and self-fulfilling prophecy.

Fair and consistent treatment

The motivation derived from healthy self-esteem and growth potential can be negated by unfair or inconsistent policies and practices under which employees work. These include vacations, sick leave, benefits, overtime, pensions, retirement plans, rest periods, reimbursement of expenses and sexual harassment. A very important part of fair and consistent treatment is fair remuneration. If somebody feels he is being cheated, he will be resentful and demotivated. Generally, if you have been successful in raising people's level of self-esteem and if they are excited about their growth potential within the company, nothing more than *fair* remuneration is required. However, if these first two qualities are absent, you might need to increase the remuneration to retain the level of motivation, or to even retain the person at all (and, in the long run, even this won't work). It is very important to have a personnel manual that clearly states all personnel policies. I have found that it is vital to constantly review all personnel regularly to ensure their self-esteem is intact, that they are motivated by future potential and that they feel they are being treated fairly.

Every human being has the potential to perform at levels *much* higher than their normal day-to-day levels, given the right stimulation and motivation. If you can find the right *buttons to push*, you will be surprised by what people can do. When people enjoy coming to work, and don't even notice when it's quitting time, you know you've done something right.

I. CORPORATE SOUL

In most business situations, it is very easy to get engrossed in the *nuts and bolts*, and focus on real issues like sales, expenses, budgets, cash flow, etc. However, there is another side to business—one that is very often neglected, and that is crucial to the company's success. I refer to that as the *Soul* of the organization.

The soul of a business encompasses many areas, which include its philosophy, ethics, self-image (that is, how the people within the organization perceive the organization, and themselves within the organization), attitude to risk-taking, method of dealing with failure, quality standards, safety standards, environmental standards and social and neighborhood standards. Some people refer to this as *Corporate Culture*. I believe that the term Soul goes far deeper then Corporate Culture, because it goes to the root of the company's *spirit*.

A corporation without Soul is unlikely to survive the test of time. Soul is what gives it the resilience to overcome seemingly insurmountable hurdles, the creativeness to achieve true breakthroughs in efficiency and technology, the team spirit to stick together through thick and thin and the motivation to reach for the stars! As you slowly start to nurse your corporate patient back to health, you need to be spending as much energy on the company's Soul as on the *Nuts and Bolts*. It is much harder to focus on this area, as it is a lot less visible and the payback is long-term. However, just as the building without strong foundations will not survive a big storm, a corporation that is not constantly cultivating its Soul will not be truly strong.

A good example of Soul Power is the amazing turnaround of Harley-Davidson, the manufacturer of motorcycles.

"At the start of the 1980s, few people gave Harley-Davidson much chance to survive. The last U.S. motorcycle maker was being battered by the Japanese. Its share of the super-heavyweight motorcycle market had fallen from 75 percent in 1973 to less that 25 percent. Yet today the Milwaukee-based company, 86 years old and still running full throttle, has nearly 50 percent of the market."

Fortune, September 25, 1989

In addition to many cost-saving techniques, like product redesign and just-in-time inventories, Harley created a unique environment of total employee and customer involvement in the whole turnaround process. For the company's 85th birthday, the company arranged for 40,000 bikers and company employees (including top management) to ride from all corners of the U.S. to Milwaukee for a big party. The ride also raised over $500,000 for charity. This type of total involvement, and the company's outstanding results, demonstrate the impact of *Corporate Soul*.

Will to live

The most important belief to instill throughout the organization is the unquestioned faith that the company *will survive and prosper*. This is fundamental and essential to any recovery process. A seriously ill medical patient that doesn't have the will to live probably won't—so too with a corporation. If you display unquestioned confidence in your company at all times, and you demonstrate the leadership, strength and vision that will inspire your employees to join you in your belief, you will be starting the process of building your corporation's Soul and will to live! From there you need to make clear to every employee with whom you come into contact (and in the initial stages of a turnaround, you should be talking to a lot of people) your belief in and commitment (and hence, the corporation's belief and commitment) to the following qualities: self-esteem and respect for all employees, integrity in all business dealings, the highest ethical standards, constant awareness and pursuit of safety, commitment to a clean environment, a social conscience and providing value to your customers.

Your role in this process is that of a missionary. You should be constantly talking to people at all levels in the company—explaining the philosophy and strategy, listening to their concerns and fears and reassuring them. No matter what other functions you delegate to others, you cannot delegate building corporate Soul. This is the Chief Executive's responsibility, not only during the turnaround process, but at all times in the company's life.

Ten Corporate Commandments

As an aid in developing and building Corporate Soul, it is always helpful for the CEO to communicate to his employees, customers, lenders and suppliers what the company stands for. This should be transmitted by his actions and by every form of communication that emanates from him.

The box on the next page contains an example of the type of simple and concise statement that a CEO could make to communicate his *Soul* message. In practice, every CEO must develop his own statement that works for his organization. This type of statement helps employees understand the true *personality* of the organization, and gives them a standard by which to evaluate and judge everyday decisions and problems. While not replacing detailed operating procedures and policies, such a statement can provide the framework around which the detailed procedures can be structured.

Ten Corporate Commandments

(Not in order of importance)

1. Protect the company's assets.

2. Treat the company's employees fairly and consistently, and with respect.

3. Conduct the affairs of the company in a lawful manner.

4. Maximize the ultimate return to the company's shareholders.

5. Protect the physical safety, health and well-being of the company's employees, customers and all parties and environment that come into contact with the company or its products.

6. Provide the highest value, quality and service to the company's customers.

7. Strive to reduce waste and inefficiency.

8. Be on the alert for changing circumstances and new opportunities, and be ready to respond to them.

9. Encourage individual action and initiative.

10. Conduct the company's business in a spirit of teamwork and mutual respect.

J. REASON TO SURVIVE

In order to survive and thrive in the long term, a business must have a *reason to survive*. That is, the business must have a sustainable competitive advantage that will enable it to earn a rate of return on its capital that will appropriately reward its shareholders. Without a sustainable competitive advantage, the business will be just *one of the pack*, and will ultimately die.

248

Many businesses take a long time to die (sometimes as long as 15 years), which often gives their owners and operators a false sense of confidence. When I analyze most of my clients, it is usually clear that they have been in decline for many years—primarily because they did not have a reason to survive.

Sustainable competitive advantages include:

- Genuinely being the *low-cost producer*, e.g., Wal-Mart
- A strong patent, e.g., Nutrasweet (however, this advantage has a limited lifespan)
- A desirable trademark or intangible asset, e.g., Mickey Mouse
- Superior product development talent, e.g., Microsoft
- Powerful market franchise, e.g., Coca-Cola
- Distribution muscle, e.g., Procter & Gamble
- Control over raw materials, e.g., DeBeers Diamonds
- Superior quality, e.g., Maytag
- Status symbol, e.g., Lexus
- Cleanliness, e.g., McDonald's

In designing the long-term turnaround strategy for your business, focus on building competitive advantages: Without at least one, you might unwittingly be beginning another (perhaps lengthy) downward spiral. Note, however, that a competitive advantage today may not be there tomorrow. With changing conditions, competitive advantages must be continually reviewed and adapted.

ACTION STEPS

› Explore and implement ways to enhance profitability

› Make customer satisfaction the number one priority

› Enhance and promote *non-financial* reasons for customers to buy from you

› Consider whether your sales manager has the *street smarts*, empathy, and profit orientation to effectively lead the company's sales thrust

› Always look for, and eliminate, *sacred cows*

› Look for ways to unleash *people power*

› Implement a continuous improvement philosophy, through measurement and enhancement of critical efficiency factors

› Consider whether growth by acquisitions is appropriate for your company

› Examine your pricing strategies to identify ways to fill up excess production capacity

› Develop an interactive management approach

› Critically evaluate whether you have the skills to lead your business back to health

› Place a strong emphasis on motivating your employees

› Take the time to build *Corporate Soul*

› Always strive to create and enhance competitive advantages

CONCLUSION

CONCLUSION

Eight weeks had passed since the meeting between Peter Jones, the Chief Executive Officer of Excalibur, Inc., the fictional company referred to in the Introduction, and Ted Rogers, the workout officer of ABC Bank. Since that meeting, Jones had been working intensively with Charlie Benson, the turnaround consultant.

Jones was initially surprised and intrigued by the approach Charlie Benson took in analyzing Excalibur. Jones felt that their initial emphasis should be placed on developing a strategy to increase sales. Benson's response was quite different.

"I'm not worried about sales at this point," he said. "With $22 million in total sales, that is more than enough to work with."

Jones was confused. He had always been taught that sales and market share were the first priorities of any business.

"When a business is in a crisis," Benson continued, "there are short-term, medium-term and long-term priorities. Growing sales can be an important long-term goal, but contrary to what you may expect, could be detrimental to the business in the short term."

"Why is that?" Jones asked.

"Because," Benson responded, "preservation and generation of cash is the most important short-term objective, and growth in sales often requires a build up of inventory and receivables, which consumes, rather than generates, cash."

"At this stage," he continued, "our most important priority is to find ways to produce enough cash so that the business can survive over the next 90 to 120 days. As part of this, we will be exploring ways to reduce the break-even point of the business, so that it is easier to earn a profit at your current sales level."

"I find it hard to believe," Jones replied, "that we will be able to reduce the break-even point by enough to return us to profitability. During this fiscal year, we are expecting to lose nearly $500,000. We have already cut out a significant amount of expenses, and I can't imagine that we will eliminate enough costs to get back into the black. In addition, I just can't see how we can generate enough cash to survive the next 30 days, let alone 120 days!"

"You are correct," Benson responded, "except that we are going to examine the business from a different point of view, and we're going to determine areas of strength and weakness. With this information, we should be able to develop a plan to significantly improve the business, by working smarter rather than harder."

"I'm all for that," said Jones, "but, to be quite honest, I don't understand what you mean."

"It has to do with a concept called ROAM or Return On Assets Managed," Benson replied. "Let me explain. This is vitally important to the success of any business. Not understanding this is a major cause of business failure."

Jones, now more confused, listened intently.

"Your balance sheet is responsible for the situation you are in," Benson stated. "Over the years, you have made many business decisions that have resulted in the balance sheet you have today. This has caused you to invest capital into assets, which has resulted in corresponding liabilities to finance those assets. While you may not have realized it, these decisions are the reasons why your business has run out of money."

"How can you tell that the balance sheet is my problem?" Jones interrupted.

"If you recall," Benson replied, "I asked you whether you could provide me with an analysis of your assets by division and product line. When you told me you could not, I knew that's where your problem lay."

"But why would an accounting report be so important to the success of the business?" Jones queried. "Surely, issues like quality, service and market share are more important."

"The key to success of a company is ensuring that every facet of the business earns an adequate ROAM," Benson responded, "And, when you told me that you could not identify the assets for every part of your business, I knew that you could not be earning an adequate return on all of those assets."

"How can you tell that we are not earning an adequate return, just because we don't know the break-down of the assets?" Jones asked.

"Because *efficiency doesn't happen by itself!*" Benson replied, "You have to make it happen by coaxing it out of every part of the businesses. To do this you need two pieces of information: First, you must know the assets employed in every division and product line. Second, you need to be aware of the target ROAM."

"What is target ROAM," Jones inquired, "and why is it so important?"

"The target ROAM is the profitability the business must achieve, as a percentage of the assets it is utilizing, in order to ensure that business has enough cash to maintain and build itself," Benson responded. "When we know the target ROAM for the business as a whole, we can then determine the target ROAM for individual divisions and product lines. This is done by an analysis called the Corporate Treadmill Test."

"How will this help us improve our situation?" Jones inquired.

"When we know the actual ROAM for each division and product line, and we can then compare that to their respective target ROAMs, we will then know which areas of the business are doing better or worse than target. With this information, we will be able identify the areas of the business that are underperforming. That is, those that are failing the Corporate Treadmill Test," Benson replied.

"I still don't see how this solves our problem," Jones said. "How do we use this information?"

"Once we know the areas of the business that are not earning an adequate ROAM, we have two options: First, we will explore ways to improve the ROAM of that area. If we cannot find any way to improve the ROAM to the point where that area of the business passes the Corporate Treadmill Test, we will give serious consideration to selling or liquidating the assets employed in that area. Without compelling reasons to the contrary, it makes no sense to retain assets that are expected to significantly underperform for the foreseeable future. It makes far more sense to redeploy the cash tied up by those underperforming assets to areas of the business that earn higher returns," Benson replied.

"How do you improve the ROAM of a division or product line?" Jones asked.

"Fortunately," Benson responded, "because ROAM is a two-dimensional concept, a little improvement in both dimensions will yield significant results. ROAM is the amount of profit in relation to assets employed. To improve ROAM, we will explore ways to increase profit, in addition to trying to reduce assets employed. Improvements in both of these components will generate significant cash flow, and will contribute to lowering your break-even point."

"How will we improve profits in these areas?" Jones asked.

"We will focus on improving margins and operating efficiency," Benson replied. "We will explore ways to improve margins through a careful analysis of what you earn from every product. We will then try to improve margins by promoting higher margin products. We will also make very aggressive efforts to negotiate better prices from your suppliers for raw materials, and all other significant goods and services. We're also going to improve operating efficiency, by finding simple and inexpensive ways to do things easier. This could include minor modifications to machinery or plant layout that could result in significant improvements in efficiency. Lastly, we're going to involve your workers in the process. This will achieve two objectives: First, some of the best ideas for improvement will come from non-management employees. Second, they'll feel good about being involved, and as such will be willing to work harder to help you achieve the turnaround."

"So," Jones said, "if I understand this process correctly, the Corporate Treadmill Test will give us targets to shoot for in every area of the business. This will enable us to identify the real problem areas, and to focus our energies on fixing the areas most in need."

"That is absolutely correct," Benson confirmed, "and with this approach, it is rare that significant improvements cannot be achieved."

Peter Jones and Charlie Benson arrived at the offices of ABC Bank to provide a status report and turnaround plan to Ted Rogers.

After exchanging pleasantries, Jones said, "Ted, I'm pleased to tell you that during the eight weeks since we last met, we have made major strides. With Charlie's help, we have gained an understanding of the true strengths and weaknesses of our business. With this information, we have been able to develop a strategic plan that appears to have a good probability of success. In addition, we have been able to implement several strategies that have significantly eased our cash crisis. Some of the most beneficial of these include the liquidation of slow-moving inventory, the acceleration of collection of receivables, the improvement of inventory turnover in some areas, the reduction of our work force by 15 people and the reduction of some key raw materials and other goods and services."

"That sounds like some worthwhile changes," Rogers commented, "I would be interested in seeing how they impact your cash flow projection. I am also interested to know how you plan to deal with your past-due balances owing to unsecured creditors."

"We have proposed a compromise agreement with unsecured creditors," Benson interjected, "whereby Excalibur will pay 60 percent of past-due balances, over a three-year period, with an initial payment of 20 cents. While the creditors were initially not enthusiastic about this, when we explained the company's financial status to them, including the fact that creditors would likely not receive any distribution if the company was to be liquidated, most of them acknowledged the merits of our proposal. So far, three of the five largest creditors have indicated they will approve the plan, and we believe that we will be able to obtain acceptance from creditors owed at least 80 percent of the total unsecured debt."

"Where will you get the funds to make the initial 20 cents payment to creditors, and how do you intend to deal with the arrear payments to ABC Bank?" Rogers asked.

"The analysis we performed with Charlie showed that a major portion of our assets are unproductive. We were surprised by the result. Because we were only focusing on profits, we were all expecting to find the new sports equipment division to be the worst performer. Instead, we found that the retail side of the bicycle division is performing far worse in relation to the assets employed. We explored several techniques to improve its performance, but could not find a way to raise the division to a level where it would pass the test Charlie developed for us. As a result, we have decided to sell the retail store division, which we estimate will generate enough cash to retire its line of credit, take care of our past-due tax and bank obligations, as well as make the down payment to unsecured creditors. We also believe that the elimination of this division, which was taking up a lot of management time, will free us up to focus on improving the rest of the business," Jones explained.

"How do you plan to improve the rest of the business?" Rogers inquired.

"We have implemented a program to improve operating efficiency at all levels," Jones answered, "which starts with the regular measurement of certain critical efficiency factors, and includes the development of an incentive plan for our workers. We have also, with the involvement of our plant employees, identified some low-cost changes to plant layout and equipment that are expected to improve efficiency significantly. Further, we are training our workers to inspect their own output, which we expect to result in the elimination of the inspection department, the improvement of quality and the reduction of scrap."

"Well," said Ted Rogers, "this certainly is an impressive response to your situation."

"We are pleased you approve," replied Benson, "and, in fact, we will still need your help in achieving this plan."

"What did you have in mind?" inquired Rogers.

"First," responded Benson, "we will need the bank to waive all of Excalibur's prior covenant defaults. Also, our cash flow projection indicates that for the next four to six months—that is until we can conclude the sale of the retail division—we will not be able to pay the bank principal payments. As such, we are requesting a six-month moratorium on principal payments. We have carried out a liquidation valuation of Excalibur, and it is our conclusion that, in a liquidation, ABC Bank would be undersecured by several hundred thousand dollars. We, therefore, believe that it would be in the best interests of the bank to provide Excalibur with the breathing space it needs, so that the bank can be confident of an ultimate full recovery of its loan."

"I believe a total moratorium of principle will not be acceptable to the bank," Rogers responded. "However, I think it might be possible to arrange a partial moratorium. If you think you could manage reduced principle payments, I would be willing to recommend that the bank agree to your request. I will need to see a complete turnaround plan and cash flow projection. I would also like to see a copy of your liquidation valuation. As I mentioned at our last meeting, Peter, we will also probably charge a fee for our forbearance agreement."

They shook hands, and Jones and Benson headed for the elevator. "That seemed to go pretty well," Jones commented, "thanks to your efforts, Charlie."

"No!" retorted Benson. "I was a catalyst, but you are responsible for this. Going through this process, and being willing to make the necessary changes, is not easy for a Chief Executive Officer. I have seen many people ruin a turnaround effort because they were not willing to implement true change. You faced the issues directly, and made the tough decisions!"

BIBLIOGRAPHY, APPENDICES & INDEX

BIBLIOGRAPHY

The National Directory of Corporate Distress Specialists. New York: Lustig Data Research, Inc. (1992-93)
>   Provides lists of corporate distress specialists including:
>   Accounting and Valuation Consultants
>   Attorneys
>   Financial Advisers
>   Financing Sources
>   Investors in Distressed and High-Yield Securities
>   Real Estate Managers & Consultants
>   Turnaround Managers & Consultants
>   Workout Officers

Pratt's Guide to Venture Capital Sources. Needham, Mass: Venture Economics, Inc. (Published annually)
>   Provides a list of venture capital companies.
>   Includes description of how to raise venture capital.

Silver, David A. *The Middle-Market Leveraged Financing Directory and Source Book.* New York: Harper, 1990
>   Provides lists of sources of:
>   Asset-Based Loans
>   Mezzanine Capital

Turnaround Management Association, 1991 Directory of Members & Services. Arlington, Virginia: Turnaround Management Association (Published annually)
>   Provides a listing of the members of the Turnaround Management Association.

APPENDIX I

Table 1

EXCALIBUR INC
CASH FLOW PROJECTION

{See attached notes}	Week 1	Week 2	Week 3	Week 4	Total Month 1	Week 5	Week 6	Week 7	Week 8	Week 9	Total Month 2	Month 3	Total Quart. 1
SALES (1)													
Bicycles	220	250	280	300	1,050	250	250	250	250	275	1,275	1,150	3,475
Sports equipment	120	120	120	125	485	130	130	135	135	135	665	700	1,850
	340	370	400	425	1,535	380	380	385	385	410	1,940	1,850	5,325
CASH RECEIPTS													
Accounts rec.	375	395	400	425	1,595	440	430	430	430	440	2,170	1,950	5,715
Fixed asset sales					0				50		50	50	100
Other					0					50	50	50	100
Total receipts	375	395	400	425	1,595	440	430	430	480	490	2,270	2,050	5,915
CASH DISBURSEMENTS													
Weekly payroll	40	40	40	40	160	40	40	40	40	40	200	165	525
Bi-weekly payroll	46		46		92	46		46		48	140	95	327
Payroll and other taxe	90	22	10	22	143	30	22	10	22	10	93	92	328
Benefits	32				32	32					32	42	106
Utilities			20		20				20		20	20	60
Vendors													
-Current purch.	100	100	110	110	420	110	110	110	120	120	570	500	1,490
-old bals.incl.tax	30	30	30	30	120	30	30	20	20	20	120	40	280
Plant expenses	80	80	90	90	340	90	80	80	80	80	410	320	1,070
S.G.&A expenses	55	55	60	60	230	60	60	55	55	55	285	225	740
Professional serv			8		8			10			10	20	38
Insurance					0			300			300		300
Machinery purch.					0				150		150	175	325
Interest		48			48		48				48	48	144
Debt principal				25	25				25		25	25	75
Leases		20			20		25				25	30	75
Other	5				5			25			25	75	105
Line of credit (2)				20	20								20
(excess)/paydown	-18	29	11	15	38	50	43	41	36	29	200	126	364
Total disb.	460	433	435	392	1721	493	463	742	548	407	2652	1979	6352
CASH GENERATED/(USED)	-85	-38	-35	33	-126	-53	-33	-312	-68	83	-382	71	-437
OPENING CASH BAL.	10	-75	-114	-149	10	-116	-169	-202	-513	-581	-116	-498	10
CLOSING CASH BAL.	-75	-114	-149	-116	-116	-169	-202	-513	-581	-498	-498	-427	-427

APPENDIX I
Table 2

EXCALIBUR INC.
CASH FLOW PROJECTION

	Quart.1	Month 4	Month 5	Month 6	Total Quart.2	Quart.3	Quart.4	Total Year 1
SALES {1}								
Bicycles	3,475	1,300	1,600	1,700	4,600	2,800	3,500	14,375
Sports equipment	1,850	800	900	850	2,550	2,300	1,400	8,100
	5,325	2,100	2,500	2,550	7,150	5,100	4,900	22,475
CASH RECEIPTS								
Accounts rec.	5,715	1,900	1,850	1,950	5,700	5,800	5,100	22,315
Fixed asset sales	100				0			100
Other	100				0			100
Total receipts	5,915	1,900	1,850	1,950	5,700	5,800	5,100	22,515
CASH DISBURSEMENTS								
Weekly payroll	525	180	230	240	650	500	500	2,175
Bi-weekly payroll	327	100	100	105	305	300	300	1,232
Payroll/other taxes	328	125	105	113	342	296	296	1263
Benefits	106	35	41	43	119	100	100	425
Utilities	60	25	25	30	80	75	70	285
Vendors								
-Current purch.	1,490	750	875	900	2,525	1,900	1,900	7,815
-old bals.incl.tax	280	50	50	50	150	150	150	730
Plant expenses	1,070	400	430	430	1,260	1,025	1,000	4,355
S,G,&A expenses	740	225	230	235	690	650	600	2,680
Professional serv	38	15	15	15	45	45	45	173
Insurance	300				0	300		600
Machinery purch.	325				0			325
Interest	144	48	55	55	158	150	150	602
Debt principal	75	25	25	25	75	75	75	300
Leases	75	25	25	25	75	75	75	300
Other	105	40	40	45	125	130	130	490
Line of credit {2}								
(excess)/paydown	364	-130	-435	-403	-969	478	95	-33
Total disb.	6352	1913	1811	1907	5630	6249	5486	23718
CASH GENERATED /(USED)	-437	-13	39	43	70	-449	-386	-1203
OPENING CASH BALANCE	10	-427	-440	-400	-427	-358	-807	10
CLOSING CASH BALANCE	-427	-440	-400	-358	-358	-807	-1193	-1193

{See attached notes}

265

APPENDIX I
Table 3

EXCALIBUR INC.
CASH FLOW PROJECTION AND RECONCILIATION TO STATEMENT OF CHANGES {3}

	TOTAL YEAR I	(PROFIT)/LOSS	BALANCE SHEET CHANGES					
			ACCOUNTS RECEIVABLE	FIXED ASSETS	ACCOUNTS PAYABLE	DEBT	INVENTORY	LINE OF CREDIT
SALES								
Bicycles	14,375							
Sports equipment	8,100							
	22,475	(22,475) {4}	22,475{4}					
CASH RECEIPTS								
Accounts rec.	22,315		(22,315)					
Fixed asset sales	100	50		(150)				
Other	100	(100)						
Total receipts[A]	22,515							
CASH DISBURSEMENTS								
Depreciation		400{4}		(400) {4}				
Weekly payroll	2,175	2,175						
Bi-weekly payroll	1,232	1,232						
Payroll taxes	1,263	1,263						
Benefits	425	425						
Utilities	285	285						
Vendors								
-Current purch.	7,815						7,815	
-old balances	730				730			
Plant expenses	4,355	4,355						
S,G,&A expenses	2,680	2,680						
Professional serv	173	173						
Insurance	600	600						
Machinery purch.	325			325				
Interest	602	602						
Debt principal	300					300		
Leases	300	300						
Other	490	490						
Line of credit								
(excess)/paydown	-33							-33
Inventory used		8100 {4}					-8100 {4}	
[B]	23718	555	160	-225	730	300	-285	-33
NET CASH [A-B]	-1203							0

{See attached notes}

APPENDIX I   Table 4

EXCALIBUR INC.
LINE OF CREDIT AVAILABILITY {2}

	Week 1	Week 2	Week 3	Week 4	Week 5	Week 6	Week 7	Week 8	Week 9	Month 3
Accounts receivable										
Opening bal.	3,450	3,415	3,390	3,390	3,390	3,330	3,280	3,235	3,190	3,160
Sales	340	370	400	425	380	380	385	385	410	1,850
Collections	(375)	(395)	(400)	(425)	(440)	(430)	(430)	(430)	(440)	(1,950)
Closing bal.	3,415	3,390	3,390	3,390	3,330	3,280	3,235	3,190	3,160	3,060
Inventory										
Opening bal.	2,075	2060	2035	2010	1976	1958	1939	1919	1909	1890
Purchases	100	100	110	110	110	110	110	120	120	500
Used	-115	-125	-135	-144	-128	-128	-130	-130	-139	-625
Closing bal.	2060	2035	2010	1976	1958	1939	1919	1909	1890	1765
Line of credit avail.										
Receivables @ 70% {5}	2391	2373	2373	2373	2331	2296	2265	2233	2212	2142
Inventory @ 45%	927	916	904	889	881	873	864	859	851	794
	3318	3289	3277	3262	3212	3169	3128	3092	3063	2936
Line of credit										
Opening balance	3300	3318	3289	3277	3262	3212	3169	3128	3092	3063
Current available	3318	3289	3277	3262	3212	3169	3128	3092	3063	2936
Excess/(Paydown){2}	18	-29	-11	-15	-50	-43	-41	-36	-29	-126

{See attached notes}

APPENDIX I

Table 5

EXCALIBUR INC.
LINE OF CREDIT AVAILABILITY {2}

	Month 4	Month 5	Month 6	Quart.3	Quart.4
Accounts receivable					
Opening bal.	3,060	3,260	3,910	4,510	3,810
Sales	2,100	2,500	2,550	5,100	4,900
Collections	(1,900)	(1,850)	(1,950)	(5,800)	(5,100)
Closing bal.	3,260	3,910	4,510	3,810	3,610
Inventory					
Opening bal.	1,765	1744	1700	1663	1690
Purchases	750	875	900	1,900	1,900
Used	-771	-918	-937	-1873	-1800
Closing bal.	1744	1700	1663	1690	1790
Line of credit avail.					
Receivables @ 70%	2282	2737	3157	2667	2527
{5}					
Inventory @ 45%	785	765	749	761	806
	3067	3502	3906	3428	3333
Line of credit					
Opening bal.	2936	3067	3502	3906	3428
Current avail.	3067	3502	3906	3428	3333
Excess/(Paydown)	130	435	403	-478	-95

{See attached notes}

268

APPENDIX I

Cash flow projection notes for tables 1 through 5

{1} Sales projections should be derived from, and supported by, detailed projections from the sales and marketing departments. Projections should be built up from the detailed analyses by division, region, product line and major customer.

{2} Line of Credit (excess)/paydown

Appendix I, Tables 4 and 5 reflects the calculation of availability under the company's Line of Credit with its lender. This calculation determines the amount of availability projected for each period, based on the projection for receivables and inventory multiplied by the respective advance rates specified by the lender (reduced by projected receivables and inventory ineligible for borrowing (See note 5)).

For purposes of calculating the projected cash flow in Tables 1 and 2, the Line of Credit is assumed be drawn to its maximum availability each period. Alternatively, if it is overdrawn, the cash flow projection reflects a paydown of the overdrawn amount, i.e., the cash flow projection is calculated on the basis that the Line of Credit is drawn to its maximum at the end of every period, resulting in either excess availability or a paydown of the line. In practice, this usually does not happen, and the Line of Credit is only drawn to the extent of the company's cash needs. However, for projecting purposes, it is easier to do it this way, and the Closing Cash Balance available represents a combination of projected cash and any excess available under the line of credit.

{3} Table 3 provides a reconciliation of the Cash Flow Projection to the Statement of Changes, to provide a way to verify the reasonableness of the Cash Flow Projection.

The column *Total Year 1* is brought forward from Table 2. The remaining columns allocate all cash inflows and outflows to either the Profit and Loss account or to respective Balance Sheet accounts. The totals of these columns can then be reviewed for accuracy and reason ableness.

{4} Certain non-cash-flow items (sales, depreciation, inventory used), while not part of the cash flow calculations, are reflected in the reconciliation columns to provide the true accrual accounting results for comparison purposes.

APPENDIX I

Cash flow projection notes for tables 1 through 5

Continued from previous page

{5} Line of Credit availability is calculated based on the projections for receivables and inventory at the end of each period, multiplied by the respective advance rates specified by the lender.

Lenders typically lend a certain percentage of the *eligible* assets. They do not lend on *ineligible* assets, which could include:

Receivables

· balances over 90 days outstanding

· full receivable if more than 10% of the receivable from that customer is more than 90 days outstanding

· government receivables

· inter-company receivables

Inventory

· work-in-progress

· obsolete or slow-moving items

Borrowing rates usually are in the 75% to 85% range for receivables and the 30% to 50% range for inventory. For purposes of this Cash Flow Projection, we have used 70% for receivables and 45% for inventory, to give effect to projected ineligible assets.

APPENDIX II

EXCALIBUR INC.
BREAK-EVEN ANALYSIS

(See notes on next page)	P&L	{1} Variable	{1}, {2} Fixed [P&L]	{2} Fixed [Cash]	{3} Non-Recurring
INCOME					
Sales:					
Bicycles	(14,375)				
Sports equipment	(8,100)				
	(22,475)	**(22,475)**			
Fixed asset sales	50			(150)	50
Other	(100)				(100)
EXPENSES					
Depreciation	400		400		
Weekly payroll {4}	2,175	1,175	1,000	1,000	
Bi-weekly payrol {4}	1,232	182	1,050	1,050	
Payroll taxes	1,263	503	760	760	
Benefits	425	117	309	309	
Utilities	285	86	200	200	
Vendors					
-Current purch.	0			0	
-old balances	0			0	
Plant expenses	4,355	2613	1742	1,742	
S,G,&A expenses	2,680	1608	1072	1,072	
Professional serv	173		173	173	
Insurance	600	60	540	540	
Machinery purch.				325	
Interest	602		602	602	
Debt principal	0			300	
Leases	300		300	300	
Other	490	294	196	196	
Inventory used	8,100	8100		0	
NET LOSS	555				
	0				
TOTAL VARIABLE EXPS.		14737			
% OF SALES		65.572%			
VARIABLE CONTRIBUTION {5}		34.428%			
TOTAL FIXED EXPS.			8343	8418	

BREAK-EVEN SALES:
FIXED EXPS./ VARIABLE CONTRIBUTION

P&L	{6}	24233	
CASH	{7}		24451

271

APPENDIX II
Notes for table

{1} All expenses must be analyzed into fixed and variable portions. Fixed expenses are those that increase or decrease when sales volume changes. Variable expenses do change when volume changes.

{2} The column entitled Fixed [P & L] reflects the fixed expenses on an accrual basis of accounting. The column entitled Fixed [Cash] reflects the fixed expenses on a cash basis. In a turnaround situation, where cash is so important, the fixed expenses on a cash basis are more relevant.

{3} Non-recurring items of income and expenditure are not taken into account in determining the break-even point, as they are not relevant to future operations.

{4} Weekly payroll usually will have a substantial variable portion, although it is often less variable than might be anticipated. This is because it is usually not practical or efficient to lay off hourly workers in direct proportion to sales. Most companies must keep a certain minimum core group of skills even if volume does drop significantly. Bi-weekly payroll, on the other hand, is predominantly fixed.

{5} Variable Contribution is the percentage contribution to fixed expenses that can be expected from every dollar of sales.

{6} Break-even Sales [P & L] is the sales level at which the business is expected to break even on its profit and loss statement, i.e., zero profit or loss.

{7} Break-even Sales [Cash] is the sales level required to break even on a cash basis. Non-cash charges (e.g., depreciation) are ignored, and cash expenditures for debt principal and capital expenditures are taken into account. In this example, changes in working capital have not been taken into account. If working capital changes are expected to be significant, they should be taken into account in determining cash flow break-even, especially if the changes are expected to be recurring from year to year. If working capital changes are taken into account, financing available to acquire inventory and receivables (interest and non-interest bearing) should be netted against the investment in working capital

APPENDIX III

EXCALIBUR INC
FORCED LIQUIDATION VALUE

(See notes on following page)

PROJECTED REALIZATION

	CBOC*	PR%* {1}	ABC BANK {2}	XYZ BANK {2}	UNSC*	MOV*
Assets						
Cash	10	100%	10			Actual
Trade receivables						
- Under 90 days	2,150	80%	1720			Estimated
- 91 to 120 days	490	45%	221			Estimated
- Over 120 days	810	15%	122			Estimated
	3,450		2063			
Other receivables	300	15%	45			Estimated
Inventory						
- Raw material	525	50%	263			Quotes
- Work-in-progress	610	5%	31			Scrap values
- Purchased parts	265	50%	133			Quotes
- Finished goods	675	60%	405			Estimated
	2,075		832			
Prepaid expenses	225	20%	45			Estimated
Land & buildings	600	70%		420		Appraisal
Machinery & equipment	1,200	40%	480			Appraisal
Jigs & fixtures	250	20%	50			Estimated
Office equipment	250	20%	50			Appraisal
Patents/trademarks	100	30%	30			Estimated
	8,460		**3603**	**420**	**0**	
COSTS OF LIQUIDATION						
- Operating losses			150			
- Liquidation costs			160	60		
NET LIQUIDATION PROCEEDS {3}			3293	360	0	
LOAN BALANCE OWING {3}						
- Term loan			450	350		
- Line of credit			3300			
- Unsecured					3250	
OVER/(UNDER-SECURED)			**-458**	**10**	**-3250**	

* CBOC = Current balance at original cost
PR% = Projected realization percentage
UNSC = Unsecured creditors
MOV = Method of valuation

APPENDIX III
Notes for table

{1} Projected realization percentage represents the estimated percentage of realization that will be achieved in a forced liquidation. Such percentages will differ for every business, based on the circumstances.

{2} The projected realization amount for each asset that is collateral of a lender should be listed in the column for that lender.

{3} Net liquidation proceeds represents the estimated amounts to be available from the liquidation of the assets, after the costs of liquidation. This amount is then to be allocated to creditors in their order of priority: First to secured creditors, based on their loan balances outstanding. If there are any proceeds left over after allocating the proceeds to the secured lenders' balances outstanding, such funds would be available for other unsecured creditors. Priority claims (e.g., taxes) may have to be paid before unsecured creditors.

APPENDIX IV

EXCALIBUR, INC.
Strategic Turnaround Plan example

This is an example of a Turnaround Strategic Plan for the fictional company described in the introduction, Excalibur, Inc. It should be borne in mind that every turnaround situation is different, and that a strategic plan must be designed to suit the circumstances of the specific company.

PART I	Responsibility	Date of Completion
1. Determine reasons why business is underperforming	P.J./Consultant	4/10
2. Complete a Corporate Treadmill Test analysis, to determine target Return On Assets Managed (for company, divisions and product lines) needed to achieve Positive Cash Flow	P.J./Consultant	4/15
3. Prepare a Financial Health Analysis by division · Profitability · Asset efficiency · Financial efficiency · Product and departmental efficiency · Future capital needs	B.C./E.D./ Consultant	5/10

PART 2—VITAL SIGNS

1. Prepare cash flow projection for next 12 months.	B.C./Consultant	4/01
2. Determine break-even levels.	E.D./Consultant	4/10
3. Prepare detailed analysis of all assets.	M.C.	4/20
4. Prepare detailed analysis of all debts and other obligations.	B.C.	4/20
5. Prepare a schedule and obtain copies of all reports currently being generated. Consider whether adequate management information is available.	J.M.	4/20

PART 2—VITAL SIGNS

	Responsibility	Date of Completion
6. Review costing system to determine reliability and accuracy of costs.	E.D./Consultant	4/25
7. Review capabilities, strengths and weaknesses of managers and key employees.	P.J./K.M./ Consultant	4/25
8. Determine status of relationships with lenders, employees, key suppliers and shareholders.	B.C./Consultant	4/25
9. Conduct a brief telephone survey of customers to determine their feelings about the company's products, service, quality and image.	Consultant	4/30
10. Prepare a Market and Competitive Analysis.	D.B.	4/30
11. Prepare a Revenue Analysis.	K.M.	5/05
12. Prepare a liquidation analysis of the business on a forced and orderly liquidation basis.	P.J./Consultant	4/20
13. Meet with attorneys and turnaround consultants to review status and options.	P.J.	4/20

PART 2—CORPORATE CPR

1. Develop strategy for communication with secured lenders, and request for additional lender support in form of deferment of principal payments for 12 months.	P.J./Consultant/ Attorney	5/10
2. Develop strategy to achieve out-of-court workout of debts to unsecured creditors —goal is to achieve payment of 60¢ on the dollar, payable over 36 months.	P.J./Consultant/ Attorney	5/20
3. Develop program to liquidate slow-moving inventory for the recently discontinued Model 600 rowing machine— goal is to generate $120,000 within four months.	M.C.	5/10
4. Hire additional accounts receivable collector—goal is to collect additional $300,000 within three months.	B.C.	5/25

276

PART 2—CORPORATE CPR

	Responsibility	Date of Completion
5. Meet with major suppliers to negotiate just-in-time inventory shipments whereby suppliers will maintain at least a truck-load of raw material on their floor, which can be shipped within 24 hours—goal is to reduce inventory level by $150,000.	J.P.	6/05
6. Meet with major customers to explore potential for reducing payment terms, in return for an additional cash discount—goal is to reduce receivables by $200,000.	K.M.	6/05
7. Meet with real estate brokers to explore possibility of sale of the building and leasing back the portion needed for production—goal is to generate $200,000 of additional cash.	P.J.	5/25
8. Retain investment banker to assist in efforts to identify investors.	P.J.	5/30
9. Convene a weekend get-away with key managers to *brainstorm* turnaround ideas.	P.J./Consultant	5/15
10. Review manpower levels and salaries at all levels to determine opportunities to reduce cost—goal is to eliminate 15 people within 45 days (savings of $300,000 per annum).	M.C.	5/30
11. Review purchase prices for top 20 items purchased, and obtain competitive bids from three other suppliers—goal is to reduce purchase prices by at least 5% (estimated savings of $300,000 to $400,000).	J.P.	6/15
12. Obtain price quotes for subcontracting heat-treating and plating, currently done in house—goal is to save $150,000.	J.P.	6/15
13. Obtain competitive bids on janitorial services, express courier services, travel agencies and insurance.	E.D.	6/10
14. Identify underperforming divisions or product lines based on a Corporate Treadmill analysis	B.C./Consultant	5/15

277

PART 2—CORPORATE CPR

	Responsibility	Date of Completion
15. Explore possibility of selling underperforming divisions or product lines.	P.J./Consultant	7/30
16. Consolidate shipping and receiving departments under one manager—goal is to reduce cost by $25,000.	J.P.	6/15
17. Discontinue Model 300 Bicycle line due to poor sales and profitability—goal is to generate $200,000 from liquidation of inventory and collection of receivables.	K.M.	7/30
18. Hire Quality Control Manager—goal is to improve on-time delivery to 95% and reduce scrap rates by 70%.	M.C.	6/30
19. Retain Data Processing Consultant to assist in implementation of an accounting system that will provide profitability by product line and division.	B.C.	6/30
20. Cancel order for tube-bending machine.	J.P.	5/25
21. Implement wage and capital expenditure freeze.	P.J.	5/10
22. Meet with insurance brokers to explore ways to reduce product liability insurance premiums.	E.D.	5/30
23. Convene regular meetings of all employees to keep them informed of the status of the company and the turnaround progress.	P.J.	5/05
24. Revise cash flow projection to reflect turnaround strategies.	B.C./Consultant	5/30

APPENDIX V

Turnaround negotiating strategies

Probably the most significant factor in the ultimate success of a turnaround is the competence and skill of management in a wide range of areas and disciplines. Negotiating ability is one of the most important of these.

Some of the most important resources you will need to implement your turnaround are *time* and *concessions*. You will be asking a lot of people to give you time to meet obligations (including lenders, suppliers, employees, customers, shareholders, government authorities), and you will be asking for a lot of concessions, which could include asking:

- creditors to accept less than 100 cents on the dollar
- a lender to release an asset it has security over so that you can obtain additional financing elsewhere
- employees to forego wage increases, bonuses, vacations, and other related items
- customers to pay earlier than required by normal payment terms, to provide you with cash to purchase inventories needed for production

Additionally, you may be negotiating with a potential buyer of one of your underperforming divisions or product lines, or perhaps a new equity investor.

Management's success in these transactions will be significantly impacted by its negotiating abilities. While good negotiating skills are often a natural talent, there are many principles of successful negotiating that can be learned. The following are a few ground rules that I have learned from *hands-on* experience and that I have found work effectively in a turnaround situation.

Trusting atmosphere

Establish an atmosphere of reliability and integrity. Even if you are starting poles apart in your positions, you need to convince your opponent that you genuinely believe in your position, and that you

279

are honest and reliable. This means that everything you do or say must blend together into a consistent, believable position. If at one point you make a certain statement, and at another point you contradict the earlier statement, your credibility will be in question. If you say you will do something, and you don't do it, your integrity and reliability will be questioned. If you can convince your opponent of your credibility, reliability and integrity, you will be well on the way to achieving a favorable negotiation. If you don't achieve this, all of your motives will be suspected and scrutinized more carefully, thereby reducing your chances of winning issues.

Avoid speaking first

Always listen to what the other side has to say first, before you make any offers or concessions. On many occasions, I have been willing to concede a point, but was staggered by the windfall the other side offered me before I spoke. In most negotiations, there are many *time-outs*, where one or both parties seek time to *caucus*, to privately discuss their position with their team. During such time-outs, your team might decide to concede one or more points. However, you don't know what position the other side is going to take. When you resume the meeting, always try to restart by taking the initiative and saying "Well, where are you guys at?" This gives you the very significant advantage of hearing their position first. You will then have the chance to favorably amend your response.

Keep it short

Say what you have to say clearly and succinctly, and then *keep quiet*. Never oversell your point. Silences in negotiations are great opportunities. Use them to your advantage by prolonging them. Unless your opponent is very experienced, chances are that the silence will make him will feel awkward, and that he will say something that might give you an opportunity. With this powerful approach, you will appear secure enough to state your position, and not defend it. Generally in negotiations, the less you say the better. The more the other side talks, the more you learn about its position, and the more *openings* you create. It is obviously important for you to talk enough to get your points across. However, any more talk than this just creates openings for your opponent.

Win, win

Be prepared to take two steps forward and one step back. If your opponents feel you are winning too many points, they may stop being agreeable, and may even take back points they had conceded to earlier. As such, going into the negotiations, you must have points that you are willing to trade. If all of your points are *deal-breakers*, you'll have no issues to trade, and you could run into a stalemate. This approach also requires you to psychoanalyze your opponent and identify the key points that he wants to win. If you know these, you'll be able to calculate the trading value of your points. You will then want to trade points of reasonable equivalent value. That is, if you have to concede an important point for your opponent, try to win an important point for yourself.

It is also very important to remember that most deals *close* only if both parties feel that they have *won*—or at least achieved a position that they can live with. If you keep hammering your issues to the point where your opponent feels boxed in the loser's corner, he will likely resist, and look for ways to frustrate the deal (unless, of course, you have significant and unusual bargaining leverage that forces the other side to agree to a position it is not comfortable with). So always have points you are willing to let your opponent *win*.

Hang on to your wins

Always try to *lock in* the other side's concessions (e.g., by confirming them in a letter, or by talking about them as a fait accompli) and try to avoid locking in your concessions until you have identified how many more concessions you are going to have to make. Your objective is to get the highest ratio of opponent's concessions to your concessions. As soon as you have given something away, you can't use it to encourage the other side to make more concessions. If you then want them to make more concessions, you'll have to give more. Whenever your opponent asks you to make concessions, the best answer to give is, "Let's continue until we know the full scope of these discussions—at that point I'll be in position to make a final decision on where I stand on these points." This statement gives you the chance to get the full lay of the land before you decide what you can live with. If you don't do this, you may concede issues early on that you might regret later. If you follow the strategy recommended above, when you have heard all the other side's points, you can then say, "Provided you are willing to agree to . . . , I would be willing to agree to . . . ." With this approach, you are making your concession conditional on his agreement.

If your opponent makes the mistake of giving you a concession and not extracting one or more from you in return, find a way to get off that topic as soon as possible, to avoid any chance of him revoking it or trying to use it as a bargaining chip. In most negotiations, a concession given is gone. Don't let it slip out of your hands.

Wait for your opportunities

Be patient and wait for your moments to push hard, and be ready to lie low till the right opportunities become available. Usually, in a long negotiation, you will get windows of opportunities. Look for them, and use them. Push hard, but be ready to back off if you see you are getting negative returns. If you really want to win a point, and you're not being too successful, back off for a while, and wait for a chance to bring it up again—you may have to trade another point to win this one.

In a tense and lengthy negotiation in which I was once involved, I was frustrated by my lack of ability to make progress in achieving my objectives. After several weeks, I was almost abandoning hope when my opponent suddenly and unintentionally revealed some information that immediately allowed me to go on the offensive and achieve the breakthrough for which I had been waiting.

Be the Devil's Advocate

Whatever proposal your opponents make to you, always find some things you don't like about their proposal. This puts them on the defensive, forcing them to sell their ideas to you, and gives you issues to trade for concessions from them. Some of the points you raise might seem totally unreasonable. Don't worry, it's often good to be a little unreasonable in negotiations—when you start to be even a little reasonable again, your opponent will feel a sense of accomplishment (even if it is false accomplishment).

Smart is not always smart

Sometimes, is also pays to be a little *slow* to understand your opponents proposal—even if you are very well aware of its meaning and implications. (I call this the *Columbo* style of negotiation.) Ask him to repeat and explain his position several times. Keep coming back to it. This can cause him to lose a little composure, and give you

282

openings. There is also the possibility that you truly did not understand your opponent's proposal. He may well be offering you more (or less) than you understood. By having him clearly repeat and explain his position, you will have time to ensure you don't talk yourself out of points.

Keep it simple

There is always a temptation in negotiating to get a little too *clever*. I have found that deals with too many intricacies often fall through. The simpler the concept, the easier it is for everybody to understand. If it's too complicated, people may say they understand, but often they don't. Sometimes, I have been forced to give up on a point that I would have liked to win, because I was concerned that it would push the *complexity quotient* of the transaction over the limit.

Avoid theatrics

I have negotiated with several people who have started shouting, stormed out or ripped up documents. At first I was intimidated, and their tactics almost worked. However, in every case, they came back (sometimes more than six months later) and agreed to most of the points that caused the blow-up in the first place. Generally, theatrics indicate insecurity. Don't be intimidated into making concessions because of your opponent's theatrics, and be very careful if you use them yourself—they can have a nasty habit of backfiring on you.

In a recent negotiation, my opponent started shouting, with the obvious intent of gaining an advantage in a deadlock. To his consternation I leaned back in my chair and just waited. When he stopped, I waited a few seconds and calmly said, "If you're finished shouting, perhaps we can return to finding a way that this deal can work for both sides." After this, I had a distinct advantage because he was clearly embarrassed by his unproductive outburst. To make matters worse for him, whenever we were in another deadlocked position, I took advantage of his prior weakness and said (half in jest, half with deliberate intent), "I hope you're not going to start shouting at me." This constant reminder of his failed strategy allowed me to retain the upper hand.

Salami strategy

The best negotiation results from a controlled and planned *beachhead* approach. Before you can take the mountain, you need to systematically win little hills along the way. A cool head is essential in this process.

Never put all your demands on the table at the same time. Deal with one or two issues at a time, usually starting with the less contentious issues. It is a lot easier to achieve consensus on these points, if the atmosphere is not strained by the introduction of inflammatory items. This is known as the *Salami* approach—where you *nibble* away one or two slices at a time. Say, for example, you are negotiating with a creditor to accept a settlement of an amount significantly less than 100 cents on the dollar, and you also want the supplier to start supplying you on open credit again (as opposed to Cash on Delivery or C.O.D.). Try to get the supplier to agree on the first issue, before even raising the second one. When you have locked in the first concession, you could then say that—in order for you to be able to make the payments to creditors under the (now) agreed-upon distribution plan, it is essential that you be back on open credit with suppliers, and that without open credit, the payment plan might be in jeopardy.

Negotiate in ranges

Until you have a good idea about how your opponent might react to a proposal, it is helpful to negotiate in ranges. After you've observed his reaction to the range, you will often be able to gauge which end of the range to focus on. For example, suppose you are proposing a compromise of debts owing to a major vendor, you may start off by saying, "We anticipate that we may be able to pay our creditors 20 to 30 cents on the dollar." If the vendor does not react negatively to the proposal, in subsequent discussions focus on the 20 cents and don't mention 30 cents unless the vendor brings it up. This approach enables you to test somebody's reaction to a proposal, without offending him with too low an offer, and without committing yourself to a high offer.

Play it cool

Never show you are too keen. In fact, always try to have a strong fall back position that makes you relatively indifferent to the outcome. In this position you'll be hard to beat.

APPENDIX VI

ACQUISITION STRATEGIES IN A TURNAROUND

Acquisitions represent the fastest way to obtain a stronghold in a new area or product range, or rapidly advance the size or capabilities of your company. They give you a chance to benefit from the hard work somebody else might have done to build an organization that is efficient, profitable and respected. Naturally the seller will try to make you pay dearly for his hard work. However, paying top dollar for the business won't do you any good unless you have a way of enhancing the business, and improving its cash flow. You could also buy a business where the seller has not been so successful, and in this case you would inherit his headaches, rather than his jewels. Hopefully, in this situation, you will be able to negotiate a price that reflects the state of the business. The ideal situation is where you are able to turn the seller's *headaches* into your *jewels*—allowing you to buy at a low price, and create significant *added value* for yourself.

Before embarking on an acquisition, a turnaround company should be confident that it has the resources (finance, expertise, time) to pursue the transaction. A turnaround, in of itself, is a demanding experience for a company—the added burden of an acquisition exacerbates this significantly. As such, all acquisitions, large or small, should be carefully planned, negotiated and executed. The following comments are intended to assist in this process:

Acquisition criteria

Before embarking on an acquisition campaign, I believe it is essential to clearly define the criteria you think are important for acquisition candidates. If you don't do this, you run the risk of buying something and discovering, after the fact, that it does not meet your needs.

Three or four years ago, I owned a car that was rear-wheel drive. During the heavy snowfalls of the winter, I had great difficulty getting the car up my driveway, which is quite steep. I made up my mind that my next car would be front-wheel drive. Now I have a four-year-old front-wheel drive vehicle, which has been great in the snow, but is getting up in miles. I was recently browsing through automobile showrooms, and I came across a beautiful import that was being offered with a very attractive lease program. Soon afterwards, an effective salesman had me giving serious consideration to the deal—but I had this nagging feeling that I couldn't identify. Just before signing the papers, I remembered to ask about front-wheel drive and discovered that the car I was about to lease did not have this important feature. Had I walked in with my criteria sheet, I would have saved myself a lot of time and disappointment.

When buying a business, every buyer will have different criteria for what he or she is looking for. However, the following criteria are those that I believe are always important:

- The business should have good accounting and information systems. Without this, you cannot have a high degree of reliance on the information provided to you to assess the business, and you will likely have to incur significant funds and time after closing to upgrade the information systems. Good systems should extend to providing information by division, branch, product line, individual product, cost center or departments. Information should include sales, margins, operating expenses and assets employed.

- Its cash flow should be predictable. If the cash flow is not predictable, you cannot have a high degree of confidence that the price is appropriate. If the business is highly dependent on the winning of large bids, its cash flow cannot be predicted because one successful or failed bid can have a huge impact on cash flow. This does not mean you should not buy a company with negative cash flow— it means you should be able to predict how negative it will be, and build that into your price and projections.

- No single competitor should have a dominant market share. If you buy a business that has a competitor with a dominant market share, that competitor could have the ability to squeeze you out of the market. Further, there will likely be less opportunities for you to build market share through acquisition because there will be fewer smaller competitors. If, however, the industry is fragmented, your opportunities for becoming dominant are greater.

- The company should have an established and strong market franchise. In most acquisitions, this is the most important asset you will acquire. Franchises are rarely built overnight; if a company's franchise is not well developed and strong, you will have a long and hard road ahead building or rebuilding it. While underdeveloped franchises are hard to build, negative franchises take an even longer time to overcome.

- Capable, independent and entrepreneurial management should be in place or readily available, i.e., you should know that you can locate appropriately qualified management.

- The business should be operating in an industry and geographic area with growing economic prospects. It is always significantly easier to prosper in an environment of economic growth. This does not mean one cannot be successful in a depressed area or industry—it is just harder, unless the negative conditions scare off enough competitors.

- There should be opportunity for growth and synergies by acquiring competitors in existing or new markets, or similar or complementary companies (See below for comments on synergy.)

- The business should *not* have good efficiency management systems. If you buy a business that has good information systems, but no efficiency systems, it should be relatively easy for you to install efficiency systems and thus lower costs significantly. If the business is already efficient, there will be less opportunity for you to create value for yourself.

Synergies

There are many reasons for doing acquisitions, with one of the most common justifications being *synergies*, i.e., the savings or efficiencies that will result from the combination of two businesses. Experience has shown me that synergies are rather elusive prey that have to be stalked and trapped do not expect them to surrender to you. Many acquisitions have been tripped up by rosy synergy forecasts in their cash flows. Don't get me wrong—profitable synergies are possible you just have to be very patient and do a lot of homework and analysis. The trick in identifying synergies is to do a thorough evaluation of the operations, systems, procedures and paper flow of *both* businesses. Yes, yours too! (Most people overlook this part. Often they end up knowing less about their own procedures than those of their target's.) You then need to do an integration plan of the two businesses, and identify overlaps and redundancies. This exercise is almost impossible to do effectively before the acquisition—it takes too long and you usually don't have sufficient access to the information. Prior to the acquisition, you can do a preliminary integration plan and, for this reason, it's best to be extremely conservative about synergy projections.

Profits vs. cash flow

When you buy a business, you are really buying the rights to the future cash stream that the business will generate. In this situation, it is very important to differentiate between cash and profits. For example, assume you buy a business that is generating sales of $5 million per year, and is making $400,000 profit before taxes. If you could borrow money at 10% interest cost and you were not concerned about cash flow, you could theoretically pay $4 million for the business and break even ($400,000/10%).

In practice, however, the situation is much more dependent on cash flows. In addition to knowing how profitable the business is likely to be, you need to analyze the cash dynamics of the business, and factor these into your calculations. For example, assume that the seller of the business described above deliberately delayed paying his suppliers for a few months before you bought the business, and that the business owed suppliers $500,000 beyond its normal credit terms. To continue to operate the business effectively after you have acquired it, you will need to bring the suppliers' balances back within their payment terms, resulting in your paying $500,000 more for the business—and getting absolutely nothing more for it. Alternatively, the business may have run down its inventory levels to generate cash prior to its sale, which will require the buyer to rebuild inventories just to maintain normal production levels. In a business, there are many other cash-sensitive items that need to be examined before you can truly assess what the business is worth to you. Examples include:

288

- working capital required to fund growth of the business (receivables, inventory, etc.)
- capital expenditures required to maintain and/or grow the business (additions or major repairs to machinery or buildings, additional space or equipment, vehicles, etc.)
- timing of tax payments (current or deferred taxes)
- timing of major expense items (insurance, etc.)

In contrast to this, there are many opportunities where businesses have the capacity to generate cash that can have the effect of lowering the price you pay for the business. For example:

- if the business always pays its suppliers promptly, and you can negotiate increased terms at no additional cost, you will generate a permanent inflow of cash
- surplus assets can be sold off to generate cash
- unprofitable divisions can be closed to generate cash from liquidating receivables, inventory or fixed assets

Valuation

There are several methods that are used to value businesses, including discounted cash flows, multiple of earnings, multiples of cash flows, book value, adjusted book value and liquidation value. In practice, a combination of some or all of these techniques can provide the basis of what is ultimately a judgment call. It is important that you focus on what the value is to you. That is, what cash stream will it provide for you? The answer to this will depend not only on the expected cash flow of the business, but also on the changes to cash flow that can be generated from your involvement in the business.

Before determining the appropriate price to pay for a business, a Corporate Treadmill Test (See Part 1: Section II) should be performed on the target. This test will tell you how much profit (Return On Assets Managed) the business will need to generate in order to justify the purchase price and ensure positive cash flow. Then, compare the Return On Assets Managed derived from the Corporate Treadmill Test to the historical performance of the business—to assess if the required returns are achievable in light of past performance, and the changes in the business you contemplate. If the difference between required and historical Return On Assets Managed is too high, rethink the purchase price or the deal structure.

A multiple of EBIT (earnings before interest and taxes) is a commonly used method for determining the value of a business. In the current economic climate, mature businesses tend to sell for between three and six times EBIT. However, very few people, if any, can explain how they selected the appropriate multiple, other than by comparing it to the multiple used in other transactions of which they are aware. In fact, this multiple is similar to the inverse of the Return On Assets Managed (ROAM) referred to in Part 1: Section II (except that ROAM is based on Earnings before depreciation, interest and taxes [EBDIT] rather than EBIT). A multiple of four times EBDIT would translate into a ROAM of 25 percent (100/4). So to determine the appropriate multiple of EBDIT[18] a business is worth, the Corporate Treadmill Test should be performed to determine the required ROAM to justify a specific purchase price. The multiple will then be the inverse of the ROAM percentage.

Note also that, in addition to any purchase price you are paying for the business, **liabilities or debts assumed are an add-on to the purchase price**. For example, if you pay $1 million for a business that has a net worth of $500,000, interest-bearing debt of $2 million and non-interest-bearing debt of $1 million, the total price you are paying is $4 million, and the Assets Managed you will be acquiring is $4 million. This $4 million will become the denominator in the Return On Assets Managed calculation.

What are you buying?

When you buy a business, two of the most important things to identify and document are: What you are buying and what is the exact method of calculating the price? Without these issues clearly defined, you could find yourself in the same position as the buyer who takes possession of a house that he has just bought, only to find that the seller has removed the curtains and light fixtures (which he thought he had bought, too, but neglected to stipulate in the agreement). Everything must be spelled out in great detail; otherwise you will likely be disappointed. If your agreement says that you will take

---

[18] I don't believe a multiple of EBIT is the most appropriate valuation measurement, because EBIT is an accounting measurement that includes non-cash charges (e.g. depreciation). A multiple of EBDIT reflects cash flow, which is a more accurate measurement of value

possession of the business on a certain date, there might be nothing to stop the seller paying himself a big bonus before closing, or selling an asset and paying himself a dividend. So make sure the agreement is specific about what assets you will be getting, what condition those assets will be in, what liabilities you will be assuming, what happens to those assets and liabilities during the period from when you start negotiating to closing, who gets the benefit of profits (or cost of losses) during that period and exactly how the final purchase price will be determined and verified.

Wherever possible, insist on a post-closing audit to substantiate the exact assets and liabilities you assumed at the closing date—with an automatic downward purchase price adjustment for shortfalls in net assets warranted. To achieve this without having to sue for a refund, negotiate for a portion of the purchase price to be held in escrow pending final post-closing verification of the price.

Value added

Before buying a business and establishing the price you are willing to pay, it is important to analyze what value you can add to that business, or what the target will add to the value of your business. If you pay fair market value for a business, and you don't add any value to it after you've bought it, you will not be able to sell it for a profit (unless overall market valuations have gone up in that period). Most acquisitions end in failure because the acquirer was not able to add value to the target. When a buyer improves the acquired business, the value of his investment will go up.

A buyer can improve a business in many ways, including:

- Increasing sales, by improving its sales and marketing effectiveness and coverage
- Reducing its costs through better purchasing, expense reductions, improved efficiency or merger with other of the buyer's operations
- Adding management, know-how or technology to the target
- Giving the target larger critical mass or prestige, to obtain volume discounts, attract larger customers
- Improving margins through the elimination of a competitor

If the buyer is not able to add value to the target, serious questions should be asked as to the merits of the acquisition.

Purchasing assets vs. stock

When buying a business, it is generally better for the buyer to purchase the assets of the business, as opposed to buying the corporation that owns those assets. When you buy assets, you can be far more specific about what you're buying, and you can often avoid most of the surprises of undisclosed liabilities that a buyer of corporate stock might experience (although some liabilities, depending on individual state laws, may not be avoidable by buying assets, e.g. product liability claims). In addition, buying assets is almost always more favorable to the purchaser from a tax point of view, because the buyer will usually have a higher asset base to depreciate for tax purposes.

Right of set-off

Always try to make part of the purchase price payable sometime in the future, and negotiate the right of *set-off*, which will allow you to deduct from the amount you owe the seller any discrepancies in what you thought you were buying and what you actually got when you took possession.

This applies not only to assets that are missing, but also to liabilities that emerge for which that you did not (or thought you did not) accept responsibility. This is an area that requires very skillful attention from your lawyer. You obviously want to assign to the seller all liabilities that arise after the sale but that relate to periods prior to the sale. The seller naturally wants to sell the business, and not have any surprises at a later date. Hopefully, with the help of your lawyers you will reach a compromise that will be accurately documented. If you discover some of these liabilities after the sale, and the contract assigns responsibility to the seller, you'll be pleased if you still owe them enough money and have the right of set-off.

Representations and warranties

You also will want to get the seller to make very comprehensive representations and warranties about the state of his business. These include:

- The financial statements fairly present the financial affairs of the company determined in accordance with

292

Generally Accepted Accounting Practice, applied consistently with prior years. The consistent application of accounting principles is a very important area. Subtle changes in accounting policy or treatment can have a material impact on the *accounting* performance of the business. If you don't identify them, you can base your purchase and pricing decision on wrong information. As a result, your accountant needs to investigate and document accounting policies for at least the five previous years for all categories of income, expense, assets and liabilities. This can be a very extensive process, and should include areas such as the timing of income recognition, cost of sales, depreciation and amortization, prepaid expenses, deferred expenses, work-in-process, capitalization of expenses, accrual of liabilities, contingent liabilities, goodwill, valuation of inventory and accounts payable. All of these areas, and many more, present the potential for many different methods of accounting. If you are not aware of these subtleties, and even worse, if they're changing, you are not going to know what you're buying.

- The business will be conducted only in the ordinary course, and there will be no material adverse change in the business. This is a very important representation, and one that must be very carefully worded by your lawyer. This wording should be strong enough to let you back out of the contract if you discover something significant about the business that had you known about it before signing you would not have gone ahead with the deal.

- No disposals of assets, dividends, excess remuneration, etc.

- All assets reflected in financial statements exist, and have values that equal or exceed their stated values, and are in a fit and merchantable condition for their intended use (inventory may be merchantable, but not for the use you intend it for in the ordinary course of business).

- No unrecorded or undisclosed liabilities.

- No undisclosed liens or encumbrances.

- No environmental problems.

293

- No actual, pending or threatened litigation.
- No unfunded pension liabilities.
- Seller has filed all tax and other returns, and is up-to-date in all tax and other withholding payments, and has no pending regulatory audits or assessments.
- Seller is responsible for warranty and other similar claims relating to goods shipped prior to closing.
- No undisclosed material facts or circumstances that, if buyer was aware of, would cause him not to proceed with the transaction.

Contingent purchase price

Although not always easy to negotiate, it is always advantageous to the buyer if part of the purchase price is dependent on the future profitability of the business. This is known as an *earn-out*. You should always, however, try to get the seller to warrant (i.e., guarantee) the collectibility of his accounts receivable. This means that if you cannot collect a receivable, it is for the seller's account and not yours. This is a very helpful clause for you to have.

Due diligence and integration

While negotiating and documenting the deal are very important processes, they are no more important than the stages of *due diligence* and final *acquisition integration*. Due diligence is the process whereby the prospective buyer tries to find as much as possible about every aspect of the business firstly to assess whether he wishes to go through with the deal, and at what price, and, secondly, to establish the plan to smoothly integrate the acquired company into the buyer's organization. It is very easy to underestimate the difficulty of this integration process. In general, you would probably go through an information-gathering process very similar to any *turnaround* situation (See Part 2: Phase I: Vital Signs), except that you would then have to establish how to link the systems, controls, communications and cultures of the two organizations. Even companies that appear very similar will have many differences, and will be very hard to integrate.

One of the major objectives of the due diligence process is to identify any unusual, extra-ordinary or abnormal income or expense items included in the company's historical financial statements. The company may show that sales increased 20 percent

294

over the prior year, but you may discover that all of that increase resulted from a one-time unusual transaction that is not likely to recur. Similarly, with expenses, you may discover that rent expense in the past was reduced, because part of the building was subleased to a company that has since vacated the premises and is not likely to be replaced. You need to uncover as many of these types of transactions as possible, and adjust the historical numbers to eliminate the abnormal items. You also need to perform a similar analysis on the future projections to try to confirm that they represent reasonable, realistic and achievable targets. Carefully examine every line of the projection and investigate any significant changes in amounts or trends, compared against the other years in the projection, and against the historical numbers.

The existence, usefulness and value of all assets should be carefully investigated to identify any obsolete, damaged, redundant or inefficient assets or uncollectible receivables. This analysis should be extensive and in-depth to avoid any surprises after the transaction is completed.

Another important purpose of due diligence is to review key areas of the business, to assess whether actions taken in the past, whether inadvertently or intentionally, can result in liability for the future. These would include, for example, environmental contamination and claims from employees for personnel-related issues like wrongful dismissal and discrimination. A potentially expensive, and often incorrectly handled area is sales tax. Many companies incorrectly do not charge their customers for sales tax for many reasons, which include interpretation of the law or perceived exemptions. Often, in hindsight, the government will reassess for sales tax that should have been collected from customers. While you may be covered by representations and warranties from the seller, the seller may not be around to recover from. It pays to check these issues carefully before getting involved.

Legal Due Diligence

This is an area that also requires significant attention, to ensure that the company is in compliance with all laws, regulations, contracts and agreements, and that there is no significant likelihood of exposure due to the breach of any such situations. It is also important to search for litigation (pending, threatened or actual) that the company may not have disclosed to you. One attorney I have retained in the past made a practice of looking through all of the target's filing cabinets (with their consent) during the due diligence process. During this time, he uncovered files on several subjects of which we were not previously aware. Your attorney should perform extensive due diligence, which should include a thorough lien search against the target's real estate and other assets.

Marrying Cultures

Corporate culture is an area that almost always presents areas of differences that are very often difficult to reconcile. After most acquisitions, there is a battle for power, and the respective cultures often try to *annihilate* each other, many times with the objective of *taking no prisoners*, i.e., on a department-by-department basis, the victor culture takes over almost completely, and the conquered culture virtually disappears. Surprisingly, it is not always the acquiring company's team that is the victor. Often, one of the major reasons for acquiring the target is its pool of talented people, who may be perceived to be more competent than your own people. The insecurity of being acquired often inspires these managers to *pillage* even more aggressively. This is often exacerbated by the fact that in the integration process, you spend so much time getting to know (and wooing) the target's staff that you unwittingly neglect your own staff, who may begin to resent the whole process. (This is very similar to how an older sibling might feel when you bring home a newborn). For these reasons, you need to pay particular attention to the cultures and needs of both staffs. To ease the culture-issue, decide and announce early in the process, the philosophy and approach you intend to adopt, and make it clear to all that you expect them to work within the framework you have laid out—and that you will take decisive action against people that don't!

Because of the tenuous nature of the finances of a company either in, or emerging from, a crisis, extensive care must be taken to improve the probabilities that the acquisition will be a success. The whole acquisition process is extremely complicated and requires the involvement and input of experts from several disciplines. It is a subject that, to be covered comprehensively, would require a book of its own. This section has attempted only to introduce some very broad concepts that I believe are important in acquiring businesses. Other very important, extensive and complicated areas that must be addressed in every acquisition are legal and tax structuring, accounting, pricing, valuation and appraisal and financing.

APPENDIX VII
REFINANCING BANK DEBT

As indicated in Part 2: Section III-F, understanding the process and mechanics of obtaining bank financing is very important to a company emerging from a turnaround. Because *you only get one chance to make a first impression*, it is important that you approach this phase of your development with a professionalism and competence that gives prospective lenders a feeling of confidence that you are in command of your business, and that the company's problems are history. The following is intended to give a broad outline of the process and mechanics of refinancing debt in a turnaround.

Terms and revolvers

Most traditional asset-based bank loans are of two types: revolving facilities to finance current assets, such as inventories and receivables; or term loans to finance fixed assets such as equipment, vehicles, buildings, etc. Availability under revolving loans fluctuates regularly, based on the movement in the current assets that collateralize the loan. The borrower is entitled to make periodic draw-downs against the availability, and must make repayments if the amount outstanding exceeds availability. Some lenders require that all cash collected be deposited into their bank account which has the effect of reducing your loan outstanding and increasing your availability. Reporting and documentation to lenders for revolving lines is often quite extensive and can be costly. Term loans are usually for a fixed amount, with a fixed repayment schedule (usually five to eight years), with minimal reporting to the lender.

Over-advances

In addition to the typical asset-based loans, it is sometimes possible to negotiate additional funds over-and-above the collateral formulas. These are known as *Over-advances*. They are usually shorter-term loans and often must be repaid within three to 18 months. Over-advances will only be made in exceptional circumstances, and only if the business demonstrates cash flow strong enough to repay these loans in a short period of time. The bank will usually charge significantly higher interest rates on an over-advance.

In a turnaround, it is more likely (but not easy) for an existing lender to agree to an over-advance (in the hope that it will strengthen its overall position) than to convince a new lender of its merits.

Process

The process of getting a bank loan is usually quite lengthy (anywhere from two to six months). In general, the process will proceed along the following path:

Business Plan

Before approaching lenders, the company must produce a comprehensive and professional business plan. This plan should include:

- A detailed narrative of the history of the company
- Its legal and corporate structure, a description of the activities and operations of the business, including its products, locations, special attributes, strengths and risk factors
- Its strategic plan for the next five years, encompassing its strategies for marketing, manufacturing and product development, manpower development and cost and expense management
- An analysis of the company's markets, and the characteristics, strengths, sizes and weaknesses of its competitors
- The company's audited financial statements for the preceding five years
- Projected financial statements for the next five year including income statement, balance sheet, cash flow and statement of changes in cash
- Management organization chart, and résumés of key managers
- Key business issues and risks, including questions and concerns that the lender will likely need to know about. It is far better to answer a lender's question before he asks you. If your business plan anticipates the lender's questions and concerns, he will usually receive a favorable impression of management's grasp and control over the business. With this approach, however, you run the risk of answering a question or focusing on a concern the

lender might not have considered. If you believe in the success of your company, this risk is usually worth taking. If you still believe caution is prudent, be prepared to answer the question with confidence if it is asked.

- Last, but definitely not least, management should demonstrate to the bank that it has contingency plans, and fall-back positions to cope with situations that don't turn out as planned which shows that management has not looked only at the rosy forecast, but has also considered what could go wrong, and how the company would deal with these issues. Again, this approach shows the lender management's capabilities in all situations. If you can convince a lender that you have a *downside* plan that works, your task will be a lot easier.

Approach to Lenders

When the business plan is completed, a list of potential lenders should be created. In doing this, you should probably seek input and advice from a variety of outsiders who could help you develop a complete list. This would include lawyers, accountants and other businesspeople. You should end up with a short list of at least five suitable lenders who are likely to be interested in loans of the type and size you will be seeking. Try to avoid direct approaches to bankers you do not know. It is far better to be introduced through an intermediary whom the banker knows and respects—a lawyer, accountant, consultant or friend.

Be wary of only approaching one lender, even if you think you have a great relationship with that lender. If a banker knows he's the only *game in town*, you might not get the best deal possible. Competition between banks encourages them to offer opportunities and pricing that might otherwise be unavailable.

When you have finalized your short list, telephone all of the prospects; tell them briefly about your financing plans, and ask them if they would like to see a copy of your business plan. It is rare for them to say no. Tell them you will contact them in a few days after they have received the plan to set up a meeting to discuss it in more detail. If a banker agrees to review the plan, it does not necessarily mean he is interested; he may do it out of curiosity, or to learn about the activities or strategies of his competitors.

In the case of larger loans, many banks, including large ones, will want the ability to *syndicate* your loan; i.e., sell off part of the loan to

299

one or more other banks. Syndication is very common, and gives banks the ability to spread their risk. One bank will become the *agent* who will do the due diligence and negotiation, and the others will rely substantially on the agent. From the borrower's point of view, syndication has some pluses and some minuses. It can make it easier to get the loan if the bank can pass off some of the risk to others, and still earn good fees for doing the deal. However, it may mean more work for you in that you will likely have to make presentations, and answer questions, for the other banks.

Romancing and Due Diligence

If the bank is interested in your business plan and funding request, they will try to get to know you and your business better, convince you they are the bank for you and check you out at the same time.

Your contact at the bank at this stage, while often called a *lending officer*, is usually a quasi-salesman—somebody interested in bringing in new business for the bank. He will focus more on the positives than the negatives, and will try to find ways to make the deal work (often because he earns a commission if the financing closes).

At some stage, as you get deeper into the deal, the lending officer will tell you that he needs to bring in the bank's auditors for an audit of your books. The auditor's emphasis is very different from that of the lending officer. Auditors get no credit for sound deals, but they don't look good when loans turn sour. As a result, they do not look at your business through *rose-colored glasses*. They dig deep and ask a lot of very relevant (and, sometimes tough-to-answer) questions. The lending officer and the auditor often end up in a *good guy and bad guy* routine, in which the lending officer uses the auditor's negative attitude toward your company to extract a better deal from you

Proposal Letter

After the audit, if the bank is still interested in pursuing the transaction, you will likely receive a Proposal Letter, which outlines in very general terms the type of deal the bank might be willing to entertain. (Some banks issue the Proposal Letter before doing the audit.) The Proposal Letter is usually subject to so many things that, for your purposes, it serves as nothing more than a letter of intent that puts in writing the key terms the bank is considering which might help avoid a subsequent misunderstanding.

While the Proposal Letter is almost always not binding on the bank, it sometimes binds you on some things, that could include the bank's out-of-pocket expenses (for which they usually require a deposit) and appraisal fees. In some cases, banks try to get you to commit to a *work fee* or even a *break-up fee*. A work fee is an amount you pay over-and-above their expenses to get the bank to consider your loan. A break-up fee is an amount you commit to pay if the bank issues a *commitment letter* (i.e., agrees to make the loan) and you subsequently elect not to accept the loan.

Paying the bank's out-of-pocket and appraisal expenses is standard in all proposal letters, and you have little chance of negotiating out of this. Work fees are not standard and you should fight hard to negotiate this out of the Proposal Letter. Break-up fees are also not standard, and completely unfair and unjustified in a Proposal Letter that does not clearly state all material terms and conditions of the loan. How can you agree to a break-up fee if you reject a loan because of unacceptable terms and conditions that you didn't know about? Yet, many prospective borrowers agree to break-up fees because they are not skilled enough to negotiate with the bank.

All Proposal Letters—no matter how unbinding they seem— should be reviewed by a skilled attorney, with experience in dealing with lenders. You might find that there are many seemingly innocuous points that could prove expensive to you. Know exactly what you are agreeing to before signing.

Commitment Letter

After the proposal letter is signed, due diligence begins in earnest. The bank really delves deeper, because this is its last chance to find the skeletons in your closet. It may ask for endless information and analyses on issues ranging from environmental issues to how your business fared in the high interest rates era of 1981/82.

If you pass all of its tests (including rigorous, dispassionate and out-of-sight loan committee reviews), a Commitment Letter will likely be issued, which is the bank's commitment to lend you the money subject to certain specified conditions. Your lawyer needs to scrutinize these conditions very carefully, because once you sign the Commitment Letter, you are usually facing significant expenses, with no looking back. The proposal letter will often contain a *commitment fee* that is payable when you accept the Commitment Letter. It is not beyond the realms of possibility that you might pay this (usually substantial) fee, and then find the bank back out of the deal because of a breach of one of the conditions in the Commitment Letter; e.g., a material adverse change in their understanding of the business. In such circumstances, you might not be able to recover your commitment fee.

Again, with the Commitment Letter, you are faced with the problem of having to sign a contract that binds you, but you still don't know what all the terms and conditions are going to be, because the bank's lawyer hasn't even started drafting the loan agreement. Despite this, break-up fees are very often present in Commitment Letters. The only thing you can do to protect yourself is to demand that the bank spell out all material terms and conditions in the Commitment Letter, and agree that you will not be bound if they insist on any other material terms and conditions not contained in the Commitment Letter.

This is the time you will be very glad that you are talking to more than one bank, because only if the bank believes that it has competition will it be likely to agree to such *unusual* requests.

Of course, in any Commitment Letter, one of the most important issues is the cost of the loan, including up-front fees and interest. The up-front fees can often be very significant and must be weighed very carefully, and negotiated where excessive. Another potential (and often very expensive) cost is a *pre-payment penalty*; i.e., you will be required to pay an often substantial fee if you want to pay the loan off early. These also need to be weighed carefully, and negotiated where excessive. Many companies agree to onerous or expensive terms of a loan because they have no choice at the time. A year or two later, when the company's fortunes have improved significantly, and when a significantly better-priced loan can be obtained, they may find that the prepayment penalty on the existing loan negates the benefits of the lower costs of the new loan.

Interest is obviously the biggest cost in the loan and you should ensure that the rate you are agreeing to (usually fluctuating prime plus a certain fixed margin) is competitive and reasonable. The margin over prime is not your only exposure, though the risk of interest rates skyrocketing are potentially disastrous for your business. Most banks today can offer sophisticated protection against such exposures. You could either buy *swaps* or you could agree to a *collar and cap* that ensures that your interest rate stays within a predefined range. These are very important (and complex) issues that you should be negotiating with your bank. Another method available to give you an opportunity to improve your interest cost is the option to convert your loan to a LIBOR (London Interbank Borrowing Rate) based loan. This option, generally only available for larger loans, gives you greater flexibility to take advantage of worldwide interest rate fluctuations. LIBOR is essentially the rate paid by banks to borrow US dollars in London. At times, LIBOR is higher than US prime rates, and at other times, it is lower. Having the flexibility to switch between the two gives you valuable opportunity to minimize your interest cost. Bankers are often reluctant to tell you about this option, because it might reduce their profits. However, you are fully entitled to ask for it.

Loan Agreement

Once the Commitment Letter has been signed, the bank's attorneys will start drafting the Loan Agreement, most of which is technical and relatively unintelligible to the layman. Your skilled and experienced lawyer should, however, review these documents very carefully, and should fight hard to protect your interests.

The following are some items that will be in the Loan Agreement that you should understand thoroughly:

- **Events and Consequences of Default**

  Default of a loan agreement is a very serious matter. It gives the banker significantly increased powers, and can be very costly to the borrower. It is important that you know intimately what the *events of default* are, and whether you can live with them especially under adverse circumstances. You should also know the consequences of default. Your lawyer should try to negotiate, wherever possible, that you have the right to be given notice of an event of default, and that you be given a specified time to cure the default.

  The most common events of default are failure to make payments as agreed or a breach of a *covenant*. The most common consequences of default are the lenders' right to foreclose, and usually some form of expensive penalty interest. In general, it is safe to say that you will want to avoid events of default like the plague. So, negotiate hard to get *events* that you can live with.

- **Covenants**

  Covenants are specific actions or performance criteria you agree to fulfill. Covenants are usually important to lenders. They are the borrower's representations about how it will operate the business. These include:

- when how promptly to report to the lender
- performance goals, usually derived from the borrower's projections
- minimum working capital and net worth levels
- agreements not to give security interests to other parties
- agreements to limit withdrawal of funds from the business
- agreements to protect the lender's collateral

Every month your Chief Financial Officer will probably be required to send a signed statement to the bank demonstrating your compliance with all covenants. Noncompliance is usually an event of default. As such, it is very important that you review the required covenants very carefully, and evaluate your likely compliance under adverse, and optimistic scenarios. Banks will try to get you to agree to tough covenants, and they may try to make them tougher as time goes on. Resist this—and try to keep them within realistic ranges that give the bank reasonable protection, but don't strangle you.

Representations and Warranties

The bank will ask your company to represent and warrant certain things about the business, financial condition and other matters. Read these very carefully, and make sure they are true. If you fail to do this, you may have very serious problems if the loan goes bad, including possible personal liability.

In general, it is important not to agree to any terms, conditions, events of default, covenants, representations or warranties that you do not feel you can realistically live up to. On the other hand, lenders resent borrowers' attempts to negotiate otherwise reasonable terms, just for the sake of winning one over the bank.

APPENDIX VIII

SAMPLE LETTER TO CREDITORS
AT START OF WORKOUT

_____ ____, 19xx

Ms. H. Smith, Credit Manager
XYZ, Inc.
1500 Third Avenue
Cleveland, Ohio 44114

Dear Ms. Smith:

As you may be aware, we have been experiencing cash flow problems during the last few months that have resulted in delayed payment of our accounts payable. The primary reasons for these problems are

We are currently conducting an analysis of our business to determine the overall impact of this situation, and to develop a payment plan for you and our other creditors. To assist us with this process, we have engaged the services of _____, an independent consulting firm specializing in these matters.

We expect to complete this analysis within _____ to _____ weeks, and will submit a plan to you by that time. At this time, unfortunately, we will not be able to make immediate payment on past due indebtedness. However, we will continue to pay for current services and supplies as they become due. As such, we would appreciate your continued patience to give us the time to develop the plan. We believe that this cooperative approach with you and our other creditors will improve our ability to achieve the maximum payments for all entitled parties on a fair and consistent basis.

We know this is not an easy time for any business, and we sincerely regret adding to your problems. However, we are committed to diligently dealing with this situation promptly, and to keep you informed of our progress.

With our sincere best wishes and thanks,
Yours Very Truly,

APPENDIX IX

EXAMPLE OF CREDITOR COMPROMISE LETTER AND AGREEMENT

Ms. H. Smith, Credit Manager
XYZ, Inc.
1500 Third Avenue
Cleveland, Ohio 44114

Dear Ms. Smith:

In my letter of _____ _____, 19xx, I advised you that Excalibur, Inc. ("Excalibur") is experiencing cash flow problems, which have resulted in its not being able to pay its past due obligations. In that letter, I promised to submit a proposal to you by _____ _____, 19xx, outlining Excalibur's plan to deal with this situation. This letter and the accompanying agreement are that proposal. Together with our independent advisers, we have formulated what we believe is an extremely favorable proposal, already supported by our lenders and a substantial number of our unsecured creditors with claims totalling $_____.

Introduction
The keys to the proposal are that it:
1. Is fair and equitable to all unsecured creditors;
2. Capitalizes on Excalibur's going concern value;
3. Provides Excalibur with temporary relief with respect to cash disbursements, thereby enabling it to stabilize and rebuild itself.

In essence, the creditor compromise provides that all past due unsecured claims (which total approximately $_____) will receive ____ cents on the dollar payable as follows: ____ percent of the reduced balance within two weeks of the acceptance of the composition ("Commencement Date") by creditors holding at least ____ percent of the unsecured claims and the remaining balance in equal monthly installments without interest over ____ months. At

306

the conclusion of this payment plan, the unpaid ____ percent of the unsecured debt shall be released.

Creditors with balances of $_____ or less will be paid in full on the Commencement Date. Creditors with balances greater than $_____ can elect to accept $_____ in full and final settlement of the claims.

The financial and other information contained herein has been prepared by Excalibur to the best of its knowledge, information and belief.

Background

Excalibur commenced business in 19xx and is now primarily in the business of manufacturing and selling bicycles and sports equipment. A summary of Excalibur's Income Statement for 19xx is attached as Exhibit A, and a summary of its Balance Sheet as of _____ ____, 19xx is attached as Exhibit B.

While Excalibur's wholesale bicycle and sports equipment businesses have continued to perform satisfactorily, we have determined that the retail bicycle division is not generating an adequate return. (This determination was not previously available due to inadequacies in our accounting system). As such, we have decided to sell this division and have retained _____ to represent us in this divestiture. Management now intends to refocus its efforts on the wholesale businesses, and believes it can regain a dominant position in certain niche markets. Plans have already been implemented to discontinue an unprofitable product line, reduce expenses by $_____ and improve quality significantly. Our management team has been significantly strengthened with the addition of a new Chief Financial Officer and Production Manager. With these changes, we believe that Excalibur can be returned to profitability within ____ months. To demonstrate, we are attaching as Exhibit C management's financial projections for the next five years.

Survival Strategy

The management of Excalibur and our advisers believe that Excalibur cannot survive and continue as a productive business with the existing debt burden. The alternatives to the creditor compromise offered in this letter and the accompanying agreement are twofold: 1) liquidation, or 2) Chapter 11 bankruptcy reorganization. As you will see from Exhibit D, a liquidation leaves unsecured creditors with little or no net proceeds. Alternatively, although a Chapter 11 reorganization may indeed prove effective as a means for accomplishing a restructuring of Excalibur, the costs of a Chapter 11 case (potentially in excess of $_____), as well as the time delay and potential adverse impact on our customer base would, we believe, likely reduce the value to be received by unsecured creditors to something substantially less than the ____ cents on the dollar offered by this plan. Accordingly, we strongly believe that the proposed creditor compromise is in the best interests of creditors and Excalibur.

Bank Claim, Other Secured Claims, Taxes, Utilities and Ongoing Contracts

As we indicated, Excalibur's two secured lenders have agreed to extend their current revolving line of credit and term loan facilities, which have balances as of _____ ____, 19xx of $_____, for 12 months (through _____, 19xx) if the composition agreement is accepted by the creditors.

In addition to the bank, Excalibur has several other secured creditors possessing liens on dies, molds or inventory (in the creditors' possession). Their collateral each has a value in excess of the debts owed to these secured creditors. Excalibur will continue to pay these secured creditors according to ordinary business terms.

Similarly, because of the unique nature of taxes and utilities, Excalibur will continue to pay these creditors according to ordinary business terms.

Summary of Composition and Conclusion

In summary, Excalibur is proposing that its unsecured creditors agree to reduce their claims by ____cents on the dollar. The reduced amount will be paid by an initial payment in the amount of _____ percent, with the balance of the reduced amount payable in equal monthly installments over ____ months without interest. The composition proposal in this letter and the accompanying agreement will be effective if ____ percent (in amount) of our total unsecured debt of $_____ accept this proposal. To accept this proposal, you should sign and date a copy of the enclosed agreement and return the signed and dated copy to us in the enclosed postage-paid envelope. Agreements should be postmarked no later than _____ ____, 19xx. If we receive signed agreements postmarked by that date or earlier from unsecured creditors holding claims of at least ____ percent of the total amount of unsecured debt, we will proceed to implement the composition proposal. At the time of this writing, our proposal has already been accepted by unsecured creditors holding $_____ of claims, which constitutes ____ percent of our total claims. Those accepting the composition already include:

1._____

2._____

3._____

If you have any questions concerning this letter, the enclosed agreement or your claims against Excalibur, we would be happy to put you in touch with our financial adviser, or our counsel.

FINALLY, WE URGE YOU TO VOTE IN FAVOR OF THIS PROPOSAL; THE ABILITY OF THE CREDITORS TO ACHIEVE A SUBSTANTIAL RECOVERY AND THE ONGOING VIABILITY OF EXCALIBUR, INC. REQUIRE THAT THIS PROPOSAL BE APPROVED.

Very truly yours,

Excalibur, Inc.

THIS AGREEMENT, made as of _____ ____, 19xx, between Excalibur, Inc. (the "Company"), and those of its creditors who become parties hereto by signing this agreement (the "Creditor").

Recitals:

A. The Company is indebted to the Creditor in the amount set forth on Exhibit A to this agreement (the "Debt").

B. The Company is unable to satisfy and discharge the Debt in full, and has offered to compromise these debts by the payment of ____ cents on the dollar in the manner hereinafter stated.

C. The Creditor has agreed to forebear from exercising its rights against the Company with respect to the Debt so long as such payments are made as specified herein.

It is therefore agreed:

1. Composition. The Company shall pay to the Creditor ____ percent of such Creditor's total present claim, as set forth on Exhibit A to this agreement, such payment to be made by the payment of ____ cents on the dollar on or before _____ ____ 19xx, and the balance in ____ equal monthly installments (without interest) of ____ cents on the dollar, the first installment to be made one month after the initial payment.

2. Acceptance. The Creditor shall accept from the Company ____ cents for each dollar owed by the Company, such amount to be paid in the manner specified in paragraph 1. So long as the Company pays the compromised amount in the manner specified in paragraph 1, the Creditor shall not at any time sue or take any other action against the Company or against its property in connection with the present claim of such Creditor against the Company.

3. Release. In exchange for receipt by the Creditor of the amounts specified in paragraph 1, at or before the times therein stated, the Company shall be completely released and discharged from all present claims of the Creditor against the Company, and the Creditor shall surrender to the Company all notes and other evidences of indebtedness now held in connection with the present claims.

4. Default. If the Company shall default as to any Creditor in making the payments specified in paragraph 1, at the times therein stated, the full amount of the present claim of such Creditor, less payments received under this agreement, shall immediately become due and payable, and each Creditor shall have the right to pursue any remedy then available to him as if this agreement had never been made.

5. Effective Date. This agreement shall become effective only upon its acceptance by ____ percent of the unsecured creditors of the Company in amount, such acceptance to be evidenced by the signature of Creditor upon this agreement on or before _____ ____, 19xx. If this agreement is not so accepted, it shall be of no force or effect.

6. Amounts of Debt. The amounts set forth on Exhibit A to this agreement is the full amount of the Debt due to the Creditor from the Company.

7. Binding effect. This agreement, when effective, shall be binding upon the parties and their respective legal representatives, successors and assigns.

8. Entire agreement. This agreement supersedes all agreements previously made between the parties relating to its subject matter. There are no other understandings or agreements between them.

9. Notices. All notices or other documents under this agreement shall be in writing and delivered personally or mailed by certified mail, postage prepaid, addressed to the parties at their last known addresses.

310

10. <u>Non-Waiver.</u> No delay or failure by a party to exercise any right under this agreement, and no partial or single exercise of that right, shall constitute a waiver of that or any other right, unless otherwise expressly provided herein.

11. <u>Headings.</u> Headings in this agreement are for convenience only and shall not be used to interpret or construe its provisions.

12. <u>Governing law.</u> This agreement shall be construed in accordance with and governed by the laws of the State of

_____.

13. <u>Counterparts.</u> This agreement may be executed in one or more counterparts, each of which shall be deemed an original but all of which together shall constitute one and the same instrument.

In witness whereof the parties have signed this agreement.

Excalibur, Inc.   Creditor
By: By:

An Authorized Officer   An Authorized Officer

Exhibit A

Creditor:

Total of past-due invoices dated ____ days
or older as of _____ ____, 19xx   ___I

INDEX

R

Receivables
    Collection of   130–131
Reports
    Daily and weekly
        Examples   103
Return On Assets Managed   33, 34, 41–42
    Company branch performance   63
    In relation to debt and return on
        shareholders' eq   58, 73
    ROAM   33, 45
        Calculated   33, 51–55
Return On Shareholders' Equity
    Impact of leverage on   56–59
Revenue analysis   113–114
Revenues
    Increasing   203–219

S

Sale
    with leaseback   133
Sales manager
    and turnaround   215–216
Scapegoats
    avoiding to make turnaround work   141
Secured Party sales   200
Shareholder equity requirements   38–40
Statistical Process Control (SPC)   222
Strategic alliance
    to solve cash constraints   134
Structural change
    and expense reduction   147–150
Subcontracting
    and expense reduction   162–163
Success
    Defination   177

T

Teamwork   146
Training
    Cross
        and expense reduction   158
Turnaround
    Strategic plan   177–179

U

Undercapitalized   22
Undermanaged   18
Unsaid messages   160

V

Value added
    and improving profit margins   217–218
Vendor
    Terms
        Extending   122–123

W

Wal-Mart   218, 249

CORPORATE INTENSIVE CARE

Why Businesses Fail
and
How to Make Them Succeed

Order your own copy today!
CALL: Toll-free 1-800-247-6553
or 216/491-0231
FAX: 216/491-0251

MAIL: York Publishing Co., 16781 Chagrin Blvd., #336,
Shaker Hts., OH 44120
Satisfaction Guaranteed.
Return within 30 days if not completely satisfied.

_____ Copies @ $49.95 plus any applicable Ohio
sales tax, shipping and handling

Name _____

Title/Dept _____

Company _____

Business description _____

Address _____

_____

City _____ State _____ Zip _____

Phone _____ Fax _____

PAYMENT • Check (payable to York Publishing Co.)
• Mastercard _____ • Visa _____

Card # _____ Expires _____

Signature _____

(Required for All Orders)
U.S. funds only. Price subject to change without notice.